PENGUIN BOOKS

J.M. COETZEE AND
THE LIFE OF WRITING

David Attwell is a graduate of the University of Natal in Durban, South Africa; he completed his MA in African literary theory and criticism at the University of Cape Town, where his supervisor was J.M. Coetzee. He holds a PhD from the University of Texas at Austin and is currently a professor at the University of York, England.

J.M. COETZEE AND THE LIFE OF WRITING

Face-to-Face with Time

David Attwell

PENGUIN BOOKS

PENGUIN BOOKS

An imprint of Penguin Random House LLC
375 Hudson Street
New York, New York 10014
penguin.com

First published in South Africa by Jacana Media (Pty) Ltd
First published in the United States of America by Viking Penguin,
an imprint of Penguin Random House LLC, 2015
Published in Penguin Books 2016

The author gratefully acknowledges the permission given to quote excerpts from the following
works: *Waiting for the Barbarians*, © 1980 by J.M. Coetzee; *In the Heart of the Country*, © 1976,
1977 by J.M. Coetzee; and *Dusklands*, © 1974, 1982 by J.M. Coetzee. Used by permission of
Penguin Books, an imprint of Penguin Publishing Group, a division of Penguin Random House
LLC. *Life & Times of Michael K*, © 1983 by J.M. Coetzee; *Foe*, © 1986 by J.M. Coetzee; *The Master
of Petersburg*, © 1994 by J.M. Coetzee; *Boyhood: Scenes from Provincial Life*, © 1997 by J.M.
Coetzee; *Disgrace*, © 1999 by J.M. Coetzee; *Elizabeth Costello*, © 2003 by J.M. Coetzee; *Youth*, ©
2002 by J.M. Coetzee; *Diary of a Bad Year*, © 2007 by J.M. Coetzee; *Summertime: Fiction*, © 2009
by J.M. Coetzee; *Slow Man*, © 2005 by J.M. Coetzee; *Here and Now: Letters (2008–2011)*, © 2013
by Paul Auster and © 2013 by J.M. Coetzee. Used by permission of Viking Books, an imprint of
Penguin Publishing Group, a division of Penguin Random House LLC. *Age of Iron*, © 1990 by
J.M. Coetzee and *Stranger Shores: Literary Essays, 1986–1999*, © 2001 by J.M. Coetzee, repro-
duced by permission of Peter Lampack Agency, Inc. *Giving Offense: Essays on Censorship*, repro-
duced by permission of the University of Chicago Press © 1996 by the University of Chicago.
Doubling the Point: Essays and Interviews, by J.M. Coetzee, edited by David Attwell, pp. 59–60,
142, 248, 250, 298, 299, 363, 391, 393–4, Cambridge, Mass.: Harvard University Press, Copyright © 1992 by the President and Fellows of Harvard College. All illustrations and quotations
from the Coetzee manuscripts, with kind permission of J.M. Coetzee and the Harry Ransom
Center, University of Texas at Austin. *Roland Barthes by Roland Barthes*, translated by Richard
Howard; translation copyright © 1977 by Farrar, Straus and Giroux, Inc.; reprinted by permission of Hill and Wang, a division of Farrar, Straus and Giroux, LLC. Robert Duncan, "The Song
of the Border-Guard" © Jess Collins Trust.

ISBN 9780525429616 (hc.)
ISBN 9780143128816 (pbk.)

Printed in the United States of America
10 9 8 7 6 5 4 3 2 1

Set in Minion Pro

CONTENTS

ACKNOWLEDGEMENTS

My FIRST DEBT of thanks is owed to the Leverhulme Trust in the United Kingdom, which provided respite from the day-to-day business of academic life in the form of a research fellowship. Thanks are also due to the Department of English at the University of Stockholm, which provided a visiting professorship close to the glories of the Swedish Academy and Nobel Library, and the Stellenbosch Institute for Advanced Studies (STIAS), whose hospitality brought me to the heartlands of Cape Town and the Karoo during the early months of conceptualizing the project.

Through the good offices of Wium van Zyl and Anton Kannemeyer, I was also able to consult John Kannemeyer's papers in Stellenbosch. It is tragic that John Kannemeyer died so soon after completing the first biography of J.M. Coetzee. He deserved to see the fruits of his labours and the positive influence he has had on Coetzee studies. He and I met twice and corresponded frequently as he worked on his project in the last three years of his life, and I am grateful for his courtesy and friendship during this period. While in Stellenbosch I also received personal support from Hannes van Zyl, John Kannemeyer's editor, for which I am very grateful.

Colleagues old and new have enabled me to give parts of this work an airing at the universities of Adelaide, Cape Town, Stellenbosch,

Giessen, Stockholm, Verona and York, Queen Mary, University of London, Rhodes University and the Norwegian Literary Festival in Lillehammer. In Adelaide, my sincere thanks to John Coetzee and Dorothy Driver for their hospitality, and to Nick Jose and Brian Castro of the J.M. Coetzee Centre for Creative Practice for their interest and encouragement, not to mention the invitation to return. In Cape Town, the Centre for Open Learning and the Coetzee Collective led by Carrol Clarkson have been consistently generous during several visits over the past five years.

The staff of the Harry Ransom Center at the University of Texas at Austin went out of their way by making special arrangements to place parts of the Coetzee archive in the public domain earlier than expected. My thanks to Tom Staley, Megan Barnard, Gabby Redwine, Micah Erwin, Rick Watson and Jen Tisdale for their hospitality and professionalism during two visits to Austin in 2011 and 2012. Bernth and Judith Lindfors made these visits to Austin a real homecoming.

Friends and colleagues have endured my conversation or read and commented on this work, either in part or in some cases on the entire manuscript. I am immensely grateful to all of them and have freely made use of their suggestions: Derek Attridge, Rita Barnard, Elleke Boehmer, Christoph Buchwald, Carrol Clarkson, Eva Cossee, Jonathan Crewe, Dorothy Driver, Laura Emsley, Patrick Flanery, Ian Glenn, Irina Rasmussen Goloubeva, Lucy Graham, Michael Green, Hugh Haughton, Stefan Helgesson, Evi Hoste, Shawn Irlam, Michelle Kelly, Rob Nixon, Annalisa Pes, Hedley Twidle, Andrew van der Vlies, Geoffrey Wall, Hermann Wittenberg and Susanna Zinato. At an early stage, Kai Easton was immensely generous in sharing some of her research in the Coetzee papers. I am grateful for her help and collegiality throughout the writing of this book. Chabani Manganyi read early efforts and asked usefully sharp questions, such as 'Who in Coetzee is Dostoevsky?' Finuala Dowling lent a novelist's eye to a number of draft chapters, helping me to see the material more clearly as a writer would do. Paul Wise provided expert editorial guidance at a crucial stage of the manuscript's development. My sincere thanks to Russell Martin at Jacana Media, for his practical help and guidance and his insightful copyediting of the final manuscript.

At York I am fortunate to be in unusually collegial company. Sincere thanks to my colleagues for their interest in this project and for their support in making it possible for me to take up the fellowship. Derek Attridge, in particular, has been unstinting in his support and I have frequently had to rely on his good counsel.

Finally, I would like to thank John Coetzee, for his conversation, his help in enabling me to gain access to the papers, his willingness to grant permission for me to quote from them, and, most importantly, his forbearance over the results. To his many deserved accolades I would add another, for courage under fire.

Early versions of some of this material have been published in *Ex-centric Writing: Essays on Madness in Postcolonial Fiction*, ed. by Susanna Zinato and Annalisa Pes (Cambridge Scholars, 2013); in an issue of the journal *Life Writing* (vol. 11, no. 2, 2014); and in Norwegian translation in *Bokvennen Litterært Magasin* (no. 3, 2013).

CHRONOLOGY

1940   John Maxwell Coetzee born in Cape Town, 9 February. His father, Zacharias (Jack), is an attorney; his mother, Vera, a schoolteacher.

1942   Jack joins up, serves with South African forces in the Middle East and Italy.

1943   David Coetzee born early in the year.

1945   Jack returns, the Coetzees settle in Pollsmoor, Cape Town. John starts school at Pollsmoor Primary.

1946   Jack takes a job with the Cape Provincial Administration. The family moves to Rosebank. John attends Rosebank Primary.

1948   Jack made redundant. He takes a job with Standard Canners in Worcester. The family moves into Reunion Park. John attends Worcester Primary from April 1949.

1952   Jack opens a legal practice in Goodwood, Cape Town. The family settles in Plumstead. John enrols at St Joseph's College, where he matriculates in 1956.

1957 –   John attends the University of Cape Town (UCT). Completes
1961   a BA, and separate BA (Honours) degrees in English and Mathematics. Attends 'imaginative writing' classes arranged by R.G. Howarth, publishes poetry in university magazines.

Leaves by ship for Southampton in December 1961, graduating *in absentia*.

1962   Secures job as a computer programmer with IBM in London. He receives a bursary on the strength of his results, enrols for an MA at UCT on Ford Madox Ford, using the Reading Room of the British Museum. Experiments with computer-generated poetry.

1963   Returns to Cape Town, renews acquaintance with Philippa Jubber, whom he had met as a student. They marry on 11 July. Completes and submits the Ford thesis. Applies for jobs in England, first as a schoolteacher, then as a computer programmer. Enquires about PhD programmes in the United States.

1964   Returns with Philippa to England by ship in January. Works for International Computers and Tabulators, Ltd (ICT) while living in Bagshot, Surrey.

1965   Applies for admission to American doctoral programmes as well as UCT, which offers him a place for a PhD on modernism, which he declines. Secures a Fulbright scholarship and, from a range of offers in the United States, chooses the University of Texas at Austin. John and Philippa embark for New York by ship from Southampton in August. John enters PhD programme in linguistics and literature at Texas.

1966   Nicolas is born, 9 June.

1968 – While completing his dissertation on Samuel Beckett in
1969   Austin, John secures visiting assistant professorship at the State University of New York, Buffalo. Visa restrictions limit the duration of his contract. He applies for posts in Canada and Hong Kong, receives and declines an offer from the University of British Columbia. Keeps petitioning for an extension of his visa. Gisela is born on 10 November 1968.

1970   Starts writing *Dusklands*. Hayes Hall incident in Buffalo. Arrested, with 44 other members of the faculty, in a campus

protest against university management and police presence
on campus. Convicted of criminal trespass and contempt,
but with leave to appeal. In December, Philippa returns to
South Africa with children.

1971   Unable to extend his visa, John teaches out the Spring
semester, returns to South Africa in May. The family
reunited, they live at Maraisdal, near the Coetzee farm,
Voëlfontein. The conviction is overturned on appeal, but
there is little prospect of being granted a re-entry visa to the
United States.

1972 –   Appointed lecturer in English at UCT, January 1972.

1973   Completes *Dusklands*. Manuscript is rejected by several
publishers, then accepted by Ravan Press in Johannesburg,
published in 1974.

1974 –   Begins 'The Burning of the Books'. Abandons it after a

1976   year. Begins *In the Heart of the Country*, published in 1977.
Publishes in 1975 *A Posthumous Confession*, translation
of the Dutch novel *Een Nagelaten Bekentenis* by Marcellus
Emants.

1977 –   Writes *Waiting for the Barbarians*. Completes the novel

1979   while on sabbatical leave in Austin and Berkeley, California.
Begins *Life & Times of Michael K* on return.

1980   John and Philippa divorce. *Waiting for the Barbarians*
published. John works on series of essay-length studies of
South African writing, eventually published in 1989 as *White
Writing: On the Culture of Letters in South Africa*. Begins
seeing Dorothy Driver, who becomes life partner.

1982   Begins writing *Foe*, completed in 1985.

1983   *Life & Times of Michael K* published, wins Booker
Prize. Publishes *The Expedition to the Baobab Tree*,
translation of Wilma Stockenström's Afrikaans novel *Die
Kremetartekspedisie*.

1984   Appointed to full professorship at UCT, delivers inaugural
lecture, 'Truth in Autobiography'.

1985   Mother, Vera, dies 6 March.

1986   *Foe* published. Publishes *A Land Apart*, collection of South
African poetry, co-edited with André Brink. Visiting
professorship at Johns Hopkins University, Baltimore. Begins
work on *Age of Iron*, completed 1989.

1987   Begins, then abandons, a memoir, which he later returns to
as *Boyhood*.

1988   Father, Jack, dies 30 June. Begins work with David Attwell on
Doubling the Point: Essays and Interviews.

1989   Nicolas dies, 21 April. Another visiting professorship at
Johns Hopkins.

1990   *Age of Iron* published. Philippa dies, 30 July.

1991   Begins writing *The Master of Petersburg*. Embarks on series
of essays on censorship. Visiting professorship at Harvard.
John and Dorothy make extended visit to Australia.

1992   *Doubling the Point* published.

1993   Appointed to Arderne Chair at UCT, the post once held by
his mentor of student days, R.G. Howarth.

1994   *The Master of Petersburg* published. Begins writing *Disgrace*.

1995 – Writes *Disgrace*, which he completes in 1998. Begins
1998   Elizabeth Costello stories (including Tanner Lectures at
Princeton, published as *The Lives of Animals*, 1999). Returns
to *Boyhood*. Visiting professorship at James Michener
Center, Texas. Begins regular visiting professorships (until
2003) in the Committee on Social Thought, University of
Chicago. In March 1995 he begins legal inquiries about
emigration to Australia. Publishes *Giving Offense: Essays on
Censorship*, 1996. Regularly publishes reviews in the *New
York Review of Books* and elsewhere; a number are collected
in *Stranger Shores*, 2001. *Boyhood* published 1997.

1999   *Disgrace* published. Wins second Booker Prize. In April
2000, ANC refers to *Disgrace* in its submission to South
African Human Rights Commission hearings on racism in
the media. Novel is discussed in Cabinet.

2001   Receives immigration visa from Australian Embassy in
        Pretoria. Retires from UCT in December.

2002   Moves to Australia. He and Dorothy settle in north Adelaide.
        Youth published. In November, John is hospitalized after
        cycling accident in Chicago.

2003   Nobel Prize for Literature. Publishes *Elizabeth Costello*.

2004   Writes *Slow Man*. Publishes translations of Dutch poets
        in *Landscape with Rowers: Poetry from the Netherlands*.
        John and Dorothy hosted as visiting professors at Stanford
        University. Begins work on *Summertime*.

2005   *Slow Man* published. Awarded South African national
        honours in Pretoria, Order of Mapungubwe. Begins work on
        Diary of a Bad Year.

2006   Becomes naturalized Australian citizen, 6 March.

2007   *Diary of a Bad Year* published. Reviews written between
        2000 and 2005 published as *Inner Workings*.

2008   Begins collaboration with Paul Auster.

2009   *Summertime* published. Omnibus edition of fictionalized
        memoirs published, 2011.

2010   Seventieth birthday celebrated at festival at De Balie,
        Amsterdam. John receives national honours, Ridder van de
        Nederlandse Leeuw. Later that year, his brother, David, dies
        in Washington, D.C.

2012   Begins *The Childhood of Jesus*.

2013   *Here and Now: Letters 2008–2011* (co-authored with Paul
        Auster) published. *The Childhood of Jesus* published.

PREFACE

The Coetzee Papers

J.M. Coetzee and the Life of Writing is a critical biography whose purpose is to read the life and the work of its subject, the novelist J.M. Coetzee, together. By concentrating on Coetzee's authorship, what I have called the life of the writing – it could equally be the life *in* the writing – I focus on just one aspect of the life of the man John Maxwell Coetzee, the part that makes him publicly known and to which he has devoted himself most fully. It is not the whole story, and aspects of Coetzee's life that have little bearing on his authorship have little relevance to this book.

This is therefore not a biography in the conventional sense. Nor does it pretend to be an intellectual biography. If by an intellectual biography we mean an account of the growth and development of Coetzee's ideas and their expression in his fiction and other writings (including the translations, reviews, scholarly essays and books), then such a task would be beyond the scope of what is offered here. The book is mainly an account of my reading Coetzee's manuscripts, which have been made available to the public in the Harry Ransom Center at the University of Texas at Austin.

The background to my reading Coetzee's papers is a relationship with his work that began in 1974, when as a student in Durban I read his first novel, *Dusklands*. Since then I have followed Coetzee's career closely and have either taught or written about each of the novels at some stage. In the early 1980s, I began to get to know something of the man when I worked under his guidance as a Master's student at the University of Cape Town, preparing a thesis on African criticism and theory. Then, over a period of three years from 1988 to 1990, when I was in the doctoral programme at the University of Texas at Austin, Coetzee and I worked together on a book entitled *Doubling the Point: Essays and Interviews* (1992).[1] *Doubling the Point* is an intellectual *auto*biography, which collects a body of Coetzee's academic essays and some ephemerally published pieces and links them together with a series of written dialogues. Soon after *Doubling the Point* I produced a work of literary criticism, based on the thesis submitted to Texas, on the six novels that Coetzee had published up to that point, entitled *J.M. Coetzee: South Africa and the Politics of Writing* (1993).

Now, twenty years later, I take an entirely different approach, a step back in order to look again, this time not as a literary critic would, which is to say at the finished works, but at the authorship that underlies them: its creative processes and sources, its oddities and victories – above all, at the remarkable ways in which it transforms its often quite ordinary materials into unforgettable fiction.

The five weeks spent exploring Coetzee's papers could easily have become five months, or five years, if I had had the time and means to continue, but the experience was astonishing enough – both unsettling and illuminating – for me to proceed with an account of it. I could not have done this if I had not been so deeply immersed in the published fiction for so long. Coetzee's papers will keep scholars busy for many years – few, if any, living authors attract as much critical attention as Coetzee does – but I have found enough for an entirely different account, one that I would like to record before the spell dies.

One element of the magic I must confess to and dispel quickly is sentimental. As a doctoral candidate in Austin himself in the late 1960s, Coetzee had read Samuel Beckett's papers there; in my own student days in the 1980s, in the same library, I pored over the papers of writers whose formation had taken place in South Africa: Olive

Schreiner, Herman Charles Bosman, Alan Paton, Roy Campbell (whose exaggeratedly unhandsome bust is still there). I did this because it connected me with home, South Africa, though in ways that home could not easily appreciate or accommodate.

Coetzee had indulged himself in a similar way when, in his twenties, he had taken time out from his studies of Ford Madox Ford in the Reading Room of the British Museum in London to look at the textual traces of early European explorers in South Africa, notably William Burchell. Coetzee's hand-drawn map of Burchell's travels is now in Texas, where I came across it. Circles within circles: the stuff of middle age, perhaps, and of the autobiography that seems to be embedded in the work of biography.

Certain essentials of a literary biographer's craft, such as a writer's most private letters, are not currently available to researchers on Coetzee. They are housed in Austin, but under restricted access until after his death. I doubt if I will go looking for them, should I live that long. I can't envisage taking pleasure in reading Coetzee's most personal papers after he has gone, so it will fall to others to find out how he might have used diaries when writing his partly fictionalized autobiographies, or whether his intimate correspondence played any role in the lives of the people who inhabit his novels. Aspects of his personal life that are elided in the autobiographies, such as his marriage to Philippa Jubber and the birth and early years of their children, Nicolas and Gisela, do occasionally surface in the papers, but for the most part they are off stage.

For a man who is known to protect his privacy, the collection housed at Texas is remarkably complete. In addition to the extensive business correspondence, speeches, awards, citations, press clippings, photographs, family memorabilia, and the author's well-preserved research materials, for the fiction and the non-fiction alike, it includes the manuscripts of all the novels from *Dusklands* (1974) to *Elizabeth*

Costello (2003). After his relocation to Australia in 2002, the drafts consist mainly of computer printouts. Most of the manuscripts are written on blue examination books lifted from the University of Cape Town, where Coetzee lectured for most of his academic career – one can imagine him collecting unused exam books at the end of an invigilation session.

The manuscript entries and revisions are meticulously dated, fortunately for those who wish to follow their development. The dating and self-archiving would have served the creative process, enabling the author to move blocks of text around and to recover discarded fragments. Coetzee works with the roughest of outlines. Typically, the earliest drafts are sketched quickly, provisionally, determinedly. Writing as often as he can, daily if possible, he is in search of his subject: the voice especially, embedded in a distinctive genre and a distinctive history. The plot is the least stable of the elements, always subserving the voice, and continually revised.

Contrary to a widely held assumption that Coetzee's novels are spun from quotations drawn from literary theory, the allusions to other writers (some theorists, but more often than not novelists, poets and philosophers) are brought in only once the work has found its own legs. He records possible titles throughout the drafting process, but decisions about them are postponed to the very end. He is content to call a work by a number ('Fiction No. 4') until the right title makes itself known.

Such methods are built on absolute faith in the creative process, on tenaciously working through the uncertainties (which are real and made explicit, as we will see) towards a distant goal until an illumination arrives, providing direction and momentum for the next phase. Of course, this process involves revision and more revision – by hand on manuscripts, by hand on typescripts, and by retyping. Twelve, thirteen, fourteen versions of a work are not unusual. Taking full advantage of hindsight, I refer at times in the chapters that follow to a 'writing event', which is the point at which a quantum leap is made, when the draft becomes more like the novel it wants to be.

Of particular interest are the pocket-sized notebooks that Coetzee would have kept when he was not at his desk. From a comparison of the reflections, self-corrections and sources jotted down in these notebooks with the more extended exam-book manuscripts, a story emerges of Coetzee's creativity, its changes of direction, insecurities, periods of confidence and fluency. Once the computer takes over, as it does in the later, Australian-based writing from *Slow Man* (2005) on, the evidence of the creative processes is less intimate, but the patterns are still discernible.

Until 2011, the manuscripts of the early fiction up to the mid-1990s were held in the Houghton Library at Harvard, where Coetzee had lodged them for safekeeping. They were available to researchers, among whom was John Kannemeyer, Coetzee's first biographer. Between 2009 and 2011, Coetzee gave interviews to Kannemeyer and provided access to many of the papers he kept at his home in Adelaide, Australia. The result was *J.M. Coetzee: 'n Geskryfde Lewe* ('A Written Life'), written and published in Afrikaans and simultaneously published in English translation as *J.M. Coetzee: A Life in Writing*, by Jonathan Ball in Johannesburg (2012).

Kannemeyer's biography is a feat of collation, monumental in scale and full of information about Coetzee's genealogical background, childhood, education, close relationships, academic career, dealings with publishers, censors and filmmakers, and the publication and reception of each of the novels.[2] The work is all the more useful for being empirically minded, indeed conservative in its approach to biography. Since Coetzee is uncooperative with most enquirers, in the absence of reliable knowledge a good deal of anecdote is in circulation, much of it embellished, a malaise that Kannemeyer has largely dispelled. Given that, by admission, his attention was trained on Coetzee's life rather than the work, Kannemeyer was unable to pay more than cursory attention to the manuscripts.

All good writers dread biography, of course, even when it is not contemptuous. Biography is one of the ways in which the present generation puts the previous one firmly in the past. Lytton Strachey, the man who started the trend by pouring irony over his Victorian subjects, eventually became a victim of it himself. Coetzee was anticipating this kind of treatment when, in *Summertime* (2009), he invented the English biographer Vincent (a conquering name), who was going to write a biography of the departed John Coetzee.[3]

But while he was still writing *Summertime*, history dealt Coetzee a surprising card in the form of the arrival of John Kannemeyer, whose purposes were not to overthrow the past at all but to archive the present in a spirit of generational fellow feeling, and out of respect for Coetzee's contribution to South African and world literature. That this could happen is related to the fact that while Coetzee's work is intellectually anchored in the cultural metropoles of Europe and the United States, it also belongs to a regional literature whose canons are barely known outside South Africa.

In being cooperative with Kannemeyer, though without authorizing him (Coetzee would not authorize any biography), he would have understood that biography is an inescapable consequence of success. Whether they like it or not, successful authors, especially Nobel laureates, have to come to terms with biography, as much as they have to endure migraines and toothache. And when, as Ian Hamilton shows in *Keepers of the Flame*,[4] writers try to ghost-write or in some cases even *write* their own biographies, or try to do so by remote control from the grave, the results are usually mixed. Coetzee said much of what he needed to say about biography in *Summertime*, which, as an autobiography, uses as its fictional pretext a biography-in-the-making. On these terms, it takes pre-emptive evasive action. Nevertheless, Coetzee gave John Kannemeyer courteous attention, assistance and, most importantly, a free hand.

Most ordinary readers, among whom I include myself, remain fascinated by biography, especially the insights it affords into the creative processes that produce the fictions we treasure most. When

I introduced *J.M. Coetzee: South Africa and the Politics of Writing* twenty years ago, I said that I was uncertain whether the book was a tribute or a betrayal, 'infinitely wishing' that it were the former. I am caught in the same quandary today. I respect the novels as public documents no less than I did then, but my admiration has undergone a major change, from the finished work to the immense labour, and the openness to the difficult and the strange, that have produced one of the exemplary authorships of our times.

1

AN ALPHABET OF TREES
Autobiography – The uses of impersonality

Her books teach nothing, preach nothing; they merely spell out, as clearly
as they can, how people lived in a certain time and place … they spell
out how one person lived, one among billions: the person whom she,
to herself, calls she, and whom others call Elizabeth Costello.[1]

IF WE THINK of Coetzee as a cerebral writer, a weaver of clever pal-
impsests, then the ordinariness of his fictions' beginnings will come as
a surprise. Typically, the novels begin personally and circumstantially,
before being worked into fiction. The Coetzee who emerges from his
papers turns out to be a little more like the rest of us: more human or,
at least, less Olympian, though only up to a point, because the question
remains: if he started *here*, how on earth did he get *there*?

My subtitle, *Face to Face with Time*, is taken from a draft of *Life &*
Times of Michael K, the novel for which Coetzee won his first Booker
Prize in 1983.[2] The relevant passage sees K escaping from his captors
by retreating into the Swartberg mountain range where he muses,

I have retreated and retreated and retreated, till I am on the highest
mountaintop and there is nowhere more to go save up into the heavens.
Now I am face to face at last with time: everything else is behind me,

only the huge block of the day is before me everyday when I wake, and
will not go away. Now there is nothing for me to do but live, through
time, like an ant boring its way through a rock.[3]

There is much here that is suggestive of Coetzee's authorship: the
inwardness and isolation of the voice; the sense of being embattled;
the desire for meaning, even when it is thwarted. The ant boring its way
through rock is a good metaphor for all of Coetzee's writing.

'Face to face with time' conveys the way Coetzee puts fiction between himself and history, between himself and his mortality. It does
this in highly self-conscious ways, with the result that Coetzee criticism
is filled with commentary on the novels' metafictional qualities – the
writing about writing. The most trenchant of the purposes of Coetzee's
metafiction, however, is that it is the means whereby he challenges
himself with sharply existential questions, such as, *Is there room for me,
and my history, in this book? If not, what am I doing?* The book must
in some sense answer to the mystery of its author's being. Coetzee's
writing is a huge existential enterprise, grounded in fictionalized
autobiography. In this enterprise the texts marked as autobiography
are continuous with those marked as fiction – only the degree of
fictionalization varies.

Each text in the trilogy of Coetzee's autobiographies, *Boyhood*
(1997), *Youth* (2002) and *Summertime* (2009), is subtitled *Scenes from
Provincial Life*. The omnibus edition containing all three of these texts
has this as its main title. It goes a long way towards explaining the
existential emphasis.

Writing about C.P. Cavafy, the Greek poet from Alexandria who is
one of the many poets Coetzee has followed, Orhan Pamuk remarks,
'For those who lead a provincial life, life and happiness are always
to be found elsewhere, in another city, in another country' – a place
'perpetually out of reach.'[4] In Coetzee, the condition Pamuk describes
involves perpetual anxiety, too, the source of which would be related
to the fact that for the thirty years that Coetzee lived and wrote in
Cape Town, he did so without being comfortably settled. He was forced

to return to South Africa from self-imposed exile in 1971 and never fully got over it until he left for Australia in 2002. The result, which is equally an expression of Coetzee's temperament, was a fear of living inauthentically, a brutal honesty about facing up to the conditions of one's existence.

The other side to this story is an equally strong desire for self-masking. Coetzee is always deliberately present and not present in his work. The desire for self-actualization is a function of needing to bear witness to one's existence in a situation in which one is in danger of culturally disappearing; but the culture in whose terms one wants to be recognized also regards such acts of self-testimony as crude, gauche. The solution is to vacillate: knowing that one can't simply return, and embrace with conviction the fate of being provincial (as Cavafy did, in living out most of his life in Alexandria), one has to remind the dominant culture that its representations *are* representations. Self-consciousness about language is often related to the problem of not-belonging.

Two of Coetzee's most powerful forebears are T.S. Eliot and Roland Barthes. These mentors arrived in Coetzee's developing artistic universe at different times, though at the right time in each case, and in the right order. The cumulative effect was to confirm, and provide a language for, Coetzee's preference for impersonality. But the important point is that, for all three, impersonality is not what it seems. It is not a simple repudiation of self in the name of art; on the contrary, it involves an instantiation of self, followed by an erasure that leaves traces of the self behind.

It is important to grasp this if we are to follow the creative paths left by such writers in their papers. Despite all the taboos, we continue to read biographically, not in order to limit the truth of the work to its biographical sources, but in order to understand how the self is written into the work and then written out, leaving its imprint as a shadowy presence. As Pamuk puts it beautifully in the same essay on Cavafy: 'Great poets can tell their own stories without once saying "I", and in doing so, lend their voice to all of humanity.'5

To continue with Coetzee's autobiographical writing: in June 1993, with seven of his novels behind him, Coetzee returned to the manuscripts of *Boyhood*, which he had started writing in 1987 and then suspended. Why he stopped would probably have had to do with other projects that were in play at the time, *Age of Iron* and *Doubling the Point*. It is also clear from the early manuscripts that he had not yet resolved the formal questions he was wrestling with.

Looking back on the years of his childhood spent in rural Worcester that he was about to describe, he wrote in his notebook: 'Deformation. My life as deformed, year after year, by South Africa. Emblem: the deformed trees on the golf links in Simonstown.'[6] He was referring to the pines on the Simonstown golf course in Cape Town. These are alien trees that have been exposed to the south-easterly wind blowing perpetually from the southern Atlantic Ocean. Planted to mark the fairways and give shade, they have assumed contorted shapes, as if in mockery of the club's wistful founders. Simonstown's pines are certainly gloomy emblems to choose for the effects of place and history on one's character, but in the writing of his memoirs Coetzee would find affirmation, too, in being a child of South Africa.

The context was a private argument that he was conducting with Barthes, and in his notebook he wonders how he will navigate around Barthes's influence. In his autobiography, *Roland Barthes par Roland Barthes*, Coetzee says, Barthes is a father figure who not only wrote the kind of autobiography he, Coetzee, now wishes to write, but who also stands in his way. Worse, Coetzee worries that Barthes would have 'no interest in recognizing a rude colonial offspring'. Despite the misgivings, Coetzee feels that he has a trump card to play over Barthes: 'something different and welcome' – 'a solidity to my concerns, a world-relevance'.[7] The Simonstown trees, symbols of malformation though they are, are also emblems of distinction, of a feeling for history *in extremis*, of a life arguably less sheltered than Barthes's was from the prevailing winds of the modern world-system.

'Emblem: the deformed trees on the golf links in Simonstown.'

Barthes, too, used images of trees to mark his autobiographical passage. The first part of *Roland Barthes* includes photographs of his childhood printed alongside reflective and self-quizzical captions. Then, as the text takes over from the photographs, in a section headed 'Towards Writing', Barthes includes a photograph of palm trees and a poem by Heinrich Heine. In the poem, the speaker is standing near a hemlock tree in a frozen northern climate, but daydreams about 'a palm tree/ That far in an eastern land/ Languishes lonely and silent/ Upon the parching sand'.[8]

Barthes is implying that as his writing takes over from the photographs – a new beginning marked by the inclusion of Heine's poem – the self is more obviously refashioned and transformed: it becomes the product of a desire that flows with the energies of the writing. Barthes glosses the poem as follows: 'According to the Greeks, trees are alphabets. Of all the tree letters, the palm is loveliest. And of writing, profuse and distinct as the burst of its fronds, it possesses the major effect: falling back.' The falling back of the palm frond is Barthes's way of drawing attention to writing's ability to unfold luxuriously, and also to double back and reflect upon itself.

All of this would have been agreeable to Coetzee. Like Barthes, he would believe that what is written as autobiography is only the 'figurations of the body's prehistory – of that body making its way toward the labor and the pleasure of writing'. The period covered by the narrative of autobiography, Barthes continues, 'ends with the subject's youth: the only [auto]biography is of an unproductive life'.[9] This would accord with Coetzee's choosing to *end* his autobiographical trilogy just at the moment when he *begins* to publish his fiction: the last of the trilogy, *Summertime*, is organized around the publication of *Dusklands* (1974). Thereafter, Coetzee's autobiography is the fiction itself.

Famously, in 'The Death of the Author', Barthes wrote of literature's ability to invent a 'special voice' that consists of 'several indiscernible voices', voices to which 'we cannot assign a specific origin'. The voice of the words on a literary page is 'the trap where all identity is lost, beginning with the very identity of the body that writes'.[10] Barthes's example is Balzac, but he writes about Mallarmé in the same vein. He might also have been writing about Flaubert, who with more than a hint of intellectual bullying chided his lover, Louise Colet, on her enthusiasm for *L'Éducation sentimentale* by saying, 'What I'd like to do is a book about nothing, a book with no external attachment, one which would hold together by the internal strength of its style, as the earth floats in the air unsupported.'[11] What in Flaubert is a style so distinctive that it floats free of all attachments becomes in Barthes a play of 'indiscernible voices' to which we cannot assign an origin.

What looks like a mid-twentieth-century anti-bourgeois polemic in Barthes's 'The Death of the Author' was therefore already a late-nineteenth-century anti-bourgeois manifesto in Flaubert, who in the same letter to Louise Colet writes, 'There are no beautiful or sordid subjects and one could almost establish it as an axiom that, from the point of view of pure Art, there is no such thing as a subject, style being solely itself an absolute way of seeing things.'[12] Art for art's sake was Flaubert's solution to an embarrassing problem: the perfection of style provided the licence that he needed to work with a subject, adultery, which he had already judged to be sordid and mundane.

Barthes's polemic was in a longstanding tradition of French modernism. Aimed at the idea of dismantling the author as a cultural institution, his essay should not be confused with what he had to say about the psychic and existential demands of authorship itself. In *The Preparation of the Novel*, the posthumously edited collection of notes for seminars he gave at the Collège de France, he says that writing is a compulsion – the result of an interruption in the normal course of a life. To illustrate the point he quotes the opening lines of Dante's *Inferno*: 'Nel mezzo del cammin di nostra vita' ('In the middle of the journey of our life').[13]

A bereavement would do the trick, as it did for Proust, who lost his mother, and for whom writing then became a matter of the '*use of Time before death*' (Barthes's emphasis). The monument to Proust's desire to write was, precisely, *À la recherche du temps perdu* (*In Search of Lost Time*).[14] In Barthes's own case, he recalls exactly the date on which he decided to begin writing: 15 April 1978, in Casablanca. (It is surely his resolve, unfulfilled, to write fiction, since he had written so much else by then.) For Coetzee, the critical date came on 1 January 1970. In Coetzee, bereavements would also play their part. Once the novel is under way, continues Barthes, then its own priorities soon take over. He writes, 'In reality, it's not memory that creates [the novel] but its *deformation*' (his emphasis).[15] The triggers for Coetzee are similar to those described by Barthes. In his notes for *The Master of Petersburg*, Coetzee writes, 'A story is like a road. What do we hope to find at the end of the road? Oneself. One's death.'[16]

In one of the interviews in *Doubling the Point*, Coetzee famously says, 'all writing is autobiography' and 'all autobiography is storytelling.'[17] These aphorisms are now much quoted as general truths. While critics have applied them in discussions of *Boyhood*, *Youth* and *Summertime*, with their third-person treatments of the autobiographical persona, they have not been much discussed in relation to Coetzee's fiction.

Coetzee himself tells us in these aphorisms that the self is always present, but as narrative rather than as raw truth. If we are to understand the equation created here between what is revealed and what is hidden – that is, if we are to understand Coetzee's creative processes – first we need to see the self inside the fiction, and then we need to see how, in telling the story, Coetzee reaches for the aesthetic and achieves something larger and more representative.

A law of diminishing returns is also operative here, of course: the more rigorous and resourceful the *ars poetica*, the more elusive the self is likely to prove. The difficulty in our generally failing to grasp this has been Coetzee's famed impersonality, which is a distinguishing feature of his authorial signature. He disappears behind those masks. Many readers feel rightly that the disappearances are a game, that he is deliberately both there and not there at the same time. The several 'Coetzees' of *Dusklands*, the 'JC' and 'Señor C' of *Diary of a Bad Year*, 'John' of the autobiographies, 'John' in the stories in *Elizabeth Costello*, are all, in some measure, Coetzee himself, but because they appear in fictional or partly fictionalized works, we are inclined to distrust them as tokens of identity.

Even the authorial name, formalized and depersonalized by the initials 'J.M.' in place of 'John', makes us think twice about ascribing the same signature to the living author. His Nobel Lecture, 'He and His Man', which is based on *Robinson Crusoe*, addresses this question in terms of an allegory of the relationships between authors and their creations.

As a younger man Coetzee had cultivated this self-masking through an affinity with his modernist forebears, although he has always insisted that there is more to impersonality than it seems. He said of Eliot, 'for a poet who had such success, in his heyday, in importing the yardstick of impersonality into criticism, Eliot's poetry is astonishingly personal, not to say autobiographical'.[18]

Eliot's most famous statement on the subject is this: 'Poetry is not a turning loose of emotion, but an escape from emotion; it is not an expression of personality, but an escape from personality.' The less frequently quoted corollary, in the same essay, is just as important: 'But, of course, only those who have personality and emotions know what it means to want to escape from these things.'[19] When these two statements are put together, this is what they add up to: in Eliot's own words, 'What happens [to the poet] is a continual surrender of himself as he is at the moment to something more valuable. The progress of an artist is a continual self-sacrifice, a continual extinction of personality.'[20]

This was congenial to Coetzee. In a lecture given in 1974 at the University of Cape Town, he quotes one of Eliot's letters to the effect that 'the creation of a work of art is a painful and unpleasant business; it is a sacrifice of the man to the work, it is a kind of death'.[21]

Impersonality is not an a priori quality inherent in a work of art, nor is it simply a function of the aesthetic. It is an *achievement*, an effect of labour in which the self is partially but not wholly buried beneath the superstructure. It is an effect that was sought after and prized in modernism of an erudite kind, with Coetzee's forebears T.S. Eliot and Ezra Pound leading the way.

Coetzee was drawn initially to Eliot's version of impersonality not only because it suited his personality, but also for cultural reasons. Later, his training in linguistics enabled him to bring a certain academic detachment to his search for an entrée into fiction. From the linguistics of the period when he was a graduate student, the late 1960s, when American structuralism was giving way to transformational grammar, he derived the broad idea that we have limited power over the cultural systems we inhabit, that language speaks through us. That view was reinforced in the 1970s and 1980s by the post-structuralism of Barthes and of Jacques Derrida and others whom Coetzee followed, and with whom he was often in ideological sympathy.

A passage in the drafts of *Youth* is especially revealing because it points to ways in which Coetzee's adoption of impersonality contributed to his deliberations when weighing up a vocation in poetry as against the novel.

There are certain dicta in T.S. Eliot that he clings to because they are all there is to prove that he is still a poet. Poetry is an extinction of personality. Only people who … [*sic*]. He has a horror of spilling emotion on to the page. Once it has begun to spill he will not know how to contain it. It will be like cutting an artery and watching his lifeblood pulse out on to the floor.

Yet the driplets of feeling that emerge are so weak, so colourless, that he knows he will never find his salvation in the medium. He will have to turn to prose. He has never written prose, but he sees it as a more tranquil medium, each page a virtual lake on whose surface he can tack about unhurried, finding his way, where there will be space, lots of space, but no storms, no high waves.[22]

Like Eliot, Coetzee finds impersonality convenient, but the difference is that while Coetzee inherits it from Eliot like furniture from an ancestral home, he has too much appreciation for the volatility of psychology, and the sheer capriciousness of language, to take it too seriously. It *is*, in part, a game. He is also, like Eliot, just as interested in irony, and irony's ability to pull the rug from under one's feet, although even this is a position in which he does not invest too deeply.

I suspect that Coetzee would prefer to think of himself as a writer of dark, ironic comedy, rather than, say, as a diagnostician of the postcolonial condition. His comedy can, at times, be very dark indeed, unbearably so. The reason for this has everything to do with the quality that he once thought gave him the edge over Barthes: the history that he has lived through, the history that has marked him – the 'world-relevance'. Those trees on the golf course in Simonstown.

2

RECUSANT AFRIKANERS
Identity drift

COETZEE HAS speculated that he might not have a mother tongue. He pursues this line of thought in the voice of JC in *Diary of a Bad Year* (2007) and again in his own, more direct voice in *Here and Now* (2013), the volume of letters with the Brooklyn novelist Paul Auster (in particular, the letter dated 11 May 2009).[1]

These reflections were prompted by Jacques Derrida's *Monolingualism of the Other* (1996), where Derrida claims that although he was brought up monolingual in French (and Coetzee politely interpolates a remark here about the other languages Derrida knew), French was not his mother tongue. Coetzee feels that this description matches his own relationship with English. He adds that living in Australia, which is almost wholly monolingual, has made him realize just how much he does not share 'the Anglo weltanschauung'.[2] The question is worth pursuing for what it reveals about Coetzee's family and cultural background. Coetzee would not be the writer he is if he had not always written in English, but the situation is far from simple.

The phrase 'recusant Afrikaners' is Coetzee's own, from the drafts of *Boyhood*. 'Recusing' oneself is a well-known practice in legal and institutional situations, but 'recusance' is a much older concept, referring originally to English Catholics under the Tudor monarchy who refused to play along with the Established Church. Recusance was a form of undeclared rebellion, though not so quiescent in the case of the recusants living in France. By lifting the term from this historical context and applying it to the nuances of his parents' Afrikaner identity, Coetzee is being especially astute in the language whose *Weltanschauung* he supposedly does not share.

The phrase captures an anomaly. Coetzee's grandparents were Afrikaans-speaking anglophiles. The result was that instead of being moulded by Calvinism and ethnic nationalism, which was more typical for Afrikaans-speaking families of the early to mid-twentieth century, both his and his parents' generations were, in the words of a draft of *Summertime*, 'left to run wild', like feral domestic animals. Not that they were embraced by English-speaking South Africa either: what it was that formed the English, Coetzee says he has no idea.[3] His parents were bilingual with a good command of English, which entitled him, in his childhood view of things, to count himself English, but 'he is intimidated by more mystical definitions of Englishness that exclude him'. The child of *Boyhood* who is described here is working on the question whether identities can be freely chosen, and he is discovering that they can't be, or not entirely.[4]

The historical background is as follows. Coetzee's paternal grandparents were born in 1868 and 1884 in small towns of the rural Cape Colony: his grandfather, Gert, grew up in Aurora, near Piketberg; his grandmother, Lenie (Gert's second wife, born De Beer), in Prince Albert. Their first language was Afrikaans but they spoke good English and had probably been schooled in English. Gert was a lover of cricket and, when he was the mayor of Merweville, he was known to run up the Union Jack on Empire Day. His father had a close friend and business associate in Cape Town called Maxwell and named his first son after him, Gerrit (Gert) Maxwell – which is the origin of J.M. Coetzee's middle name.

Coetzee himself believes that the nine children of his paternal grandparents had a tutor who was English. Later, they were sent to boarding school, the girls to Wynberg Girls' High in Cape Town, the boys to Caledon or to Paarl Boys' High. Gert's anglophilia did not mean that the children became English-speaking, however; all of them spoke

Afrikaans as their first language and all, bar one, brought up their own children with Afrikaans as the home language. The exception was Coetzee's father, Jack.[5]

This exception, and why Jack's children, John and David, were brought up speaking English at home, had everything to do with their mother, Vera. Vera's parents, Piet and Louisa Wehmeyer, were from the Uniondale district of the Cape. Louisa was the daughter of a Polish clergyman and missionary by the name of Balcer Dubyl, a name he Germanized as Balthazar du Biel, and Anna Brecher, the child of a Moravian missionary. Balthazar and Anna met in what became German South West Africa (now Namibia) through their association with the Rhenish and Moravian church missions respectively. Soon after marrying they left for the United States, where they ministered to German immigrants in the Midwest, and then they returned to southern Africa. There were three children from the marriage: Albert (who was to become a fairly successful Afrikaans novelist of the 1920s), Annie (the Aunt Annie of *Boyhood*, a schoolteacher who translated her father's religious writing from German into Afrikaans), and Louisa. Louisa was born in the United States; Albert and Annie may have been too.

Unlike her siblings, Louisa developed a strong dislike of Afrikaners: she gave her children English names (Roland, Winifred, Ellen, Vera, Norman and Lancelot) and brought them up speaking English. For J.M. Coetzee the writer, the maternal line from Balthazar through Louisa to Vera completed the switch from German and Afrikaans to German and English. Balthazar's sojourn in the United States was decisive in bringing this about, just as Coetzee's own sojourn in the United States opened *his* English to an expansiveness that was invaluable in his writing, especially for someone whose English was not the natural result of being born into the Anglo-Saxon fold.

Unlike the provinces that were the former Boer republics – the Orange Free State and the Transvaal – the Cape, particularly the rural Cape, was freely bilingual by the early twentieth century, and the children of parents like Piet and Louisa Wehmeyer could drift towards being either

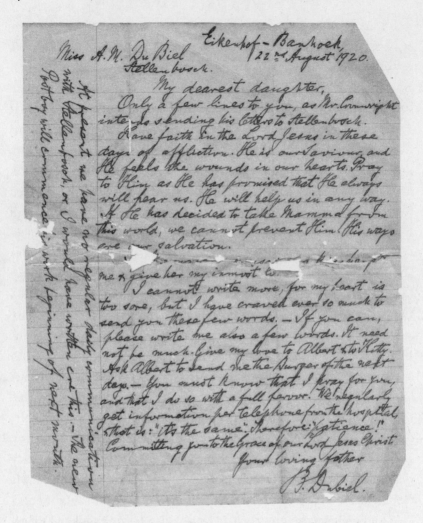

Letter in English from great-grandfather Balthazar du Biel to daughter Annie, concerning his wife's declining health, 22 August 1920.

culturally Afrikaans or culturally English. Not infrequently, Afrikaners of this background were not hostile to the British Empire: under the leadership of Jan Smuts they could imagine an accommodation within it, retaining an Afrikaner distinctiveness without sacrificing their loyalty to the Empire or Commonwealth. After 1948 this outlook became politically untenable as Afrikaner nationalism won power in the country and took on a more virulently republican colour. Afrikaans-speakers who were accommodating to a loosely defined imperial identity, such as Coetzee's parents, were referred to as 'Sappe' (from the SAP, Smuts's South African Party). Called recusants by Coetzee, they were regarded as *volksverraaiers*, traitors, by more militant Afrikaners.

Coetzee's father spoke excellent English but with an Afrikaans accent. Coetzee remembers him doing the *Cape Times* crossword, and doubts if he could have managed the Afrikaans equivalent in *Die Burger*. His reading was in English and included Shakespeare and Wordsworth. The conversation between Jack and his brothers and sisters on the family farm was bilingual; they would switch languages from one sentence to the next and use English words in Afrikaans sentences. In *Boyhood*, Coetzee recalls these conversations fondly by comparison with the rigidity of the Afrikaans promoted by his school in Worcester. Among Coetzee's cousins, Afrikaans became dominant.

Vera's English was even better than Jack's. She spoke good Afrikaans but used English informally and read and taught in English. Both parents would have associated English with high culture and Afrikaans with low. (Afrikaans was a *kombuistaal* for this generation, a language of the kitchen, distinct from Dutch.) Coetzee's schoolteachers, like the Mr Gouws who taught him in Standard Five (the last year of primary school), who is remembered in *Boyhood*, would have had similar dispositions. Mr Gouws had no university education but an excellent command of English grammar, according to Coetzee.

To an English-speaking South African ear, Coetzee's spoken English is unlocatable. It could be textbook Received Pronunciation, but his consonants have an American softness. (He uses American spelling in his manuscripts.) Part of the explanation for this lies in the high-cultural associations of the English spoken by his parents, and part in his particular relationship to English as the language of academic life and the currency of a global literature. The neutrality of Coetzee's spoken English, one would have to conclude, is a function of his cosmopolitanism and his election of world culture over regional or national culture.

*Electing traditions: John Coetzee at the grave of an ancestral Dubyl relative,
near Odolanów, Poland, July 2012.*

'Elective tradition' is a suitable name for this outlook, and the family
precedents for it were Balcer Dubyl, who chose to become German and
Protestant rather than remain Polish and Catholic, and grandfather
Gert Coetzee, who saw no contradiction in choosing to associate himself with the British Empire while being Afrikaans-speaking.

The studied quality of Coetzee's English, written and spoken, lends
credence to his suspicion that English can't be his mother tongue. When
Coetzee lived in England in the early 1960s, he carried with him the
high-cultural associations of the English of his home life and schooling.
He evidently felt like an outsider, sensing that he knew English better
than the English themselves. He could not accept the contemporary
orthodoxy of a multitude of equivalent Englishes, noting in the drafts
of *Youth*, 'Example of [Renaissance] humanist classical scholarship:
better Athenians than the Athenians.'[6]

But Afrikaans could not fill the role of mother tongue, either.
Coetzee was never hostile to the Afrikaans language: indeed, he was

proud of doing well in it at school, and in his matriculation year he was the only boy who took the Afrikaans language examination of the Akademie vir Wetenskap en Kuns (the Afrikaans-oriented Academy of Sciences and Arts). Nevertheless, he did not read Afrikaans books and magazines for pleasure, and would not have wished to think of himself as culturally Afrikaans, for being an Afrikaner meant accepting the terms of post-1948 nationalism, with its identikit of strict linguistic, religious and political loyalties. The overall effect was a form of identity drift: neither the one nor the other. In a draft of *Summertime* he writes,

> He was born into English, it was 'his', though without a thought. Then gradually in adulthood he has lost that happy unawareness. More and more the language becomes a foreign body which he has to enter. He becomes, in his mind, a person without a language, a disembodied spirit.[7]

Coetzee's English is rather like his mathematics; or, in another exaggerated comparison, it is something like what French became to Samuel Beckett. The peculiarity in Coetzee's case is that, though he had been born into English (unlike Beckett, whose French was acquired), its naturalness was gradually lost. Coetzee's is therefore an English shorn of the identity markers of Englishness.

The textual traditions which Coetzee assembles in 'The Narrative of Jacobus Coetzee', the second part of *Dusklands*, are pan-European, consisting of Portuguese, Dutch, English, German, Swedish and French travel writing, ethnography and linguistics, but the culture into which these streams coalesce is undoubtedly Afrikaner in conception. The novel's fictitious father, S.J. Coetzee, lectures at Stellenbosch University on the early explorers of the Cape, in the years when political Afrikanerdom was ascendant, 1934 to 1948. The organization that publishes the historical editions which the novel parodies is the Van

Plettenberg Society, after the late-eighteenth-century governor of the Cape, Joachim van Plettenberg, which is in turn an echo of the actual Van Riebeeck Society, a historical publications society named after the first Dutch colonial governor, Jan van Riebeeck.

On the subject of whether he has ever seen himself as an Afrikaner, Coetzee has expressed himself clearly: Afrikaners would never accept *him*. But there is some distance between that position and *repudiating* Afrikanerdom. He says, 'Is it in my power to withdraw from the gang? … is it in my heart's desire to be counted apart? I think not … not really.' He concludes by referring to *Dusklands*: 'I would regard it as morally questionable to write something like the second part of *Dusklands* – a *fiction*, note – from a position that is not historically complicit.'[8]

Dusklands is so strong an indictment of the violence perpetrated on the indigenous people of the Cape, and of the archival erasure of that violence in the interests of white nationalism, that to expose it from the outside would feel morally questionable. The position he places in question is the judgementalism of the outsider – an objection often levelled at British attitudes to South Africa, although English-speaking South Africans were certainly capable of this view of Afrikaners during the apartheid years.[9]

Coetzee felt this to be the case with Nadine Gordimer. In the drafts of the entry on Harold Pinter that appears in *Diary of a Bad Year*, he ruminated on the subject of writers using their cultural capital to confront others, whether writers or public figures. Pinter used the Nobel platform to confront Prime Minister Tony Blair over his actions in Iraq. Coetzee finds no comparable taste for confrontation in himself, and he attributes some of this to the after-effects of disagreements he had with Gordimer.

While he acknowledges that an essay of his comparing Gordimer with Turgenev is 'not entirely flattering', it was Gordimer, he believes, who had chosen to confront *him* in the full sense – in the 1988 controversy over the invitation to Salman Rushdie to visit South Africa, and in her review of *Life & Times of Michael K*, a novel which she 'in effect criticized for lacking in political courage'.

Behind the lingering resentment here is a sense that when Gordimer adopted the role of prophet, she went off key: it is not the *sincerity* of the position that Coetzee questions, but the fact that it was mixed with contempt:

> I always felt that Gordimer disliked and despised and (most hurtfully of all) dismissed Afrikaners, and that her dislike and contempt and dismissiveness came out of ignorance. Not that I thought Afrikaners did not merit dislike and contempt; but (I thought) only people like myself who knew them from the inside qualified to dislike and despise them in a properly measured fashion. As for dismissiveness, I don't believe that anyone deserves to be dismissed, particularly in the *de haut en bas* manner that Gordimer came to cultivate.

He adds,

> Perhaps it is a comparable sense of being dismissed – dismissed from the banquet table of history – that fuels the hatred of young Muslim nationalists for modernizers and the West.[10]

How do matters stand today? The changed dispensation in South Africa has taken the edge off the issues and the labelling has different implications. The burden of historical guilt carried by Afrikaans-speakers remains, but it is fast diminishing and it is easier to speak of the plurality of identities that has in fact always been intrinsic to the history of Afrikaans and its speakers, particularly the racial diversity of the language, the aspect that white nationalism sought to disavow. White people are in the minority as mother-tongue speakers of Afrikaans in South Africa today.

One effect of Coetzee's Nobel Prize is that prominent Afrikaner spokespersons have sought to bring him back into the fold. Kannemeyer quotes correspondence written in Afrikaans between Coetzee and a friend, the historian Hermann Giliomee, soon after the announcement was made.

'The Afrikaans press is calling you an Afrikaner. Is that true?' Coetzee replied: 'About group identity I've always said: you can't just pick and choose, you also have to be picked and chosen. If they want me, they can have me.' To which Giliomee replied: 'We really want you. You'll just have to decide: a hybrid Afrikaner (Athol Fugard), an ordinary Afrikaner or a dyed-in-the-wool Afrikaner. I myself am an otherwise Afrikaner.' Coetzee's response to this was: 'A doubtful Afrikaner, perhaps.'[11]

Giliomee's word for 'otherwise' is *dwars*, meaning 'across' or 'oblique'. Coetzee's 'doubtful', which is *twyfelagtig* in the original, could also mean 'ambivalent' or even 'dubious'. The exchange signals a rapprochement. By July 2012, when talking about his origins to a Polish audience at a graduation ceremony, Coetzee could speak confidently of being 'an Afrikaner in an historical sense'.[12]

That Coetzee has a deep relationship with the Afrikaans language is apparent from his writing. 'There are those of our people who live like Hottentots, pulling up their tents when the pasture gives out and following the cattle after new grass.'[13] The syntax here is less English than Afrikaans, in which language it might read, *Daar is van ons mense wat soos Hottentotte lewe*, or, *Daar is dié onder ons mense wat soos Hottentotte lewe*. A more idiomatic English rendering would be, 'Some of our people live like Hottentots ...' The implied Afrikaans could be appropriate to the character, but if so it is not sustained in all of the speech given to Jacobus Coetzee, and so the effect is incongruous.

It is not just any kind of Afrikaans that Coetzee is attached to, however. The code-switching Afrikaans of the Karoo farms of his childhood is what is remembered in *Boyhood*:

> Greedily he drinks in the atmosphere, drinks in the happy, slapdash
> mixture of English and Afrikaans that is their common tongue when

they get together. He likes this funny, dancing language, with its particles that slip here and there in the sentence. It is lighter, airier than the Afrikaans they study at school, which is weighed down with idioms that are supposed to come from the *volksmond*, the people's mouth, but seem to come only from the Great Trek, lumpish, nonsensical idioms about wagons and cattle and cattle-harnesses.[14]

If this is light Afrikaans, then in *Youth* it is a heavy Afrikaans that John is anxious about using on the streets of London, where it sounds like 'speaking Nazi'.[15] Throughout *Boyhood*, the natural spring that gives the farm its name (Voëlfontein, 'bird spring') is never referred to as a spring but instead as a *fountain*, the English word lexically closest to the Afrikaans *fontein*, but an 'incorrect' translation.[16] Coetzee handles the colloquial intimacies of Karoo speech that span the divide between masters and servants – the language of the women who manage the kitchen, and the farmers, farmhands and shearers who manage the sheep – with a delicate touch, as he also does in *In the Heart of the Country*. John in *Boyhood* becomes anxious when he hears the adults talking about a threat from the government to force boys with Afrikaans surnames to attend classes in Afrikaans, but this does not diminish his affection for the kind of Afrikaans spoken on the farm.

The tug of this familial Afrikaans is consistent, enduring into *Summertime*. It is strong in Margot's narrative in that book: in her inflections, idiom and jokes, and in allusions to Afrikaner intellectuals like Eugène Marais and Totius – so much so that it seems implausible that the Englishman Vincent, the fictional biographer and supposed author of Margot's text, would be able to pick up the subtleties of her speech. No mention is made of Vincent using a translator: he 'transcribes' her Afrikaans, we are told, and has a South African colleague check the Afrikaans words, but this implies that he has done the translating himself.

How, then, could this Englishman know just how appropriate it would be for her to use the term *slaughter-lamb*, which, together with *slaughter-sheep*, is not part of conversational English, at least not to the extent that *slagskaap* is in contemporary Afrikaans? Or how would he know to approximate the word order of Afrikaans in constructions like 'it has rained not a drop in the past two years', which is closer to *dit het die afgelope twee jaar nie 'n druppel gereën nie* than idiomatic English (which would typically use the noun 'rain' rather than the verb, as in 'There has not been a drop of rain in the past two years')? Similarly, the severity of 'the fault is mine' is closer to *die fout is myne* than to the equivalent colloquial English acknowledgement, 'It's my fault.' When Margot complains that there is little love in John, she says, 'And what is the point of cutting oneself free of everyone and everything? What is he going to do with his freedom? *Love begins at home* – isn't that an English saying?' It is of course *charity* that begins at home – could Vincent confect this mistake? Vincent is surprisingly adept at capturing Margot's tone of theological distress as she contemplates the decline of the farm:

> If, in God's vast, benign design, it was never intended that this part of the world – the Roggeveld, the Karoo – should be profitably farmed, then what exactly is His intention for it? Is it meant to fall back into the hands of the *volk*, who will proceed, as in the old, old days, to roam from district to district with their ragged flocks in search of grazing, trampling the fences flat, while people like herself and her husband expire in some forgotten corner, disinherited?

Such sensitivities would surely be beyond the Englishman, even if he was schooled in Thomas Hardy, a near-equivalent. The sticking point here is *volk*: to a (British) English ear, the word would refer not to the Khoikhoi, of whom Margot is speaking, but to Afrikaners themselves with their Germanic connections. It is odd that, as someone who is supposedly a cultural intruder, Vincent is able to produce such a convincingly Afrikaans Margot. Coetzee's relationship with his origins has introduced an implausible element in his representation of character.

Another version of *volk*, namely *volkies* ('little people'), was decisive in taking Coetzee to the bilingualism of his second novel, *In the Heart of the Country*. In a work renowned for anti-realism, Coetzee made surprisingly assiduous efforts to be authentic, and the Afrikaans dialogue serves that function. In the earliest drafts – which are entitled 'Home' – the dialogue is written in English. The switch to Afrikaans came ten days into the writing, on 10 December 1974, with the sentence, "'The mistress is truly an angel to her <u>volkies</u>," they say to me.' In this sentence, Magda is imagining her family speaking about her reputation among the servants. The full idiomatic sense of *volkies* is untranslatable, so Coetzee writes the sentence on the verso page in Afrikaans: 'Die mies is 'n ware engel aan haar volkies.' By August of the following year, Coetzee was writing the dialogue exclusively in Afrikaans.

That Coetzee saw himself positioning his second novel obliquely in relation to English is clear from a note that reads, '*The Story of an African Farm*. Ordentlike mense.' This refers to Olive Schreiner, whose character Lyndall is a forerunner of Magda with her surging inner life on a colonial farm. Coetzee is pointing specifically to Schreiner's inadequate grasp of Afrikaans and Afrikanerdom; Schreiner's Tant Sannie is a stereotype of a Boer woman who is easily duped by a passing Irish rogue. 'Ordentlike mense' (respectable people) is a post-imperial gesture.[17] These sensitivities around the Afrikaans touches in the text of *In the Heart of the Country* led to some steely correspondence with the editor at Secker & Warburg in London when the book was being prepared for publication.[18]

In *Summertime*, Julia puts her erstwhile white South African male lovers behind her by saying how inappropriate it is that they should think of themselves as 'the Jews of Africa', or 'the Israelis of Africa: cunning, unscrupulous, resilient, running close to the ground, hated and envied by the tribes they ruled over. All false. All nonsense.'[19] In so far as Julia's judgement of white South African men is Coetzee's – and there is good reason to believe it is – it is Afrikaners who tended to think of themselves this way, not the English. English-speaking South Africans thought of themselves unselfconsciously as world citizens, protected by an imperial past.

In an essay on 'The Great South African Novel', Coetzee remarks that English 'has a most uneasy relationship with the natural world of southern Africa'. Whereas Afrikaans has succeeded in naturalizing itself, he argues, English remains a language of '*downs* and *woods*, of *badgers* and *stoats*, of *cuckoos* and *robins*'.[20] The description is wide of the mark for the period when it was written, the 1980s, though it may have been true for the English of Coetzee's parents' generation. As with all languages when they take root in a new environment, English has been indigenizing itself for generations by means of rampant appropriations from African languages and indeed from Afrikaans, as the *Dictionary of South African English on Historical Principles* makes abundantly clear.

It would be truer to say that it is Coetzee who resists English's becoming national, a process that by the 1980s was well under way. In *Disgrace*, he puts this resistance into the mouth of David Lurie, who, when he hears Petrus speaking English, fears that 'Stretches of English code whole sentences long have thickened, lost their articulations, their articulateness, their articulatedness. Like a dinosaur expiring and settling in the mud, the language has stiffened.'[21] It is the loss of a *literary* language that Lurie fears, as English is adapted, simplified, code-switched and phonetically blended into the speech patterns of (African) second-language speakers. There is little room to move between Lurie's and Coetzee's views here: the evidence suggests that for the latter, the proper destiny of English is as an international lingua franca that renews itself through its range of reference – a local creolized English has little appeal.

What, then, is the language of the heart for Coetzee, the language of Coetzee's heart? It could be the Afrikaans of the rural Cape as it was spoken in the 1940s and 1950s. The trouble is that few people speak it any longer, and certainly not Coetzee himself.

1 JANUARY 1970
The beginning – *Dusklands*

Every morning since 1 Jan 1970 I have sat down to write. I HATE it.[1]

'1 JANUARY 1970' is a myth of origin. Asked when he started writing, more than once Coetzee has offered this date.[2] It is not true, of course. Long before then, he had written and published poetry, and well into his twenties, in the mid-1960s, he still sought a poetic career, while briefly experimenting with prose. The point of the date is that it was a moment of real crisis and self-confrontation, the origin of a resolve that has stood firm.

On that date, shortly before his thirtieth birthday, Coetzee carried out a New Year's resolution by locking himself into the basement of his house at 24 Parker Avenue in Buffalo, New York, wearing boots and a coat, and vowing that he would not emerge until he had written a thousand words. He was determined that he would write every day until he had a manuscript. The daily word-count soon came down, but the resolution held. Using materials that he had been accumulating for years, though without a clear sense of the shape they would eventually assume, he began writing what would become *Dusklands*.

Fictionalized autobiography in Coetzee actually starts here, at the beginning of the oeuvre, with *Dusklands* – not with *Boyhood*, in other words, where the genre is explicitly taken up. Coetzee's points of departure in fiction *are* his origins. They lie in his historical roots

24 Parker Avenue, Buffalo, New York, c.1970.

and in his contemporary and actual present – they are, in actual fact, himself.

Getting to 1 January 1970 involved having to overcome a series of procrastinations, a state of 'guilty self-betrayal' that took the form of at least five years of elaborate note-taking from archival sources and then a series of formalistic studies (relating mainly to Beckett) that he had begun as a graduate student in Austin, Texas.[3]

What Coetzee wrote on that date was the first salvo of a project called 'Lies', the purpose of which was to open the can of worms that came with being a white South African seeking to put his background behind him and get on with living in, or with, America. He wrote: 'Among those heroes who first ventured into the interior of Southern Africa and brought back the news of what we had inherited, Jacobus Janszoon Coetzee has hitherto occupied an honorable but minor place.'[4]

The positionality of this opening speaks volumes. The boots and coat tell us that the basement of 24 Parker Avenue was unheated. In icy, post-industrial Buffalo, Coetzee projected himself back into his warm, semi-desert home. But the homesickness, if that is indeed what it was, had soured, had become conflicted, and it is the resulting

Jan. 1, 1970
(1)

Among the heroes who first ventured into the interior of Southern Africa and brought us back news of what we had inherited, Jacobus Coetzee has hitherto occupied an honorable but minor place. He is known to students of our early history as the discoverer of the Orange River and the giraffe; but from our ivory towers we have also indulgently smiled at the credulous hunter who brought back to Governor Rijk Tulbagh those fables of long-haired men living in the far north that led to the expedition of Hendrik Hop (1761-62). Various Circumstances have conspired to maintain this stereotype and thus to hide from us the true stature of the man. The most notable of these has been the truncated account of Coetzee's exploration which has hitherto been current. This account, the work of a Castle servant who heard out Coetzee's story with impatience and wrote down a hasty précis for the desk of the Governor, has hitherto been received as definitive. *1 It records only such information as would have been of interest to the Dutch East India Company, that is to say, information about the disposition of mineral ores and about

---

**1 This, prepared by the Political Secretariat at the Castle of Good Hope on November 18, 1760, the document has been transcribed from the archives by E. C. Godée Molsbergen and published in his Reizen in Zuid Afrika in de Hollandse Tijd (vol 2 (1916)), pp. 18-22.

First draft of 'Dusklands', 1 January 1970.

confusion of feeling that gives us the true point of origin.

The origin was in fact about being betrayed by one's origins. In the spirit of Dostoevsky, the position is full of double thoughts: an accuser of some kind, unrepresented but present, lays on historical guilt; an equivocal voice replies to the accusation in a spirit of self-exculpation, a voice we hear on the surface of the text; *behind* this voice, in ironic rebellion, stands Coetzee himself: youthful, bitter, sardonic, repressing the desire for absolution, repressing the love of family.

Coetzee makes common cause with his accuser, but since he is on the *inside* of conquest, the guilt is not easily shaken off, and the culture of the forefathers is turned inside out. This is what he would have meant by the need to 'dislike and despise … in a properly measured fashion', in his remarks about Nadine Gordimer mentioned in the previous chapter.

'I have high hopes of finding whose fault I am,' says Eugene Dawn, another of *Dusklands*'s narrators. Given the scale of the mountain that Coetzee was climbing in this first work, it is not surprising that his start was delayed; what he sought had huge conceptual reach, a linking of self and history on a grand, world-historical scale.

This is apparent from his note-taking, which includes a chronology of all of colonial history, starting with Portuguese mercantile adventures in 1470 and continuing at twenty-year intervals until 1955. It includes major events and cultural transitions, starting with the Reformation and continuing with English colonial history, the founding of the settler colonies and American history. He takes notes from all the major accounts and compilations of travellers to the Cape, Namaqualand and Namibia: L. Schultze, Olfert Dapper, Willem ten Rhyne, J.G. de Grevenbroek, O.F. Mentzel, Anders Sparrman, Henry Lichtenstein, John Barrow, William Burchell, Robert Jacob Gordon, Henrik Jacob Wikar, E.C. Godée Molsbergen. He reads W.H.I. Bleek's *Comparative Grammar of South African Languages*, noting clicks and noun suffixes and making vocabulary lists in Nama. He reads G.M. Theal's *History and Ethnography of Africa South of the Zambesi*. It is in Theal that he finds the story of Jacobus Coetzee's expeditions. The

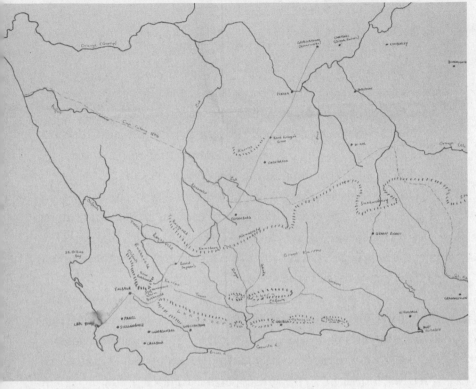

J.M. Coetzee's map of Burchell's travels in southern Africa.

account in *Youth* of reading William Burchell in the Reading Room of the British Museum is understated: in fact, he is so absorbed in Burchell that he draws a map of Burchell's journey.

Apart from the ethnography and cartography, the terrain on which Coetzee was establishing himself was the German Romanticism of Oswald Spengler, whose *Decline of the West* (1926) gave him the title of this first novel. Spengler was drawn to Goethe's idea of a life's work comprising a single great confession. Coetzee, reading Spengler, writes in the draft,

No man confesses himself with the inward certainty of absolution. As the need of the soul to be relieved of its past remains urgent as ever, all higher forms of communication are transmuted, and in Protestant countries music and painting, letter writing and memoirs, from being modes of description become modes of self-denunciation, penance, and unbounded confession.[5]

This is certainly not frivolous: all of art since the Reformation is self-denunciation, penance and unbounded confession. It is not even particularly modernist, although in formal terms the text that was emerging was avowedly so, perhaps postmodern in its playfulness.

But Coetzee was not writing *personal* confession, either of a religious or of a secular kind. Later, in the mid-1980s, he would turn his attention to the specific traditions of confessional writing with an essay on Rousseau, Tolstoy and Dostoevsky, but in this first work the introspection is directed at the problem of identity: not at the question of *who* I am, as much as that of *what* I am.

If the confession was not personal, then what was there to confess? The answer that comes from *Dusklands* is that to be a white African is to be the heir of an expansionist colonial philosophy of violence fuelled by Western rationalism and the delusion of one's own election. Coetzee's American formation could have played a role here, but Spengler, who also had Europe's African empires in mind, writes, 'The expansive tendency is a doom, something daemonic and immense, which grips, forces into service, and uses up the late mankind of the world-city stage, willy-nilly, aware or unaware.'[6] Jacobus Coetzee and Eugene Dawn, the protagonists of the two novellas that make up *Dusklands*, are intelligent and crazy people in the service of imperial cultures. Spengler writes approvingly of Cecil John Rhodes; Coetzee puts his characters into an acid bath of parody.

The point of departure in Coetzee's writing is a gesture of refusal. *Summertime* puts this more expansively: writing is 'a gesture of refusal in the face of time'.[7] There is almost a lifetime of work between *Dusklands* and *Summertime*, of course; in the later book, the confrontation with one's past is less a matter of historical guilt; nevertheless, the connection between writing and self-confrontation is consistent throughout.

⌘

To give flesh to this account, it may be necessary to fill in more of the historical background. The first Coetzee settler to arrive from the Netherlands, courtesy of the Dutch East India Company, was Dirk Couché. Later he spelt his name Coetsé – by the fourth generation in Africa, it was Coetzee.[8] Title deeds dating from 1682 show that Coetsé acquired land in what became the more patrician parts of Stellenbosch: the farm Coetzenburg (now the main sports venue of the University of Stellenbosch, and revered as the home of South African rugby) and the farm Assegaibosch in the lush valley of Jonkershoek.

In 1721 Coetzenburg passed to Dirk's son Gerrit, with whom it remained until 1753 when ownership was transferred to the town council. The name Gerrit, after the Dutch Gerard, was the dominant name in the male line of the Coetzees for the next three generations, eliding to Gert by the time of Coetzee's grandfather. It was Gert Coetzee who in 1916 bought and developed Voëlfontein, in the Koup region of the Karoo.

The Jacobus Coetzee of *Dusklands* was born in 1730, one of the second generation of Coetzees born in Africa, the son of Johannes Hendrik Coetsé and Anna Elizabeth Paal. Like his father, Jacobus was a *vryburgher*, a free burgher, a citizen-farmer no longer directly employed by the Dutch East India Company. Johannes farmed cattle to the north of the settlement, in border territory guarded by a military outpost near the present town of Piketberg. In time, Jacobus acquired a farm nearby that had belonged to an uncle, Johannes's brother Cornelius.

In 1760, at the age of thirty, Jacobus secured permission from Governor Rijk Tulbagh to explore what is now the Northern Cape, the home of the Khoikhoi. His explorations took him further than previous expeditions, across the Gariep River (also called the Great, and later the Orange, River) into what is now southern Namibia. When he brought back reports of a clan called the Damroquas living in the far north who had long hair and wore linen clothing, a follow-up expedition was commissioned under Captain Hendrik Hop, with Jacobus as guide and interpreter. Jacobus's *Relaas*, the account of his journey, was taken down by a scribe of the Dutch East India Company and signed with an X, indicating Jacobus's illiteracy.

The *Relaas* was among the documents that John Coetzee collected as a graduate student at Texas. As it happens, John is not a direct descendant of Jacobus (as the criticism has tended to assume), but he is related.[9] *Dusklands* turns the *Relaas* into 'The Narrative of Jacobus Coetzee', a collection of quasi-historical documents. They include the original text, which is subtly amended to make it conform to Coetzee's own rewriting of it; a greatly amplified, first-person version of the same text (in which we get inside Jacobus's head and witness his violence and psychological deterioration); a narrative of Hendrik Hop's journey, which is rewritten as a punitive raid on the servants who deserted Jacobus on his first journey; and an afterword, a piece of nationalist hagiography written by an entirely fictional father, S.J. Coetzee.

The rebellion against the forefathers is not obvious in the earliest drafts of *Dusklands*. Only gradually does it become apparent that Coetzee is acting as a mole, undermining the tradition while pretending to be its newest representative. The following passage from the manuscript presents a surprisingly seductive picture; writing in Buffalo, Coetzee seems to have felt the temptations of nostalgia strongly at this stage:

> Thus Coetzee on his farm had laid the foundations for another of those durable relations in which the family of the farmer and the family of the servant move slowly in parallel through time, the farmer's son and the servant's son playing <u>dolosse</u>[10] together as children, then moving into the more respectful relation of master and servant with the coming of adulthood, the servant revolving around the master for the duration of his working life, the two old men that they become stopping in the

bright sunlight to exchange a cackled reminiscence, the tipped hat, the shuffle, the grandchildren playing <u>dolosse</u>. There is no word for 'Yes' in Hottentot. To signify assent to an order, a Hottentot will repeat the last phrase of the command. Although the Hottentot language has perished, one can still hear these antiphonal conversations today on the farms of the Western Cape, in Afrikaans: 'Drive them to the north camp.' 'The north camp, my baas.' In the hollow behind the trees the huts of bent wattle branches and animal skins have disappeared, replaced by mud huts with corrugated iron roofs. These are capable of a picturesqueness of their own: smoke drifting up from the open fire, pumpkins on the roof, children with tops and no bottoms, etc. There is a principle of stability at work in history which refines from all conflicts those conformations which are likeliest to endure. The quiet farmhouse on the hill slopes, the quiet huts in the hollow, the starlit sky.[11]

Writing this must have been a matter of succumbing to the nostalgia, then reining it in, succumbing, reining in again. What Coetzee began writing was in fact S.J. Coetzee's afterword to the *Relaas*. S.J. Coetzee is the mandarin of a pioneering colonial tradition, and his afterword was first published, we are dutifully informed, as an introduction in Afrikaans to Jacobus Coetzee's Dutch text. Since the line between nostalgia and irony is faintly drawn at first, the reader of the drafts who is familiar with the published text wonders when the tension will break, when the familiar violence of the novel will erupt onto the page. When Coetzee was writing it, the position of the afterword in the collage would still have been unclear; in fact, in *Doubling the Point* he refers to it as 'a memoir', a 'contribution to the history of the Hottentots' which became 'absorbed' into *Dusklands*.[12]

The violence flares up when he begins to write Jacobus Coetzee's narrative in the first person – that is, when he gives the flimsy historical *Relaas* flesh and blood by reinventing Jacobus's voice. At this point, the sepia recollections are summarily cast aside and, instead, the ancestor speaks from a dangerous, living present.

> The days are past when Hottentots would come to the back door begging for a crust of bread while we dressed in silver knee-buckles and sold wine to the Company. There are those of our people who live like Hottentots, pulling up their tents when the pasture gives out and following the cattle after new grass. Our children play with servants' children, and who is to say who copies whom?[13]

Coetzee crafts this voice mindful of the anxieties of mid-twentieth-century Afrikaners, who fear that social distances are disappearing in the conurbations of industrial South Africa. (Apartheid was invented, after all, to force apart those who were already coming together.) Exacerbating the anxiety was the decolonization of Africa, which was the ultimate nightmare that apartheid sought to resist. Accordingly, Jacobus's equanimity topples over repeatedly, into accounts of genocidal hunting expeditions against the San (Bushmen), the rape of their women, and a punitive raid whose purpose is to murder the disloyal servants.

The assessment given to such passages in *Summertime*, written thirty years later, is that *Dusklands* 'was a book about cruelty, an exposé of the cruelty involved in various forms of conquest'. This is the judgement of Julia, an ex-lover who believes that the source of the cruelty is the author himself; in her view, writing is 'self-administered therapy', an 'unending cathartic exercise'. John of *Summertime* becomes vegetarian in an effort to expunge all forms of cruelty from his life.[14]

Julia's assessment is a form of ventriloquism on Coetzee's part. It is recognizably Coetzee's own judgement, and it is consistent with the importance of confession in his work from the start. But it is not only cruelty that is being expunged through the parody in *Dusklands*; it is also anger, because *Dusklands* is indeed an angry work, the book of a young author who is angry about his origins, and angry about the role that his origins have assigned him in the world.

Coetzee began writing in Buffalo, revisiting his South African origins. By the time he began the second novella of *Dusklands*, 'The Vietnam Project', on 11 June 1972, he was back in Cape Town. There is a tidy symmetry to this: in each case, distance facilitated a reconnection and a critique.

It was while he held an assistant professorship in English at the State University of New York at Buffalo (from 1968 to 1971, during which time he applied for other academic posts and was offered positions in Vancouver and Hong Kong) that Coetzee was arrested on 15 March 1970 and convicted of trespass along with forty-four other faculty staff in a sit-in on the Buffalo campus. The group was objecting to acting university president Peter F. Regan's management of campus conflict, especially his penchant for calling in the police to deal with demonstrators, then retreating to safety himself.

For the Americans involved, the arrest had few consequences – it could be worn as a badge of honour. For Coetzee, it was a catastrophe. He did not have permanent residence in the United States because the terms of his visa, which related to his having held a Fulbright Scholarship, required him to return to his home country. He had been trying to overturn this requirement, arguing in letters to the Immigration and Naturalization Service (INS) that his professional life would suffer and that his children, as US citizens, ought not to be forced back into a country where racist socialization was the norm. With some exaggeration he claimed that his publicly expressed opinions rendered him liable to prosecution or banning in South Africa.[15]

The arguments failed to convince the INS. With the help of university acquaintances he approached a US Senator, Jacob K. Javits, who agreed to intervene on his behalf by bringing a private member's bill to have the ruling set aside. The arrest put an end to this petition, even with the strong likelihood of an acquittal on appeal.

The fortunes of a young family hinged on this crisis. In the prevailing uncertainty, John's wife, Philippa, and the children (Nicolas who had been born in Austin, Gisela in Buffalo) flew back to Johannesburg in December 1970, while he stayed on to teach out the semester until

Maraisdal, where the Coetzees lived from May to December 1971
after their return from Buffalo, NY.

May. He gave the authorities an undertaking that he would return to serve his sentence if the appeal failed, but actually the possibility of return was receding. Having taken unpaid leave from Buffalo, rather than resigning, he joined the family and they arranged to live rent-free at Maraisdal, a smallholding near Voëlfontein in the Karoo, close to the railway siding where his grandfather had once owned a butcher's shop and a hotel.

Here Coetzee completed the Jacobus Coetzee narrative. In November 1971, six months into the stay at Maraisdal, it was still not clear what shape the book would take. He wrote to the chair of English in Buffalo saying, 'I have recently completed a book-length manuscript, in the area of African Studies, and am commencing a second, a critique of linguistic stylistics. For the present I would like to devote myself full-time to this work.'[16] He was being less than candid about his circumstances, and dressing up his novel as a tame academic exercise.

That he described the American half of *Dusklands* as a 'critique of linguistic stylistics' is revealing. He had been immersed in linguistic stylistics for some years since his studies in Austin, particularly the subfield of stylostatistics, whose computational methods measured lexical and syntactic patterns as an indication of a writer's style. In stylostatistics Coetzee sought to bring together two of his academic interests, Beckett and mathematics (or computer science), but over time he had become less and less confident about what kind of knowledge the field's scientific methods could deliver about a text, over and above what we might already know intuitively. By the time he wrote *Dusklands*, the positivism of stylostatistics had even come to seem related to the mythology of the technocrats who ran the military-industrial complex. A 'critique of linguistic stylistics' is a dramatically understated description of a ferocious parody of scientific rationalism on which he had actually embarked.

The crisis of self-confrontation that crystallized on 1 January 1970 not only involved an end to the procrastination of the earlier years; it also entailed an intellectual volte-face in which the attempt to build an academic career in the safe zone of scientific rationality came to an end. 'Counting words, playing with numbers, I was doing two things, both bad. I was postponing the day of reckoning; and I was fortifying my position in academic life.'[17]

He continued publishing academic papers on stylistics for some years, but the range of his interests widened to include Chomskyan transformational linguistics, experiments with surreal metaphors, and rhetorical studies more widely conceived. By and large, after 'The Vietnam Project' the idea of bringing science and formal analysis together was abandoned. The fictional 'Coetzee' who surfaces as Eugene Dawn's supervisor is actually an alter ego that Coetzee was trying to expel from himself: when he first appears in the manuscript, 'Coetzee' is an academic seeking tenure and, according to Dawn, 'a docile little Assistant Professor who will sign on the dotted line when he is told to'.[18]

The conflict in Dawn is between his scientific pretensions, which involve efforts to be a propaganda specialist for Armed Forces Radio, and a radical insecurity. The insecurity has no specific origin, because Dawn is a representative of a modern Western neurosis which combines reason with self-doubt, a condition whose origin is attributed to René Descartes. As the text develops, this split comes out in intensely worked, exploratory writing. There are also suggestions of a Freudian structure, with Dawn's supervisor 'Coetzee' a controlling ego and Dawn as the rambling, garrulous id. The psychoanalysis is explicit and Dawn tries to keep it 'post-Marx', meaning that the internal monologue will become more and more prominent and neurotic.

The critique of scientific positivism is bitter and clearly the product of personal investment and a subsequent feeling of wasted time. In the drafts of July 1972, Dawn hopes that his son will become an 'overdog' who knows that everything would be 'as it seems to be', that 'the identity of justice and power' resides in 'a world without Judgement'. He should be 'kept away from Christianity and its encouragement of the fantasy of a final restitution of balance'. The link between reason and cruelty is brought out with ice in the veins. In a bitter piece of parody on Coetzee's part, Dawn writes that if he were given 'three fairy wishes', he would 'spend one of them on my son, and wish for him a distinguished and uneventful career designing and testing new weapons. I would even be so specific as to predict the invention which would make a name for him: the heat-seeker, a slow-flying baby missile that homes on the beats of a human heart.'[19]

Given the philosophical position with which he began, that is, the critique of Western rationality, it is clearer now why Coetzee would never completely make peace with realism, though several later novels seek to do so, as we will see. The basis of his entry into fiction was this anti-rationalism, and a revolt against what he saw as realism's unadventurous epistemology. But the sudden interest in parody in *Dusklands*, which made sense politically and philosophically in 1970, would have had the effect of imploding some of his own long-held assumptions about the novel as a form, which, as he saw it, was an invention of the realist tradition that ran from Defoe through Flaubert, Henry James and on to Ford Madox Ford. Joyce, too, was a writer of realism to Coetzee at this stage, a psychological realism that sets about building a credible representation of consciousness, though with a mythic undercarriage borrowed from Homer. All this helps to explain why *Dusklands* is such a formally peculiar work. Coetzee was actually in rebellion against himself. He wanted to write, but how could he, when his support structures were collapsing?

There are moments in the drafts of *Dusklands* when the uncertainties surface explicitly in notes to himself. 'Like everything else in this work, [the scene in the motel room] is not taking on novelistic proportions. Everything is rendered in so short a space that it reads more like something decided on ... than something being explored.'[20] He felt that he was writing a formulaic polemic, a book impatient with the task of creating a credible world, instead of a book that was open to experience. He knew it: 'there is no social or environmental depth to it, there is nothing but the narrator'. He resorts to sarcasm: 'So, why not a massive appendix, an alphabetized list of all the people and places with heavy, solid histories and <u>descriptions</u> of them.'[21]

By the time he came to write the next novel, *In the Heart of the Country*, Coetzee was no closer to making peace with the need to produce verisimilitude. Magda is a female version of Dawn: articulate, analytical, garrulous, insecure. Her narration is a series of numbered paragraphs, a device that Coetzee used to avoid the tedium of having to flesh out the realistic details. He would continue on this path, gradually making his way towards the formal security of the third novel, *Waiting for the Barbarians*, but by then he had launched a career in which suspicion of realism's pretensions would remain a distinguishing feature.

Even as he wrote *Barbarians*, wrestling its huge invented milieu into the shape of a plausible world, he was wondering,

I have been reading Robert Alter on the self-conscious novel. He correctly observes that the important question is <u>why</u> the novel should be self-conscious. His answer is that the self-conscious novel is aware of impermanence and death in a way that realism cannot be. Maybe he is on the right track.[22]

4

KAROO

The beloved landscape – *Life & Times of Michael K, In the Heart of the Country*

I do believe that people can only be in love with one landscape in their lifetime. One can appreciate and enjoy many geographies, but there is only one that one feels in one's bones.[1]

How unfortunate, how truly unfortunate that my life will not express a happier meaning – the unthinkable contentment, for example, of a settled people in love with the land.[2]

'NIETVERLOREN' is a little-known short story in which Coetzee looks back over a lifetime of deep but troubled attachment to the Karoo, and tries to bring it to order. *Nietverloren* means 'not lost'. In the lexicon of Dutch names of South African farms it would compare with *Allesverloren*: everything lost. While *Allesverloren* evokes a wistfulness in losing everything, *Nietverloren* conveys relief at having found a home. Having risked everything, you discover that nothing has been lost after all.

These names belong to wine farms in the Western Cape, but in Coetzee 'Nietverloren' has a personal meaning that is quite different from the providential implications of the name. The farm so named in the story is not in the winelands but in the Karoo, which is the semi-desert of the country's interior plateau, embracing parts of the Western,

The Coetzee family homestead on Voëlfontein.

Eastern and Northern Cape. Once a vast inland sea, the Karoo became the domain of nomadic pastoralists and hunter-gatherers when the wetlands dried up. From the mid-nineteenth century to the present, the economy of the Karoo has been based mainly on sheep-farming.

In the drier regions of the Karoo, like the Koup, each sheep requires ten hectares of grazing for a farm to be profitable. Because the country is so barren – because the life it sustains is so elemental, because of its exquisite sunsets and, above all, because it is so silent – the Karoo creates strong attachments. For Coetzee, that is the problem. It is the kind of landscape that makes things difficult for the cosmopolitan artist-intellectual who wants to escape his natal earth and country. The story 'Nietverloren' is therefore an exorcism of sorts, in which Coetzee tries to expel the Karoo from within himself.

The story brings out some of Coetzee's earliest memories although it was written when he was in his sixties, after his emigration to Australia and years after he ceased visiting Voëlfontein. The farm provides the personal memories on which the story is based, as well as a history

of agricultural practices dating from the 1920s. The starting point
is Voëlfontein's threshing floor, which is out in the open veld, some
distance from the homestead. As with all of Coetzee's autobiographical writing, this story is told in detached, third-person narration, but
the fictionalization is thin. It begins as follows:

> For as long as he could remember, from when he was first allowed to
> roam by himself out in the *veld*, out of sight of the farmhouse, he was
> puzzled by it: a circle of bare, flat earth ten paces across, its periphery
> marked with stones, a circle in which nothing grew, not a blade of grass.[3]

From the English picture books he has read, the boy assumes that this
is a fairy circle where fairies come out to dance with sparkling rods
or glow-worms to light their way, but soon enough he dismisses this
explanation because, self-evidently, fairies could not survive the Karoo
heat. Without providing all the details, his father tells him that it was
a threshing floor.

Thirty years on, he pieces the story together from old photographs.
In one of these, two young men with rifles, deceased relatives, are
photographed going off on a hunt, while in the background a pair
of donkeys yoked together are led around the threshing floor by a
farmhand. Donkeys were used to trample wheat while the wind carried
off the chaff. He makes further inquiries: the farm used to grow not
only wheat but also fruit and vegetables in abundance. Irrigation was
led from a dam, with water pumped out of the aquifer by a windmill,
supplemented by the manual labour of farmhands.

With this information, the story builds a history of decline. The
farm of memory used to be self-sufficient: its agriculture provided
eggs, milk and meat, grain, bread, fruit and vegetables, not only for
the white family in the farmhouse but for the families of the coloured
labourers in the cottages too. After the droughts of the late 1920s and
early 1930s, subsistence farming of this kind became more difficult.
It was made redundant by the increasing availability of supplies of
groceries from shops in the nearby towns, and by the 1940s it was

The threshing floor on Voëlfontein, with the farmhouse in the distance.

replaced, as it was elsewhere, entirely by commercial sheep-farming.

Coetzee is exaggerating, actually, because these modes of farming coexisted for generations on many Karoo farms, though perhaps less so in the Koup, which is so dry. Be that as it may, Coetzee's animus begins to reveal itself in the story. The perspective shifts from memory to present-tense narration, with Bill and Jane, old friends from the United States, visiting South Africa. The speaker accompanies them on a road trip from Cape Town to Johannesburg, during which they pass through the Karoo and decide to visit a farm, the 'Nietverloren' of the title, which a leaflet found at a petrol station advertises as a resort for cultural tourism. 'Visit an old-style Karoo farm, experience old-style grace and simplicity. Only 15 km from Richmond on the Graaff-Reinet road. Luncheons 12–2.' There they are served a meal of leg of Karoo lamb with sweetened vegetables and milk tart for dessert. The hostess assures them that everything has been grown on the farm.

This ersatz Karoo prompts an outburst from the speaker, which closes the distance between the character and Coetzee himself. Proper farming – that is, tillage – he says, survives only as cultural tourism; for the rest, it is now only sheep-ranching, which in the worst cases is done from the cockpit of a helicopter. It looks modern but in reality it is a matter of putting history into reverse. Humankind is supposed to progress from hunter-gathering to nomadic pastoralism and then settled agriculture, but commercial sheep-farming is a reversion to stage two, pastoralism. Not only is the sheep-farming a reversion: when farmers start stocking their lands with antelope and zebra and inviting American and German tourists to shoot them for high fees, the land is being driven back into an even earlier phase of history.

Here we reach the point of the story: if the Karoo is no longer what it was, if it has given up its true nature, which is to be a cradle of harmony and sociability, it would be better to abandon it. Settler colonialism has lost all pretensions to good stewardship of the land. The speaker feels 'bitterness of defeated love':

> I used to love this land. Then it fell into the hands of the entrepreneurs, and they gave it a makeover and a face-lift and put it on the market. This is the only future you have in South Africa, they told us: to be waiters and whores to the rest of the world. I want nothing to do with it.[4]

'Nietverloren' doesn't simply mean *not lost*; to Coetzee it means, *in turning my back on the Karoo I have lost nothing*. Karoo farming has lost its way, and so I can move on.

Is Coetzee's historical diagnosis accurate, as it is reflected in the story? Not really. But then, he is not being entirely serious. He gives rein to a degree of outrage that deliberately distorts the whole perspective. The model of history on which the story depends is both overstated and truncated: it is based on a classical model (hunting followed by pastoralism then agriculture), but by the eighteenth century it was recognized by Adam Smith that there is a stage beyond agriculture, namely the stage of the commercial market. It is the market that supports the rise of the modern state, which is funded by taxes, whereas the form of government associated with agriculture is monarchy, sustained by patronage.

While the central character in 'Nietverloren' treats large-scale commerce as an aberration in which farmers become waiters and whores, Karoo people have in fact long since adjusted to selling their produce on the market, and the wool market has been global for many years. By the late nineteenth century, most of the wool produced in the Karoo went to mills in the north of England; in the 1950s it went to Japan; currently it goes to China. Karoo farmers have been tied to global commerce for a century and a half, even if their children grew up believing that the farms were created for their pleasure.

One meaning of Coetzee's Karoo, therefore, is that it is paradisal, a place of childhood. It is, in Coetzee's own words, 'the one place on earth he has defined, imagined, constructed, as his place of origin'.[5] *Boyhood* conveys this poignantly:

> The farm is called Voëlfontein, Bird-fountain; he loves every stone of it, every bush, every blade of grass, loves the birds that give it its name, birds that as dusk falls gather in their thousands in the trees around the fountain, calling to each other, murmuring, ruffling their feathers, settling for the night. It is not conceivable that another person could love the farm as he does.[6]

This love is alloyed because his father is not the heir to the farm and neither could he be; already it has passed from his grandfather to his uncle Son, whose son Gerald is to inherit it. Coetzee's attachment to the farm is made even more tenuous by the fact that his mother is resentful of Voëlfontein, because for part of the time her husband was up north during World War II, Vera lived with her two sons, John and David, then still a toddler, in a single rented room in nearby Prince Albert on Jack's meagre military stipend. Though Prince Albert is

Remnants of tillage on Voëlfontein, April 2012.

less than two hours' drive from the farm, an invitation never arrived, according to Vera.

Whether or not these feelings were well founded, the cramped conditions, the shortage, the heat and boredom in the room in Prince Albert marked Vera's sense of her place in the Coetzee family so deeply that John, who lived intensely in her shadow, could not help being affected by it. In *Boyhood*, the child feels a conflict of two 'servitudes': bound as much to his mother as he is to the farm, 'He has two mothers. Twice-born: born from woman and born from the farm. Two mothers and no father.'[7]

The shift in the Karoo economy that is described in 'Nietverloren' took place on Voëlfontein during the tenure of Uncle Son. *Boyhood* tells us that Son took advantage of high wool prices after the war to run more sheep, which also meant growing lucerne rather than wheat to augment the grazing. The horses were sold and the pigs became pork. John remembers the last pig being shot: 'the bullet took it behind the ear: it gave a grunt and a great fart and collapsed, first on its knees, then

Remains of the Studebaker on Voëlfontein, April 2012.

on its side, quivering.'[8] The cows and ducks followed. Son's increased prosperity became evident in the purchase of the new Studebaker that was driven to town to buy groceries and used for hunting at night, with John sitting on the dickey-seat and the occasional steenbok being caught in the car's headlights before being dropped by a bullet.

The change from general agriculture to sheep-ranching was going on around John even while he roamed about the farm reflecting on his complicated attachment to it, but in 'Nietverloren' the farm in its idyllic state is retained as the point of reference. The vision is inherently wistful and pastoral, but it is an unusual pastoralism. The point of the story is its bitterness: whatever ideal the agriculture of early Karoo farms once represented, it has been lost forever.

∞

Given his family's particular circumstances, Coetzee's relationship with the Karoo has never been proprietorial, but there is a deeper conflict that has had an impact on his writing. Coetzee loves this landscape yet has sought to detach his love from the ways it has been socialized by colonial history. On accepting the Jerusalem Prize, he spoke of a 'failure of love' in South Africa: the 'excessive talk' of the country's hereditary masters about how much they love the land is always directed 'toward what is least likely to respond to love: mountains and deserts, birds and animals and flowers'.[9] How, then, does one write that love – not write about it, so much as release it – in ways that circumvent the corrupted historical forms that it has assumed? The task is to free this love as a necessarily asocial, possibly rootless energy that brings new forms of representation into being, new ways of loving the land.

The two novels that seek to do this are *In the Heart of the Country* and *Life & Times of Michael K*. They are both Karoo novels, in which the central characters are Karoo people, but Karoo people rendered strange and estranged: the lonely, murderous Magda in *In the Heart of the Country*, and the benign outlaw Michael K.

Magda's is a story of revenge in which she, as 'die heks van Agterplaas', the witch from the back of beyond, fantasizes murdering her father for taking a new wife and for having sex with his coloured farmhand's bride. As the family patriarch, he is responsible for creating her miserable life. With him out of the way, she imagines, she will be free to explore previously prohibited forms of intimacy with the servants, but in their own ways they are just as defined and confined by the past.

Michael K, for his part, is a survivor – a prodigy, idiot-sage, clown, escape artist – whose private communion with the Karoo enables him to circumvent the myriad forms of entrapment thrown his way in the civil war that is ravaging South Africa's towns and countryside. The Karoo of *In the Heart of the Country* is primarily a social space. In *Life & Times of Michael K*, it is a natural space, in which the social-historical situation is made to appear transient.

Magda's plight is captured fluently from an early stage in the manuscripts.

My father is a big, blustering man with mustachios, insensitive to the feelings of other people. My father now has a new hostess to serve him tea (coffee?) on the front stoep, and I am not wanted. I find that I cannot get serious about my father and his treatment of me, despite the fact that tragedy is looming for him, for his bride, and for me. Tragedy is looming because I am determined that I will not forever sit here in my room taking my revenge in my diary while he and she fuck cavort in the outer rooms. When the time is ripe, when I have been adequately moved, when my rage is sufficiently motivated, I will move from suffering to action, and then we will see what I will do. So I plot and plot and whip up my feelings.[10]

To the question that Coetzee poses about the Karoo in South African art and literature in his collection of essays *White Writing* – namely, how to develop an art that is responsive to 'empty' country[11] – *In the Heart of the Country* gives the answer: the Karoo is not empty, because its social textures are subtle in their own way. The drama of the inner life is as complex in the Karoo as it is anywhere.

Magda's inner life is the substance of the narrative. Coetzee had invented her as early as 1974, soon after completing *Dusklands*, but he hadn't found all the narrative elements:

> If there is any meaning to this rudimentary life I find myself leading,
> it lies in the major relationships of that life: with my father as a late
> Victorian landowning patriarch; with my stepmother as an ambiguous
> sister-mother-seductress figure; with the land itself; with the servants
> as a feudal class.

At this early stage, the book was a proposition; a thesis, in fact; not a novel. Who the 'I' actually is at this early point is ambiguous – it could be either Coetzee or Magda:

> I am simply going to lose my thread if I try too much particularism
> of the servants, just as I will lose it if I forget myself in particular

enthusiasms about the land (the particular beauty of sheep-bells in the violet dust of the evening, the particular heat of river-sand against my thighs, to name two examples). I can bring such particularities to life only in order to sound myself against them – the sheep-bells to express a ~~prescient~~ nostalgia about the desert idyll which betrays my doubt that I have any future here.

The particularities, resonant in themselves, are really only elements 'to sound myself against'. Confession overrules representation. The end result of this approach would be the Coetzee who dispenses with scene-setting altogether. There is no realist padding in the novel at all, no *mise en scène* of the kind that would give us the outlines of a credible world. Instead, we have the numbered paragraphs, each of them springing directly from Magda's tortured mind. The numbering, Coetzee said, was 'a way of pointing to what is not there between [the paragraphs]: the kind of scene-setting and connective tissue that the traditional novel used to find necessary – particularly the South African novel of rural life that *In the Heart of the Country* takes off from'.[12]

The whole novel is meant to be this mental canvas, but there is an anomaly: the dialogue, especially the dialogue between masters and servants. Hendrik's arrival on the farm to look for some work is a good example. The following version is from the manuscript, written in the year 1974:

'Wat se soort werk soek jy?' ['What kind of work are you looking for?']

'Nee, werk, my baas.' ['Anything – just work, baas.']

'Waar kom jy vandaan?' ['Where are you from?']

'Van Armoede, my baas. Maar nou kom ek van baas Kobus, baas, baas Kobus sê baas het werk.' ['From Armoede, my baas. But now I come from baas Kobus. Baas Kobus says the baas has work here.']

'Werk jy vir baas Kobus?' ['Do you work for baas Kobus?']

'Nee my baas, ek werk nie vir baas Kobus nie, ek was by baas

Kobus om werk te soek, toe sê baas Kobus baas het werk, toe kom ek.'
['No, I do not work for baas Kobus. I was there looking for work. Then
baas Kobus said that the baas has work. So I came.']

    'Wat se soort werk kan jy doen? Kan jy met skape werk?' ['What
kind of work can you do? Can you work with sheep?']

    'Nee, baas, skape ken ck, baas.' ['Yes I know sheep, baas.']¹³

It is an authentic social record. Coetzee brings the narration back to
the subject at hand, Magda's interiority, by adding, 'How satisfying, the
flow of this dialogue. Would that all of my life were like that, question
and answer, word and echo … Men's talk is so unruffled, so serene, so
full of common purpose. I should have been a man …'¹⁴

But it is in the Afrikaans dialogue that Coetzee achieves some of
the novel's most socially challenging moments, challenges that even
Coetzee's own English translation can only approximate. Magda's
appeals to Hendrik for tenderness after being raped, for example, have
a quality of anguish in the Afrikaans that the English can't fully match.
Magda is a wild being through whom Coetzee imagines life after a
change of power. Some of this was toned down in the final version,
such as the following passage, which was edited out – appropriately,
since the demagoguery is out of place:

Now listen to me, all of you. I have good news. You are free men. <u>You
are free men</u>. I personally give you your freedom here and now. You
have nothing more to fear. Your old master is dead. If you do not
believe me, I ask you to come into ~~the~~ his bedroom and see. Yes, you
hear me right: come into ~~his bedroom, which you~~ the house, which
you have never before now dared to enter except by the back door,
with your hat in your hand – come into the house as free men and see
where he lies dead. Come and see what I have done for you and your
children. I have given you your freedom. I have destroyed your master.

    But before you begin to rejoice, hear one more thing. You know
that news of your master's death will soon reach the other farms.¹⁵

Rock formations in the Swartberg mountains of the Karoo.

When social relationships fail her, Magda attempts vertical, meta-physical ones, by writing messages in faux Spanish in white stones arranged in the veld – also a Karoo practice, though not in Spanish, and reserved for mundane purposes like the names of towns.

Despite her iconoclasm and her metaphysical yearnings, Magda is rooted in the very Karoo that drives her crazy: 'I am corrupted to the bone with the beauty of this forsaken world.' She chooses 'to die here in the petrified garden, behind locked gates, near my father's bones, in a space echoing with hymns I could have written but did not because (I thought) it was too easy'.[16] Coetzee would write other swansongs to the Karoo (in *Disgrace*, in *Summertime* and in 'Nietverloren'), but the intractable love we see in Magda would never completely let go of him.

The tillage occurring on grandfather Gert's Voëlfontein found its way into *Life & Times of Michael K*, too, the novel in which K's vocation is to be a gardener. Indeed, K's gardening is more than wage-labour; it is a mode of life and an existential principle: 'It is because I am a gardener, he thought, because that is my nature.'[17] With gardening elevated to a redemptive mode of being, it comes to stand as an alternative to political liberation in *Michael K* – the turn that cost Coetzee dearly when Nadine Gordimer reviewed the novel.[18]

The source of K's gardening is Coetzee's part-remembering and part-imagining the phase of Voëlfontein's history when grandfather Gert made the desert bloom. But there is yet another sense, equally important, in which the Karoo finds its way into *Life & Times of Michael K*, and that is in its geology. Here is K reflecting on the effect the landscape has on him as he hides in the mountains to avoid the predations of officials. Contrasting the rocky Karoo with the damp earth of Wynberg Park, where he once used to work in Cape Town, he thinks,

> It is no longer the green and the brown that I want but the yellow and the red; not the wet but the dry; not the dark but the light; not the soft but the hard. I am becoming a different kind of man, he thought, if there are two kinds of man. If I were cut, he thought, holding his wrists out, looking at his wrists, the blood would no longer gush from me but seep, and after a little seeping dry and heal. I am becoming smaller and harder and drier every day. If I were to die here, sitting in the mouth of my cave looking out over the plain with my knees under my chin, I would be dried out by the wind in a day, I would be preserved whole, like someone in the desert drowned in sand.[19]

The geology of the Karoo in *Michael K* is not just scene-setting; it is part of K's conception of himself. Some of K's most distinctive qualities as a figure of elemental freedom – elusiveness, self-sufficiency, resilience – are figured in the description of the Swartberg mountains. In the following passage from the manuscript, we see Coetzee inching his way towards discovering these qualities in K.

I had come, I thought, as far as a man could come to be by himself,
to be no trouble to others, to save himself from being swallowed in
the convulsions of the times. There was no one who had reason to
cross these plains, climb these mountains, ~~comb~~ search these rocks
to find me and ~~drag me back~~ embrace me and draw me back into the
bosom of society. There were no officials with enough time on their
hands to comb their lists ^{records} and find ~~me~~ that Michael K- is gone and
send dogs or policemen ~~and~~ in helicopters after me, to the ends of the
earth, to bring me back to face the charges of escape, flight, evasion
and absence. I have retreated and retreated and retreated, I thought,
till I am on the highest mountaintop and there is nowhere more to go
save up into the heavens. Now I am face to face at last with time …[20]

More than any other character in Coetzee's fiction, K embodies a
capacity to survive the nightmare of history. It is not fanciful to suggest
that by the time Coetzee wrote *Michael K*, the Karoo had become an
essential part of the substrate of his creativity, a key element in his
poetics.

5

'THE BURNING OF THE BOOKS'

Censorship in the life of writing

'THE BURNING OF THE BOOKS' is an unrealized novel that Coetzee began writing after *Dusklands* and before *In the Heart of the Country*. This unfinished project throws new light on the story of Coetzee's relationship with censorship.[1]

In October 1972, towards the end of his first year as a lecturer at the University of Cape Town, the university registrar sent heads of department a memo asking for a report on how the country's censorship system was affecting the academic life of the university. The report would contribute to an assessment by the Committee of University Principals, a body at least nominally sensitive to the erosion of academic freedom.

In a handwritten note sent to Coetzee, the head of the English Department, David Gillham, asked him to provide a list of banned books that he would regard as essential to his research and teaching. Coetzee responded with extraordinary thoroughness, poring over the 16,000 titles in *Jacobsen's Index of Objectionable Literature*, the standard source for such information. He returned to Gillham a detailed, tightly organized report.

He begins by explaining that 'I have subjected myself to [this] dreary and dejecting task' because 'I did not want to become an inadvertent criminal' and because 'I wanted to get a clear idea of the bounds within which I have to confine myself in my reading and teaching'. '[You] may be interested to look over the following condensation of how our censors have impoverished our lives,' he proffered.[2] At the time, he was writing 'The Vietnam Project'. He doesn't say so, but the energy Coetzee put into the report shows that what he was most concerned about was how censorship would affect his career as a writer.

The report lists banned authors and works, arranged into the categories 'American literature', 'British literature', 'South African literature in English' and 'World literature'. Among the writers whose books he would expect students to read in a course on the twentieth-century American novel, Coetzee finds William Faulkner (*Sanctuary*), Nathaniel West (*Miss Lonelyhearts*, *The Day of the Locust*), James Farrell (the Studs Lonigan trilogy), Richard Wright (*Native Son*) and Vladimir Nabokov (*Lolita*, *Ada*). Among contemporary American authors he highlights Gary Snyder (*Earth House Hold*), Norman Mailer (*An American Dream*, *Why Are We in Vietnam?*), James Baldwin (*Another Country*), Bernard Malamud (*The Assistant*), Joseph Heller (*Catch-22*) and John Barth (*The End of the Road*). He appends a further list of background reading that would be inaccessible, including authors whose works were regularly banned: Norman Mailer (four books), William Burroughs (five), Henry Miller (five), James Baldwin (five), John Updike (four), Jack Kerouac (three), John O'Hara (five), R.V. Cassill (five), Gore Vidal (two) – and twenty-one others.

That Coetzee's navigation was trained on the United States rather than Britain is clear from the detail he gives to American as opposed to British authors. On the British side he mentions John Cleland's *Memoirs of a Woman of Pleasure*, D.H. Lawrence's *Lady Chatterley's Lover* and twelve other British writers (including Christopher Isherwood, Doris Lessing, Kingsley Amis and Alan Sillitoe), without specifying the number of times they were banned. The report was an opportunity to affirm, for the anglophile Gillham, the importance of American literature in the South African curriculum: 'I am convinced, in particular, the number of works by serious American writers of our day proscribed quite emasculates any course we might offer in the twentieth-century American novel.' Given the provenance of 'The Vietnam Project', the excision of American writing would have felt like an amputation.

The list of banned South African authors includes Ezekiel Mphahlele (*The African Image*, *The Wanderers*), Richard Rive (*African Songs*, *Emergency*), Alex La Guma (*A Walk in the Night*, *And a Threefold Cord*, *The Stone Country*), Bloke Modisane (*Blame Me on History*), Peter Abrahams (*A Night of Their Own*, *Tell Freedom*, *A Wreath for Udomo*), Alfred Hutchinson (*Road to Ghana*). White writers with banned works are C.J. Driver (*Elegy for a Revolutionary*), David Lytton (*The Goddam White Man*, *The Freedom of the Cage*) and Nadine Gordimer (*The Late Bourgeois World*, *A World of Strangers*).

A 'World literature' list distinguishes past writers from present, with thirteen dead authors declared undesirable (including Nikolai Gogol, the Marquis de Sade, Maxim Gorky, Alfred Jarry, Pablo Neruda and Jean Genet) and fifteen living ones (among them Fernando Arrabal, Alain Robbe-Grillet, Italo Calvino, Carlos Fuentes and Mikhail Sholokhov).

A dispiriting picture indeed, and in his overall assessment, unsurprisingly, he accuses South Africa's Publications Control Board of stupidity – on three grounds. Firstly, it works by the rule 'If I do not understand a book, ban it'. (The Russian text of Gogol's play *The Inspector-General* was banned but the English translation was not; the French translation of Neruda's *Canto General* was banned but not the Spanish original or the English translation.) Secondly, 'If I banned a work by this writer in the past, I can ban every new publication of his without reading it.' James Farrell had fifteen novels banned on this basis, and the list of those affected includes Richard Wright, Bernard Malamud, Mary McCarthy and R.V. Cassill. Thirdly, the board bans books on the basis of their blurbs rather than their contents, the most egregious example being Gary Snyder's *Earth House Hold*: the censors are 'apparently unaware of the fact that Snyder's revolution is the neolithic revolution.'

Coetzee's position was the standard one in English-speaking, liberal circles. Its pedigree was venerable, going back at least as far as John

Milton, who said that whatever lofty ideals there might be in censorship as a way of guiding public morals, they would be undone by the fact that censors would have to be dull people taking on the 'tedious and unpleasing journey-work' of reading books they hadn't chosen to read ('ignorant, imperious, and remiss, or basely pecuniary').[3]

One of the urban legends circulating in South Africa at the time was that the censors had banned the children's book *Black Beauty* by Anna Sewell on the grounds of its title. The actual story behind the banning of *Black Beauty* is more intriguing: a consignment of books arrived by airfreight in Johannesburg of which the dustcovers, labelled *Black Beauty*, were neatly wrapped around copies of Chairman Mao's *Little Red Book*. Whoever had chosen to smuggle Mao into apartheid South Africa using this title had miscalculated. The presiding customs official decided that instead of wasting the time of his clerks on checking each book, he would embargo the lot.[4] The more blunt version of the story leaked to the liberal press, where it became an example of apartheid-era lunacy.

A year later, in October 1973, with *Dusklands* in press, Coetzee began writing his second novel. For a theme he turned to his report on censorship. He worked on 'The Burning of the Books' for a full year, but then abandoned it for what became *In the Heart of the Country*. 'Burning' was to have a similar *Götterdämmerung* atmosphere to that of *Dusklands*. In some respects, it prepared the ground for the later books, *Waiting for the Barbarians* and *Life & Times of Michael K*, by imagining a revolutionary situation unfolding in Cape Town.

'The Burning of the Books' involved a young man working as a censor, living with his mother in a flat and thinking of himself as a black beetle inhabiting a part of the city where people metamorphose into strange creatures. The mood was self-detachment, à la William Burroughs by way of Kafka. Every day the man leaves his office to go out to a shed at the port where he sees to the incineration of books from the university libraries. Lorry-loads of books arrive at a desolate place of sand, wire, wind and shredded plastic. The books that pass he stamps 'goedgekeur' ('approved'). The context is a police crackdown after an uprising; there is random violence, fires flaring on the horizon. Repression is to grow and grow until – following the line from Heinrich Heine – the burning of books turns into the burning of bodies. (The motif of incinerated corpses that we find in *Disgrace* was first developed here, so the Holocaust lies behind David Lurie's incineration of the corpses of abandoned dogs.) The man is a neutral representative of his times, a Tiresias or Prufrock, but also the corporal who runs the war in *Catch-22*.[5]

Despite being highly specific in his geography, Coetzee was troubled by what he saw as a weak sense of place in this writing. The 'senses of identity and place seem to be linked', he writes. 'That is, the person with a tremulous sense of who/what he is does not have a strong sense of where "he" is.' He worries that if he named a place without using quotation marks (like Dalton or Heston, place names in *Dusklands*), he 'would feel like an imposter or a young man trying to write a novel'. He imagines a 'great liberation to be achieved by inventing a place – a galaxy, or a Buenos Aires I confess I have never seen. There is also the possibility of "lifting" a place out of someone with a secure sense of place – Paris out of Balzac.'[6]

He would test this sense of liberation by inventing a milieu for *Waiting for the Barbarians*, though not without a struggle and not before returning to the Karoo for the second novel, *In the Heart of the Country*. The torture scenes in *Barbarians* have a precedent in 'The Burning of the Books', too: in a section headed 'The Security Police', the man watches through barred windows scenes of torture taking place in nearby offices, with electric shocks being applied to testicles, and rape.[7]

A revealing feature of the drafts of 'The Burning of the Books' is that they show again the extent to which Coetzee hadn't resolved to his own satisfaction some basic questions about the kind of fiction he was after. He writes, 'Fiction, being a serious affair, cannot accept pre-requisites like (1) a desire to write, (2) something to write about, (3) something to say. There must be a place for a fiction of apathy toward the task of writing, toward the subject, toward the means.' He proceeds to cancel out what would clearly *not* work: '(1) Fiction without a subject. (2) Fiction whose sole subject is apathy toward the notion of a subject. (3) Fiction whose subject is solely an occasion for apathy toward it.' He then hits on a practice that *would* serve him throughout his career: '(4) The possibility of rewriting another novel (*Le rouge et le noir*?), or of making that rewriting into the subject of your own writing.'

For this procedure to work it would be simpler, he notes, if the original text was schematic, like a fable, something 'heavily dependent on turns in the action, which can then be investigated in all their possibilities. (The whale swallows Jonah, The whale does not swallow Jonah ...). "The Garden of the Forking Paths" [Borges]. *The House of Assignation* [Robbe-Grillet]. Chinese novels.'[8] A 'synoptic' structure interests him most, something 'that allows a variety of variegated episodes, perhaps parodic. Episode: a girl comes into Sigmund Freud's rooms and tells him her problems. He diagnoses. Episode: ... And then perhaps at a certain stage the episodes start to be mixed. And their relations start to become apparent. (But how does one know beforehand that they will have relations?)'[9]

Novels by Coetzee that rewrite other novels are *In the Heart of the Country* (Schreiner's *The Story of an African Farm*), *Foe* (Defoe's *Robinson Crusoe, Roxana*), *The Master of Petersburg* (Dostoevsky's *The Possessed*). The technique of episodic patterning, in which events are turned around and explored from different angles, he would soon take up in *In the Heart of the Country*: the father returns home with a new bride, the father then steals the bride of his black farmhand, and so on – an axiomatic approach to narrative that would have appealed to the mathematician in Coetzee.

Despite the boldness of the project in exploring the mood of its times, Coetzee abandoned 'The Burning of the Books' because he could not find a coherent focus: 'There must be a myth behind it,' he realizes. 'When I think of a story with the kind of shape that *Ulysses* or *Molloy* have, I sense possibilities, which are given by the shape of the wanderings, tests and perils. On the other hand, when I think of the story of a man sitting and censoring books, my heart sinks.'[10]

∞

The last manuscript entries for 'The Burning of the Books' are from October 1974. A month later, Coetzee took the extraordinary step of applying to be a censor himself. What possessed him to do this?

In correspondence with Peter McDonald many years later, he explained that he wanted to call the censors' bluff. Applications had been invited for 'suitably qualified persons', which Coetzee took to be 'code for sharing the government's view of the world'.[11] A parodic gesture, then? Possibly. The explanation is not entirely convincing, though, because, as the application came so soon after abandoning his novel on this very subject, it seems more plausible that he thought that if he were *engaged* as a censor, he might find the position useful, no matter how distasteful. If his purpose was more obscure than this suggests, or less instrumental than the notion that some first-hand experience might be good research, it remains extraordinary in showing the lengths to which he could go in arranging for life to imitate art – even at the risk of incurring immense opprobrium from the liberal establishment.

In November 1974, under the sardonic headline 'Censors Wanted', the *Cape Argus* reported that the Ministry of the Interior, then presided over by the conservative Dr Connie Mulder, had invited nominations for candidates for appointment to a reorganized censorship system. On 23 November Coetzee sent a po-faced letter to the Secretary for the Interior requesting the relevant forms.[12] He duly applied and later received a response dated 17 March 1975, informing him without explanation that his application had been unsuccessful.[13] There would be little point in speculating what Coetzee might actually have done if the application had proved successful, because, judging by the context, it never could have been.

Following the first banning of an Afrikaans novel, André Brink's *Kennis van die Aand* (*Looking on Darkness*), and after a commission of inquiry led by Jimmy Kruger, a 1974 Act of Parliament replaced the Publications Control Board with a Directorate of Publications, based in Cape Town. The new system was a devolved structure of panels that were intended to be more representative, with a Publications Appeal Board sitting in Pretoria. It was these panels that were to be filled by nominations, for which Coetzee had applied. Under pressure from the Afrikaner churches and the security establishment, the new system was more draconian than the previous one, its aims being to uphold a 'Christian view of life', using as yardstick 'the median of standards in the community' as 'represented by the average decent-minded, law-abiding, modern and enlightened citizen with Christian principles'.[14]

McDonald shows that the approach adopted in the legislation was expressly anti-elitist, granting literature no special status. In fact, Judge J.A.H. Snyman, who presided over the Publications Appeal Board, insisted that the directorate was concerned only with 'reading matter' and the Act stipulated 'that the members of the committees would be appointed "by reason of their educational qualifications", which … meant that the "approach must be that of the educationist, not of the literary scholar"'.[15] If Coetzee thought he might be able to call the censors' bluff because he held a PhD in linguistics and literature and was proficient in English, Afrikaans and several European languages, and was therefore eminently qualified, he was mistaken.

In the event, the new system was more concerned about the security of the state than about the morals being purveyed in the literature that came off the country's presses, or that arrived at its harbours and airports (although obscenity always remained a source of concern). The era of the directorate, which was in place by April 1975, was the most politically repressive in the history of the system: the number of submissions went up dramatically, thanks to the watchful efforts of the police, who were responsible for fifty per cent of the 2,520 submissions in 1978, followed by customs officials, who submitted thirty-two per cent.[16] Despite Snyman's disparagement of the literary elite and the overall tilting of the system towards control over political agitation, the panels that scrutinized literary publications did include a number of writers, mainly of Afrikaans, and academics who were socially connected or affiliated to conservative institutions.

It was following another banning of a work by an Afrikaans author, Etienne Leroux's novel *Magersfontein, O Magersfontein!*, in 1978, and after a long fracas, that the system's attention again became focused on literature. A special advisory panel was introduced which, as it happened, consisted largely of people who were already working for the system without being given special status. It was this group, under the chairmanship of Professor H. van der Merwe Scholtz, that made the decisions that determined the fortunes of Coetzee's early fiction under censorship from 1976 on. In 1980, when J.C.W. van Rooyen, a professor of criminal law at the University of Pretoria, replaced Judge Snyman as chairman of the Publications Appeal Board, another era began in which the criterion of judgement shifted from the average decent-minded citizen to the most likely consumer of a particular work. On this slightly more sophisticated basis, during Van Rooyen's regime there was some liberalization, although the field was still rife with contradictions. Coetzee, who came later than his compatriots André Brink and Nadine Gordimer, was treated lightly.

Dusklands came out in 1974, when Coetzee was writing 'The Burning of the Books', also the year of his odd flirtation with becoming a censorship apparatchik. *Dusklands* slipped through the net, possibly because its design and marketing made it seem innocuous, and possibly because the entire system was under review in 1974. Nonetheless, Coetzee became concerned after abandoning 'Burning', and once he was sufficiently into writing *In the Heart of the Country* to be able to see the shape that it was assuming, because on 27 June 1975 he wrote to Peter Randall at Ravan Press, the publisher of *Dusklands*, saying,

I am working on a book-length fiction which, if published in South Africa, might conceivably be banned on one or both of the grounds that (1) it impairs good race relations, (2) it is obscene etc.

(a) Assuming that Ravan Press were interested in publishing the book, and assuming that I had no objections, would you be prepared to submit the MS to the Publications Control Board for scrutiny? And if they asked for cuts, what would you do? (b) If you were not prepared, in principle, to submit any MS to the PCB, would you be prepared to publish a book which, although in your opinion of literary merit, stood a good chance of having official action taken against it? To what extent would considerations like these influence your decisions on form of publication, size of printing, etc. To what extent would the (presumably beneficial) repercussions of banning on overseas publication and sales enter into consideration? In other words, to what extent would such a risky act of publishing have to be insured by prior agreements with publishers overseas? (There is a moral tightrope one has to walk here.)

Please be assured that these questions are exploratory only, and that all I want is some kind of understanding of the economic realities of your position.[17]

He was, in reality, much further away from completing the manuscript than the letter implies. Some of its most intense scenes involving interracial sex – which the censors would be most interested in – had still to be written. He was anticipating difficulties that lay ahead, but judging from the manuscript, he seems to have continued undeterred.

Clearly, as early as mid-1975, before he had completed the second novel, censorship was a factor in a web of interrelated issues that he was pondering, including the economics of publishing and his position in relation to local and overseas readerships. He raises the question of a foreign market gingerly with Randall, suggesting that an agreement with an overseas publisher might be advantageous in the event of a ban. He had tried to interest publishers in London and New York in *Dusklands*, but without success. The ideal arrangement would have been to publish in Britain and the United States but with a local edition, preferably by a South African publisher or at least a multinational publisher with a local imprint. Elsewhere this is straightforward: rights are sold on a regional basis and, in theory, all parties come away satisfied, but in the South Africa of the mid-1970s the situation was more complicated, as the publishing history of *In the Heart of the Country* reveals.

The option Coetzee broached with Randall proved to be unworkable, and the situation more complex. Ravan was very much a local, non-commercial and oppositional press, and as such it was willing to take risks if it felt that a book mattered. The London publisher that took on *In the Heart of the Country*, Secker & Warburg, was willing, initially at least, neither to forgo the South African rights, nor to distribute it in South Africa properly if there was a threat of the book being banned. Coetzee was facing Catch-22. A tortuous negotiation developed in which Secker and Ravan walked the 'moral tightrope' that Coetzee refers to in his letter, balancing political calculation on one hand and profitability on the other.

In addition to the financial and moral issues, there was a third factor that soon entered the picture, and this was linguistic: early on in the writing of his manuscript, Coetzee had decided to switch from a wholly English text to one in which there were passages of dialogue written in Afrikaans. Aesthetically, and ethically, this was the right decision: the book deals with the entanglements of master–servant relationships, their barriers and intimacies, the textures of which could be properly reflected only in Afrikaans. During the course of drafting, his practice became to write the text first with Afrikaans dialogue, and then later, while correcting the first draft, to add the English translation on the verso side of the notebook. He stuck to this course, postponing the implications of having to have different editions for different readerships, doubtless because he imagined that an arrangement ought to be feasible with English and bilingual editions appearing side by side. In practice, however (again, initially), Secker wanted it both ways: a single-language English edition *and* the South African market. When the two manuscripts were complete, one in English and the other bilingual, Coetzee wrote to Celia Catchpole of the Murray Pollinger agency in London, which had secured the deal with Secker, to broach the subject of different editions. There is no doubt about which course of action he preferred:

> Besides the version of the novel I sent to you, I have a second version … in which all the dialogue, constituting perhaps 10% of the text, is given in Afrikaans, in a *patois* which stands in roughly the same relation to literary Afrikaans as the speech of Faulkner's crackers and poor Negroes to literary American English. In preparing the English text I was unable to find a stylistic variety which was non-regional and yet had a rural, traditional flavor; I therefore translated it into a rather colourless colloquial English. For this reason, and for other reasons, I prefer the mixed or bilingual version to the English version, though it is obviously unsuitable for publication anywhere but in this country.[18]

Secker acceded to Coetzee's wishes, allowing Ravan to bring out a local bilingual edition, but only nine months after its own English edition had been on sale in South Africa and with other conditions attached: not only should the Afrikaans be restored, but the entire text should be reset, or otherwise Secker would expect proportionate compensation.

Despite professions of goodwill on the part of Tom Rosenthal at Secker & Warburg, it was a colonial arrangement, and it is not surprising that Coetzee would reflect on this ruefully at the time in an interview with Stephen Watson, saying, 'we're in a colonial situation in that, so to speak, our literary products are flown to the metropolitan centre and re-exported to us at a vastly increased price. And this goes for me, it goes for almost any writer in this country today.'[19] It seemed to Coetzee that the price of reaching an overseas market was to have to give up the local one. For the next four novels he would resist this pattern, assisting Ravan's efforts to retain South African distribution rights. At the time *Life & Times of Michael K* was published, Rosenthal told Ravan that the economics of publishing made it necessary for Secker to have the rights to the South African market. When Coetzee was informed of this, he immediately offered to phone Rosenthal 'to throw Tom's moral rhetoric back at him'.[20]

As if Secker's conditions were not bad enough, their actions over the question of censorship proved to be even worse. Ravan and other dissenting publishers like Taurus, Ad Donker and David Philip risked the little means they had in order to get important books out, but with the Publications Control Board and, later, the directorate and the Publications Appeal Board looming over them, it was always a case of publishing beneath a guillotine.[21] One had to be nimble, to publish quietly and quickly, avoiding the commercially high-profile channels of distribution for politically sensitive books, and nurturing relationships with independent bookstores.

While Ravan was still preparing its bilingual edition, Alison Samuel of Secker sent copies of two UK reviews and a publicity notice to South African newspapers in advance of its consignment of two hundred copies of its English edition, which of course they hoped would sell quickly. Oblivious of the intricacies of Ravan's situation, the publicity trumpeted the fact that they were publishing a book that would interest the censors. The press obliged, naturally, with sensational reports, including one in *Weekend World* in which it was broadcast that Coetzee's 'sex-across-the-colour-line' novel contributed to 'calls for the scrapping of the Immorality Act and Mixed Marriages Act'.[22] The obvious conclusion, correctly drawn by Hermann Wittenberg, is that Secker sought to sensationalize in order to ensure better sales for their international edition while conveniently seizing the moral high ground.[23]

Peter Randall and Coetzee quickly entered into a damage-limitation exercise, exploring pre-emptive measures that could be taken in the face of what seemed to be an imminent banning. In the event that the censors objected to scenes of interracial sex, Ravan would publish a text with some of these scenes blanked out, so that the reader would know that the text had been expurgated, a practice that opposition newspapers had begun to adopt when faced with the banning of reports of police action. The novel's structure facilitated this solution because it consists of 266 numbered sections. Coetzee suggested three deletions, each having to do with sexual violence: section 206 (which would leave

43 blank lines), section 209 (32 lines) and section 221 (4 lines). Even with the deletions, readers would be able to gauge from contextual clues the kind of narration that was omitted. So Coetzee and Randall hung on, waiting to see what would happen to the Secker edition before Ravan produced theirs.

In the event, the book was passed by the censors and the un-expurgated, bilingual Ravan edition could go to press. Because the London edition was selling well in South Africa, Ravan's print run was reduced from a thousand to seven hundred copies. Before it came off the press there were other difficulties, including a major typesetting error in which the numbering was omitted and had to be restored. More significantly, Randall was served with a banning order, which meant that he had to relinquish his position as day-to-day manager and publisher at Ravan. His banning had nothing to do with the novel, which would have been a minor part of his role at Spro-cas, the Study Project on Christianity in Apartheid Society, of which the press was an offshoot. Mike Kirkwood, who had been a lecturer in English on the Durban campus of the University of Natal (where *Dusklands* had been boldly prescribed in 1975), took over from Randall as Ravan's publisher. Kirkwood, in turn, launched the well-known *Staffrider* magazine and a related *Staffrider* series of literary books while continuing to develop an impressive list of publications in social history and sociology. Kirkwood and Coetzee worked closely together until and including the publication of *Foe* in 1986, with Ravan bringing out local editions in their own covers of books produced by Secker & Warburg in London.

The story behind the censors' taking a benign view of *In the Heart of the Country* is remarkable. Coetzee's widely shared but stereotypical assumption that the censors were all dull, dark-suited bureaucrats has turned out to be erroneous, now that the censorship archives have become publicly available. Peter McDonald has shown that the committee that reviewed *In the Heart of the Country* consisted of two university academics (a retired professor of Semitic languages, F.C. Fensham, and H. van der Merwe Scholtz, mentioned earlier, a professor of Afrikaans and a colleague of Coetzee's at the time in a neighbouring department at the University of Cape Town) and a prominent writer, Anna M. Louw, whom Coetzee had met socially. All three readers admired the book's literary strengths, explicitly downplaying the obscenities and the transgressive sex in their reports in order to recommend unanimously that it be passed.

Louw went as far as to rework her censor's report into a book review for *Die Burger*, the Cape Town Afrikaans daily, in which she praised the novel as 'the book of the year'. Without being aware of its genesis, obviously, Coetzee even sent this snippet, based on the Secker edition, to Ravan for their blurb, so that, as Wittenberg aptly puts it, 'Inadvertently, the voice of the censor thus insinuated itself into the very book that it was subjecting to scrutiny, thereby forming a bizarre and insidious circuit of simultaneous repression and endorsement.'[24] The censors' evident understanding of their role as guardians of the literary while simultaneously serving the interests of the state, their use of aesthetic universalism in the service of a totalitarian system, is an irony of the apartheid era that unhinges the certainties of liberal views of how censorship usually works.[25]

Coetzee's negotiations with his publishers in both London and Johannesburg prior to publication are equally revealing. As a solution to the problem of risking a financial loss in the event of a ban, Coetzee proposed that a typescript of *In the Heart of the Country* be submitted to the censorship directorate for approval in advance. Randall was reluctant to countenance this idea for any of Ravan's books on the grounds that it amounted to collusion; and at Secker & Warburg, Alison Samuel and Tom Rosenthal were equally unreceptive.

So what was Coetzee thinking? He had a sharp exchange of letters with Samuel (who promptly handed all the negotiations over to Rosenthal) about the tactics of bringing the book out in South Africa. Coetzee points out to Samuel that the authorities are only too pleased if writers and publishers censor themselves by refusing to take risks. The censors are reluctant to ban literary books because there 'is invariably an unpleasant hullabaloo in the press, the size of the hullabaloo depending on the newsworthiness of the writer'. (He would have had in mind the fuss over the banning of André Brink and Etienne Leroux.) The press, he tells her, both English and Afrikaans, 'is pretty much united on the issue of censorship of serious literature', and self-censorship, he adds, 'places both Seckers and myself in an untenable moral position'. He questions the advice that Secker had taken from Heinemann South Africa, Secker's distributors, on the grounds that Heinemann's stake in the local textbook market made them unreliable. He reiterates his insistence that 'the book be placed before the censors', and 'If you are not prepared to take [this step], I will have to take it myself'.[26]

Rosenthal replies to this in conciliatory tones, insisting that Secker's position is one not of self-censorship but simply of financial prudence. In their view, since the book deals with miscegenation, 'the ultimate moral crime in the republic', it would be unwise to submit it to the directorate. He supports this view by referring to their experience with James Michener's *The Drifters*. Michener generally sold well in South Africa, but since *The Drifters* included an interracial relationship, they had submitted the book 'to the censorship boys in the hope that they would get too bored by the book's length and not reach, as it were, the dirty bits'. The strategy failed and the book was banned, although the ban was later overturned when a Corgi paperback edition was shipped in and sold well before being noticed.

Notwithstanding these efforts to dissuade Coetzee, Rosenthal concludes by saying that if he still thought it necessary, they would submit the book to the censorship directorate, but his own preference would be to get the book reviewed and make it possible for small quantities to be sold, or for individuals to order it.[27] In the end, this was the course of action that Secker embarked on, but only after Coetzee had appealed for a more nuanced view, pointing out the contradictions of the system, including the fact that the board had passed Brink's *'n Oomblik in die Wind* (*An Instant in the Wind*), which included interracial sex. Part of Coetzee's rejoinder is steely.

Finally, I must say that I will find myself placed in an unacceptable position if a situation arises in which the book is neither banned nor available in this country, while no moves are occurring in any direction, i.e. a position of stalemate. If the book is not going to be available in the only country in which it really attains its full significance, I must at least have the comfort of knowing that I am not responsible.[28]

A week after writing this letter, Coetzee played a very surprising card. Through Elsa Joubert, the writer well known for *Poppie Nongena*, he had managed to have the typescript of *In the Heart of the Country* read by her husband, Klaas Steytler, 'who doubles as a publisher and a member of one of the panels of the Directorate of Publications (the office of the censor)'. 'Mr Steytler says that in his opinion the book will be passed for distribution in South Africa. He advises that a copy be placed before the Directorate as soon as possible. He advises prompt action in order not to put the Directorate in a position in which it feels itself under any pressure, a maneuver which he regards as counterproductive.' Coetzee suggests that Tom Rosenthal make the arrangements as soon as possible through its local distribution agent, adding, 'If on the other hand you decide not to, I assure you that I will not go on pressing.'[29]

After this, Randall agreed reluctantly to submit the book to the directorate; initially, Rosenthal seemed to relent, too, because on 20 June 1977 he instructed his South African representative to proceed as Coetzee had proposed.[30] A week later, however, he must have had second thoughts, because he reversed his decision, writing on 28 June to Coetzee to say that he still preferred 'the least evil of all worlds': he would not submit the book to the censors, but instead would ship out review copies followed by a small consignment (the two hundred), hoping that these would sell and that the bookstores would order more. The 'least evil' of the options clearly included selling as many books as possible before the censors noticed, but Rosenthal was finding it difficult to make a profit and at the same time keep his conscience clean: 'I find the overall circumstances of publishing and selling in South

Africa so painful that I would not think it right to take any money from Ravan, but of course Ravan must recompense you properly.'[31]

Less than a fortnight later, the problem was taken out of his hands: his consignment was embargoed at Johannesburg airport. Customs stepped in where he had demurred, by sending the book to the censorship directorate. 'I am afraid the censorship boys have already struck on *In the Heart of the Country*,' he wrote on 19 July, 'and the book has been embargoed, so no one quite knows what will happen from now on.'[32]

How do the approaches of Rosenthal and Coetzee compare, before the state took charge? Rosenthal's phrase 'the censorship boys' is significant. In one of his early letters, when the relationship involved more courtship than business, Rosenthal recommended to Coetzee the novels of Tom Sharpe, especially *Riotous Assembly* and *Indecent Exposure*.[33] Sharpe's characteristic note in dealing with the apartheid regime was that of farce. Officials are buffoons, in Sharpe's world. By contrast, Coetzee's approach was tactical; he speaks without irony of the assistance of 'Mr Steytler'. Is this compromise? It would seem so, but from another point of view it is a case of being willing to confront the beast in its lair. Applying to be a censor, submitting work for approval rather than engaging in self-censorship, acting on inside information: these moves on Coetzee's part come from an intimate but deadly struggle with the beast. On his return to the country, Coetzee seems to have come to terms with the fact that living in South Africa meant having to make deals with the devil, but this was not going to deter him from doing what he felt most compelled to do.

During the Van Rooyen era, when the censorship regime was mildly liberalized – the official line became that decisions were based on the most likely consumer, rather than the fiction of the average citizen – Coetzee was approached by the Directorate of Publications to assist them in making a decision about William Burroughs's novel *Cities of*

the Red Night. He must have been known to members of the board as an Americanist. The request would have come, we now know, from Afrikaans-speaking literary academics who felt that Burroughs was beyond their ken. Coetzee agreed to help. He must have thought that he was already neck-deep in the system and that if his opinion led to a book's being passed, this would be preferable to keeping his conscience clean at the cost of its being banned. The reasoning is not difficult to construe, but the tone of the communication with the directorate is revealing.

In his report on Burroughs, he finds he is unable to summarize the contents because the novel 'is structured in a deliberately modernistic or avant-garde way and does not follow a narrative line' – and simplifying – 'for convenience it may be thought of as a set of interweaving fanta- sies revolving around biochemical poisoning and coloured by para- noid fears of global psychological/political control'. There are scenes that could be construed as obscene, he notes, that describe homosexual intercourse; nevertheless, 'I do not regard the book as undesirable' because the book is 'neither erotic nor pornographic'. Its spirit is, if anything, 'one of despair and disgust'. This is a function of Burroughs's vision, which is that of a materialistic universe in which 'everything is permitted' (Dostoevsky's phrase), leaving people to prey on one another. Burroughs's fascination with drug addiction stems from his view that values are determined by nothing more than 'bio-electrical transfers in the brain'.

At this point, Coetzee's assessment takes an interesting turn: although Burroughs is regarded as a significant writer, 'perhaps the major prose writer of the generation of the 1950s in the United States', Coetzee can't endorse this opinion 'because he has been repeating himself for the past twenty-five years'. The judgement has everything to do with the fact that after 'The Burning of the Books', Coetzee could not find a use for Burroughs in his own work. We know that the censors, in their role as 'the literature police', saw themselves as protecting aesthetic value; no doubt this is why they were reluctant simply to ban the novel, knowing Burroughs's reputation. Coetzee's contribution to their thinking was to say, in effect, the work does *not* have universal significance, but nevertheless *do not ban it*.

Having been cooperative, up to a point, he concludes by declining payment, writing, 'I am not convinced that the system of publications control we have is a desirable one, and do not wish to become part of it.'[34] He received a fraternal reply from the relevant official (a certain Professor A. Coetzee, as it happens), thanking him for his report and adding, 'I understand your point of not wanting to become integrated into the publication control system, although naturally, I have different views on the matter.'[35]

In the course of the 1980s, Coetzee was inclining to the view that censorship was not simply an instrument of control in the hands of the state, though it was that, too; it was an impulse, a reflex, something that had come to affect and infect the entire culture. It was this point of view that he began to develop in the essays that would be collected in *Giving Offense* (1996). Instead of writing about the pros and cons of censorship, he chose to explore its stupidity, and 'the dynamic of that stupidity, a dynamic which dictates that instead of becoming more and more pointed and conclusive, debates about censorship should become more and more dull and heated and endless.'[36] The impatience is a form of self-reproach. It continued for nearly two decades until, in the years of apartheid's last gasp, it was exacerbated by the public disagreement with Nadine Gordimer over Salman Rushdie's proposed visit to South Africa.

Salman Rushdie had accepted an invitation to a book festival in Cape Town at which he would appear with Coetzee as a fellow Booker Prize winner to discuss censorship. On 31 October 1988, in a theatre packed with an audience starved of literary celebrity by the cultural boycott of apartheid South Africa, which was by then just beginning to wind down, onto the stage walked Coetzee, not with Rushdie, but with Gordimer. She was, in fact, there to explain Rushdie's absence, and this became the evening's cause célèbre. *The Satanic Verses* had appeared on 26 September in London; it was soon banned in India and elsewhere; extracts had been faxed to Cape Town; the organizers of the festival – COSAW (the Congress of South African Writers) and the *Weekly Mail* – had been asked by local Muslim leaders to cancel Rushdie's visit under threats of violence. The organizers acceded to this demand and the invitation was withdrawn.

Into this electricity Coetzee spoke, arguing that Rushdie knew exactly what he was taking on by writing the novel; he might have been informed of the risks, including that of an unreconstructed police force stepping back to enjoy the spectacle of an attack on the left by a black religious minority; it was wrong for the organizers to project a united front at the price of acceding to the demands of fundamentalists; the organizers had, in fact, connived in a new form of censorship, and by doing so they had violated a key principle of *The Satanic Verses*, and of their own craft, namely, the protean qualities of writing, which could be taken as a model of freedom which fundamentalists of all kinds – in their insistence that after the one Book there were to be no more books – would do everything to suppress.

He was at pains to say that the problem was not specifically Islamic fundamentalism, but fundamentalism in general: 'We know about religious fundamentalism in South Africa. Calvinist fundamentalism has been an unmitigated force of benightedness in our history. Lebanon, Israel, Ireland, South Africa, wherever there is a bleeding sore on the body of the world, the same hard-eyed, narrow-minded fanatics are busy, indifferent to life, in love with death.'[37] Instead of assembling to discuss censorship, he continued, everyone present ended up being party to it, in an event that had re-institutionalized it in the name of an elusive democracy.

Coetzee also said that he was willing to accept the good faith of COSAW and the *Weekly Mail* in several respects, such as their genuine concern for Rushdie's safety, their diplomatic naivety in risking a snub, the fact that no one had thought of saying to Rushdie, 'we will do everything in our power, our limited power, to ensure your safety. You understand that we cannot call on the assistance of the police.'[38] But what he could *not* accept, he said, was that the writers' union had given everyone the full story:

> I believe, and will continue to believe, until I am otherwise convinced, that some kind of trade-off took place in a smoke-filled room, some kind of calling-in of debt, some kind of compromise or bargain or settlement in which the Rushdie visit was given up for the sake of unity of the anti-apartheid alliance and in particular for the sake of not making life too difficult for Muslims in the alliance.[39]

The goodwill of the Muslim fundamentalists had become a pawn in the struggle with the state, which had moved quickly to ban the novel, thus presenting itself as the protector of minority interests.

Unusually, for Coetzee, he found himself saying exactly what his audience wanted to hear: they were on their feet applauding. Soon afterwards, however, everything changed: the *fatwā* was declared in Iran and the seriousness of the threat was confirmed. Two years later, Coetzee said, 'In retrospect I think Gordimer, in her prudence, was right, I was wrong.'[40]

Gordimer's contribution to the evening was to give an account of the negotiations in which she had been a participant. By and large, in retrospect, she dispelled the idea of a deal struck in a smoke-filled room, but in the heat of the moment Coetzee's detached position seemed more principled; Gordimer's, from inside the discussions, seemed tainted by them. Twenty-five years later, one might open the question for a different kind of scrutiny: in the light of the willingness of the African National Congress (ANC) government to reimpose press censorship, perhaps Coetzee's warning was prescient in pointing to dangers that lay ahead. That view would exonerate his intervention in hindsight. But a less complimentary observation is also possible here: there is a contradiction between Coetzee's willingness to strike a deal when it came to the publication of his books, and his unwillingness to accept the compromise made by the progressive alliance of the 1980s over Salman Rushdie's visit.

∞

In 1996 Coetzee published *Giving Offense: Essays on Censorship*, a collection of twelve loosely related essays taking as their point of departure the changing context of South Africa's censorship laws. The volume describes the legal framework, its permutations and effects, and tracks the fortunes of André P. Brink and Breyten Breytenbach in their encounters with the system. The perspective is also international, with essays on pornography, D.H. Lawrence, Osip Mandelstam, Alexander Solzhenitsyn and Zbigniew Herbert. The most autobiographical of the essays – the one most revealing of Coetzee's own position – discusses the dilemmas of taking sides in dim-witted debates. At its heart lies a strange choice of interlocutor: Desiderius Erasmus, whose *The Praise of Folly* gives Coetzee a model, or perhaps anti-model, of how to cope in a climate of contagious idiocy.

Coetzee's argument throughout *Giving Offense* is described by McDonald as 'anti-rationalist', meaning that instead of laying out the case against censorship, for which there is already a voluminous literature, Coetzee seeks 'to understand a passion with which I have no intuitive sympathy, the passion that plays itself out in acts of silencing and censoring'. The intriguing line is that he wishes 'to understand, historically and sociologically, why it is that I have no sympathy with that passion'.[41]

'Historically and sociologically' gives a strange emphasis: what drives Coetzee more than anything else in the book is what it means intellectually (but also affectively and psychically) to live with, and under, censorship – what its effects are on the creative life of the writer. In *Giving Offense*, Coetzee tries to gain control over a volatile and distasteful problem that beset the early phase of his career; after its publication there were further perplexities, although no threats, when the apartheid-era censorship archives were revealed.

The essay on Erasmus is a meditation on what it is like to be a public intellectual in a time of violence, when reason is subordinate to contagion. It reflects on the difficulties of crafting a position out of a distrust of *all* prevailing positions, and out of the self-doubt that infects someone who fears that success, in such a climate, can only come at the price of abandoning one's principles. Coetzee turns to the figure of Moria in *The Praise of Folly* because he admires Erasmus's efforts to develop a metaphor and style of argument that fall outside the culture's own ideas of seriousness. The potential he sees in Moria lies in her sexualized mockery:

> What is *to take a position*? Is there a position which is not a position, a position … in which one knows without knowing, sees without seeing? *The Praise of Folly* marks out such a 'position', prudently disarming itself in advance, keeping its phallus the size of the woman's, steering clear of the play of power, clear of politics.[42]

The project was to craft an anti-political polemic against censorship. This purpose is one that comes from a writer who had not been forced to confront the system in the heat of battle, but who felt that he had been tainted. He says as much: 'I regard it as a badge of honor to have had a book banned in South Africa,' one he has 'never achieved, nor, to be frank, merited'. Apart from coming too late for the worst of the censorship era, 'my books have been too indirect in their approach, too rarefied, to be considered a threat to the order'.[43]

This helps to explain why, in *Giving Offense*, his approach is more psychological than political. He refers to the disagreement with Nadine Gordimer as 'unsettling'. In later reflections he asked, 'Why was it so hard to think of anything interesting to say about censorship? Did the discussion of censorship simply belong to politics?'[44] To oppose politics with the playfulness of folly is already idiosyncratic, but another peculiar presence in these essays is Freud, whose reflections on paranoia Coetzee found relevant.[45] The main focus of *Giving Offense* is the psychology of the creative mind, the dynamics of the inner 'zoo', the management of which involves 'pleasing and satisfying and challenging and extorting and wooing and feeding, and sometimes even … putting to death'.[46] The problem presented by the censor is that he (male by definition) interposes himself between the desiring subjectivity of the writer and the desired object:

> Working under censorship is like being intimate with someone who does not love you, with whom you want no intimacy, but who presses himself in upon you. The censor is an intrusive reader, a reader who forces his way into the intimacy of the writing transaction, forces out the figure of the loved or courted reader, reads your words in a disapproving and *censorious* fashion.[47]

Intimacy with the beast, which we have observed in practice, is seen here to find its way into the unconscious. Curiously, there is no evidence in the manuscripts of *In the Heart of the Country* that Coetzee was writing in the shadow of this unwelcome intimate, no obvious self-censorship, that is; on the contrary, the sex scenes involving the relationship between Magda and Hendrik are developed in explicit detail, accompanied by acutely painful dialogue exploring the psycho-sexual baggage of racial estrangement.

Was Coetzee succumbing to the reverse psychology that censorship encourages – that is, a perverse desire to engage in what is forbidden? That is possible, but readers have not accused Coetzee of being gratuitous, either; instead of acceding to the censorious interloper, in however subtle ways, what Coetzee does do is fictionalize him; for example, in the figure of the police chief, Maximov, in *The Master of Petersburg*, with whom Dostoevsky, the fictional writer of that novel, holds an intelligent if tense discussion over the reading of his stepson Pavel's jejune but violent stories.

It is typical of Coetzee's practice that he should want to externalize the threat in this way, by subjecting it to fictional representation. Elizabeth Costello is an extension of this practice. When the demand on Coetzee to become the public intellectual became more and more intolerable – with an argument over censorship playing a key, perhaps *the* key, role in clarifying this – Coetzee turned to the resources of fiction, or switched on the power of fiction, to regain control. Costello is a form of puppetry – not a ventriloquist's doll, exactly, because she does not speak for him in any simple sense, but rather an uncanny puppet through whom Coetzee is able to mirror back to society its expectations of the writer as public figure, and subject them to his own inscrutable, and occasionally unscrupulous, effects.

6

WRITING REVOLUTION
Waiting for the Barbarians

All things hold together, he says to himself: when the order of justice
collapses in the state, it collapses in the heart too.[1]

IN COETZEE's analysis of the South Africa of the late 1970s, censorship
went hand in hand with paranoia. Diagnosing the problem in retrospect, in *Giving Offense*, he turned to Freud, who explained paranoia as
a general detachment of libido from the world.[2] Freud was discussing
the case of a certain Judge Schreber, who wrote an autobiographical account of his own paranoia, which took the form of an end-of-
the-world fantasy.

After the Soweto student uprising of 1976, the discourse of the
apartheid government was certainly marked by paranoia. From the
time that P.W. Botha came to the premiership from the Ministry of
Defence, the official line was that a 'total onslaught' was being waged
against the country and against Western Christian civilization in
Africa. The government believed that the assault was cultural as well
as military and political, and it was in this period that the censorship
apparatus was extended.

Coetzee wrote, 'In the psychohistory of the white South African
in the last years of apartheid, detachment of libido from the world
took the form of an inability to imagine a future, a relinquishing of

an imaginative grasp upon it.'[3] It would not be obvious, perhaps even to Coetzee himself, but there is an element of introspection in the observation, because in his creative life Coetzee had lived through the psychohistory he describes, having tried, precisely, to imagine South Africa in the aftermath of a revolutionary war, but then found himself unable to bring such a narrative to fruition.

Instead of the novel about revolution that he set out to write, what he achieved was a novel about the failure to imagine a future, a novel about baulked desire, too: *Waiting for the Barbarians*. In the next novel, *Life & Times of Michael K*, he would return to the uncompleted project, imagining Cape Town in the grip of revolutionary energies, but again he would steer away, becoming absorbed this time in his strangely liberated protagonist, K.

Paranoia is the basic condition of the Empire in *Barbarians*. It is not a psychic motivator in the novel's magistrate, but, as we will see, libidinal withdrawal and loss of desire do play a role – both in the character and in the writing. In the notebook accompanying the manuscript of 'The Burning of the Books', Coetzee writes, 'Ever since I moved back to SA [in 1971] my attitude toward the Revolution has become more ambivalent. And in parallel with this movement, my <u>fervor</u> as a writer has waned.'[4]

Earlier he had written, 'What has happened between *Dusklands* and now is that I have become unpolitical. The revolutionary setup behind ['The Burning of the Books'] doesn't fire me. I can now see that D [*Dusklands*] was a product of the passionate politics of 1965–71, USA. I was a satirist in D – not a satirist out of moral conviction, but because I was being aroused by events in a way I feared to be aroused. Now my attitude seems to be more detached.'[5]

Also in 1974, he expresses 'resigned bewilderment about [the] <u>place</u> one <u>finds oneself</u> in. Am I in the opening of [Beckett's] *Molloy*? Or on the other hand is this *Robinson Crusoe* I am in?'[6] Place, as South Africa, had seemed unproblematic when he sat in Buffalo; now that he was in Cape Town, it was losing its hold on him. Or to look at it another way, he could not find the connection between place and the kind of fiction he wanted to write. He says, 'A tour of all the excesses available to the fictional consciousness in South Africa (parricide, rebellion, miscegenation even, <u>heimwee</u> [homesickness, nostalgia]), none of them of course being adequate to an existence without a centre.'[7] This misgiving was expressed *before* he wrote *In the Heart of the Country*, of course, a novel that could be said to accomplish everything that he declares here to be impossible. Magda undertakes all of these little journeys – parricide, rebellion, miscegenation, *heimwee* – while also undergoing a complete existential disintegration.

The question Coetzee was asking in 1974 seems to have become an answer by 1977. Nevertheless, when he began writing *Waiting for the Barbarians*, which he did before *In the Heart of the Country* had appeared on the shelves, the relationship between place and consciousness – the latter being his true subject – was still far from settled.

The reader will anticipate where this leads: to the remoteness, the lack of historical specificity, the placelessness, precisely, of *Waiting for the Barbarians*. Critics in the United States would wonder about the novel's detachment from the immediacies of South Africa in the 1970s. And while a routine move in the criticism was to imagine something equivalent (the Mojave Desert, or the northern Cape), Coetzee's stated point of view was that the milieu does not exist.

He later testified to the fact that the challenge was not to describe an unfamiliar landscape, but to construct one, from scratch. Unlike the Karoo of previous novels, 'the landscape of *Barbarians* represented a challenge to my power of *envisioning*'.[8] Actually, the Karoo did remain a point of reference, but I will come back to that. The point here is to try to understand how and why the remote setting of *Barbarians* was a solution to the problem of writing about South Africa.

Coetzee began writing *Waiting for the Barbarians* on 11 July 1977, sketching the idea for the novel in a notebook. It was not until 20 September that he began the almost daily business of drafting, at the very moment when, as far as he was aware, the censors were trying to reach a decision about *In the Heart of the Country*, which

11/7/77.   The time: The middle of a
            revolutionary war in S. Africa
(the war remains throughout in the background). The place: an island transit
camp for aliens waiting for transport out
of the country — Robben Island, the prison
now a tired hotel, with a launch
bringing out supplies daily. Planes are
not flying (no refuelling facilities, the
north too dangerous). The man + the
woman meet. Both hold British passports
and are returning to Britain (where they
have no roots). The man is 50, an
academic working on a translation + edition
of a narrative of the fall of Constantinople.
The woman is 21/22, she has left her
husband (or he is dead).
        They make love in an upstairs cell.
This becomes some kind of home to them.

First notebook entry for 'Waiting for the Barbarians', July 1977.

was under embargo at the airport in Johannesburg. It is tempting to conclude from this, circumstantially, that the displaced milieu of *Barbarians* was a tactic to evade the censors, but that inference would be thoroughly incorrect, because when he began writing it, the novel was set in a highly recognizable Cape Town. In fact, in the teeth of probable censorship this time (in the case of *In the Heart of the Country*, because it dealt with interracial sex, censorship was a distinct possibility but no more than that), he began to put together a story about South Africa after apartheid, in which Robben Island was no longer a prison for Nelson Mandela and his comrades but an embarkation station for white refugees who were fleeing the dying republic in UN-chartered ships. The manuscript begins,

> From the open window of the guardroom Manos Milis watched the refugees trudge up the road from the jetty to the that led from the jetty to the prison gates. The launch that had brought them was already half-way back to the mainland. It was plain that the crew were not talking to the people they had ferried. Otherwise who would come.[9]

The style was naturalism, of the kind that his fellow Capetonian Alex La Guma had used to describe the city, a style marked by a fastidious listing of seedy detail, with roots in Émile Zola. Coetzee had written appreciatively of La Guma.[10] In Coetzee's prison turned transit station,

> grass, nettles, thistles, clover had grown in the courtyard, splitting the flagstones. Mice had run in the corridors. In the toilet bowls the water had dried up, leaving rings of rust. The only sound had been the cry of seagulls birds. Pigeon shit caked the window ledges. Gulls swooped into the courtyard at dusk. In his lodge the watchman drank himself to sleep.[11]

This is the paraphernalia as well as exhausted tone of naturalism. To get from this to the wholly invented landscape of *Waiting for the Barbarians* was a major leap, although the published novel still plays with verisimilitude: it is realist without actually referring to the real Cape Town.

The naturalism proved to be a dead end. After several weeks of writing, each false start is marked 'ABANDONED', although elements survive from one version to another. At one stage in these drafts, Manos Milis is a forty-year-old Greek, a former teacher of ancient history, writing a book about the fall of Constantinople, assisting passengers to embark on the ship *Anaconda* at the Cape Town docks. The ship is unable to leave because there is a dispute between the UN

20/9/77

From the open window of the guardroom Manos Miti watched the refugees trudge up the road ~~from the jetty to the~~ that led from the jetty to the ~~prison~~ gates. The launch that had brought them was already half-way back to the mainland. It scudded over the grey seas. It was plain that the crew were not talking to the people they ferried. Otherwise who would come.

The prison in which they lived had not been used since a year before the war. Grass, ~~nettles,~~ thistles, clover had grown in the courtyard, splitting the flagstones. Mice had run in the corridors. In the toilet bowls the water had dried up, leaving rings of rust. The only ~~sound~~ had been the cry of birds ~~seagulls~~. Pigeon shit caked the window-ledges. Gulls swooped into the courtyard at dusk. In his lodge the watchman drank himself to sleep.

Then in the second year of the emergency ~~war, they had begun to~~ after the first great flood of refugees had dwindled, the prison had been reopened as an embarkation ~~for~~ station for the indecisive, for those who had hung on hoping that everything would be all right yet, who were now at last frightened enough to cut their ties with the dying ~~sinking~~ white republic and flee to wherever accidents of birth or parentage entitled them to go. In dribs and drabs, on Tuesday and Friday mornings, when the offices opened, they ~~passed~~ stood in line to pass through the emigration checkpoints at the harbour gates, boarded the Robben Island launch, and were ferried out ~~to~~ to the huge sandstone ~~prison~~ cube

U.N.
to wait for the charter ships, ~~flying~~ to save them.
The charter ships had taken out ~~half~~ a quarter of a million European nationals in the first year.

First page of the manuscript of 'Waiting for the Barbarians'.

and the new government about who will pay for the fuel. The most promising aspects of Milis's story are his reflections on history, his conviction that history is best written when one stops imagining that the self, or oneself, lies at its centre. Coetzee is exploring the position of the internal exile and discovering that it might be liberating: some of the later magistrate's wistfulness had been found here.

The plot of these early versions was a dark love story, with the interest falling on aggressive, unfocused desires that are unleashed by a revolution. With Robert Musil in the background, Milis is 'an explorer of the vitalities thrown up by the last days of the republic. Literally a fin de siècle book.'[12] At one point Milis is fifty; the woman he is interested in is twenty-one, twenty-two, having left her husband, or the husband having died. (Structures used later in *Disgrace* keep appearing in these drafts for the first time: the relationship between an older man and a younger woman; his absorption in a relevant intellectual project, like the opera on Byron.) The lovers have compulsive, despairing sex; they make a temporary home in a former prison cell; she withdraws physically; he becomes obsessive and sadistic in trying to restore her to life; she commits suicide. The focus is on sexual restlessness, with more than a hint of misogyny in Milis.

At times the sexuality was to be 'polymorphous perverse', Freud's description of prepubescent erotic life. Milis was to have dreams of erotic tenderness, without phallic consummation.[13] The beginnings of the relationship between the magistrate and the barbarian girl lie here – the washing of her feet – but much had still to be worked out. Coetzee was reading Jerzi Koziński's *The Painted Bird*, a disturbing picaresque novel set in World War II. In the climactic moments, Coetzee imagined that Milis would become a 'burier of the dead', another foreshadowing of *Disgrace* but also a development out of what had been planned for 'The Burning of the Books'.

Coetzee had found a tone, a mood, a situation, but not a plot. The narrative was stuck in the impasse it represented. The significant development, the event that got him writing the novel that it would become, came in the fifth version ('Version E'), to which he gave the title 'Disposal of the Dead'. Speculation about titles was frequent as the drafts progressed: at various times the novel is called 'Exile', 'Traitors', 'The Border Guard' and 'Barbarians'. The title would eventually be drawn from C.P. Cavafy's poem 'Waiting for the Barbarians', but Cavafy was not an influence at the start. It is hard to resist the inference that behind 'Disposal of the Dead' lay T.S. Eliot and the first section of *The Wasteland*, which is entitled 'The Burial of the Dead'. When Coetzee substitutes 'disposal' for 'burial', he becomes even more desiccated than Eliot himself. He was mining his poetic resources, exploring with as much force as possible the idea that white South Africa was destroying itself from within. Like Eliot's poem, the novel would use the seasonal cycle to mark the disintegration. From beginnings in naturalism, the novel was searching for a more poetic key.

The early manuscript is laboured, and Coetzee knew it: 'After 22 pages, no liftoff yet. It would seem that I can get nowhere unless the whole thing turns into a drama of consciousness a la *In the Heart*. But I cannot face the prospect of writing at that hysterical intensity again. Once is enough.' The missing ingredient, he told himself, was 'the creation of a credible beloved you', but he could not see how he was going to do this while writing realism in the third person.[14] A week later, he had got no further: 'I have no interest in telling stories; it is the process of storytelling that interests me. This man MM, as a "he" living in the world, bores me. "Creating" an illusionistic reality in which he moves depresses me. Hence the exhausted quality of the writing.'[15]

He began again, on a different tack, proposing an 'I', but this time, crucially, turning Milis into a guard on a frontier, a border post or fort. The catalyst was Robert Duncan's magnificent poem 'The Song of the Border-Guard', which begins,

> The man with his lion under the shed of wars
> sheds his belief as if he shed tears.
> The sound of words waits –
> a barbarian host at the borderline of sense.[16]

This development was an important writing event, nudging the book towards what it would become, although there was a long way to go. The setting he still kept deliberately vague: 'Sometimes it is the Amazonian jungle (Aguirre [a reference to Werner Herzog's film *Aguirre: Wrath of God*, about a conquistador]), sometimes central Asia (Buzzati [a reference to Dino Buzzati's novel *Il deserto dei Tartari*]); other possibilities South Africa, colonial N. America, Roman Europe.' But, he added, 'The position is beleaguered. They are forgotten, nevertheless they do their duty.'[17]

To solve the problem, continued from the early drafts, of the novel's not having momentum, he wanted to create 'a plan for "You" in this story. The various roles "you" (she) can be tried out in are: prisoner, camp woman, fellow inmate.' Once this 'you' is known, he writes, the next problem is to find a 'home' for her, 'in the flesh, in the word'.[18] Until the possible habitations of 'you' were found, the novel could not progress. She is Ariadne, focusing the guard's desire; but in whose lair the story was to play out was still unclear.

It would soon become clear. In the very weeks that Coetzee wrestled with these materials, South Africa became convulsed with yet another political catastrophe: the death in detention of Steve Biko, the Black Consciousness leader, followed by the inquest into its causes. Since the inquest took place in open court, the press, the liberal *Cape Times* especially, took the opportunity to cover it in great detail. Coetzee kept press clippings and followed it closely.

Biko's torture and death gave Coetzee the minotaur's lair, the 'habitation for desire' that he was looking for, the situation in which his character's obsession with 'her' could be explored: that situation was the transformation of a placid border town by a reign of terror run by police agents from the capital. The novel's emergence took the form of a simultaneous, seemingly contradictory, two-way process: both a distancing – into an unspecified empire at an unspecified moment

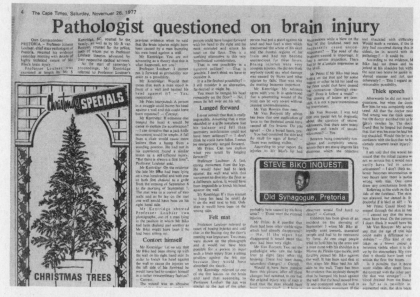

Press clipping from the 'Cape Times' kept by Coetzee about the Biko inquest.

in history – and a homecoming into the violence of apartheid in the period of its climactic self-destruction. There was no single moment of crystallization for this, but a period of intense experimentation that was full of uncertainty.

On Christmas Day 1977, Coetzee wrote, 'It is a wholly unreal enterprise I am engaged in. No matter what, this is a book that could have been written a hundred years ago. Exoticism, nothing more. There is no pressure of form on me, hence the lack of any engagement of feeling. The book comes straight out of the Western: Long-knives and Redskins.'[19] Two days later, belief returns: 'Going ok. Hard to believe I have at last found the form I wanted.'[20]

To flesh out the newly discovered setting, Coetzee began to research the geography of Mongolia for information about terrain, names, climate, flora and fauna, agriculture, diet and so on. His collection of papers and notebook gleanings on this subject is extensive, although the manuscripts also show that he was still frequently unsure of the results; unsure, specifically, that what he ought to be doing was creating a realistic portrayal at all. He regularly proposed reverting back to southern Africa, especially South West Africa, as it was known, and wondered whether he should throw in a few Afrikaans names to create a melange of situations that would emphasize fictionality – but these temptations were resisted.

A key formal discovery – perhaps the most significant one – was finding the voice of the magistrate. It surfaces most clearly on 4 December 1977, in epistolary form: in letters addressed to an official in the imperial centre, reassuring him that the rumours he has heard of an impending barbarian uprising are unfounded. In a second letter, written on the same day, this official, no longer Milis but unnamed ('X'), reports on a minor chieftain called Jargetai who has a seal from the Emperor and who represents no danger. Jargetai reappears in later drafts, along with Ölöt, Batu and 'the defiles of the Kum-tagh'.

How did this voice free Coetzee from the laboriousness of the process up to this point? One answer is technical: the change from third-person to first-person narration enabled him to emphasize the flow of feeling he had always sought, leaving him at liberty to experiment with just those external events and textual genres that served the purpose of bringing this consciousness into the open. Another answer has to do with Coetzee's own social position: he didn't have the means to create the naturalistic detail that the novel about life in Cape Town after a revolution would require. He makes the point for himself, in the notes: 'When one is living a full life and working on a book, everything is transmuted (comme on dit) and used. With a thin life, I am writing a thin book.'[21] To bring off the first kind of novel, he would have needed to be closer to the personalities, intrigues, aspirations, disappointments of lives lived on the street in times of change. Instead of this broad social canvas, what Coetzee could do was a psychological drama of displacement – and as he did not have a naturalistic context for such a project, he would have to invent one.

In a certain sense, the milieu he created *was* familiar territory, in so far as it was on the near side of revolution rather than after it; and the shift to a historically vague, Manichaean, allegorical landscape is of a piece with his frequently expressed diagnosis of colonial history as an irremediable moral crisis. 'Between black and white there is a gulf fixed,' says John in *Youth*; people like himself 'are here on this earth, the earth of South Africa, on the shakiest of pretexts'.[22] (This view also animates *Disgrace*.) It is a short step from this moral pessimism to the mythic, divided world of *Waiting for the Barbarians*.

The situation he invented would strike a chord with readers observing South Africa with mixed feelings from abroad: reviewing *Waiting for the Barbarians* for the *Times Literary Supplement* soon after it appeared, Peter Lewis contrasted Coetzee's style with the realism of Alan Paton, adding, 'Coetzee has developed a symbolic and even allegorical mode of fiction – not to escape the living nightmare of South Africa but to define the psychopathological underlying the sociological, and in so doing, to locate the archetypal in the particular.'[23] A just description.

The change of focus enabled Coetzee to draw on his resources, including, paradoxically, the Karoo. 'Make the desert more like the Karoo,' he writes in his notes, when the narrative is well under way.[24] In the manuscript there are indeed numerous Karoo-like moments, such as the following: 'Summer is wheeling to an end,' the 'orchards groan under the burden … In the sky there are a million stars. We are on the roof of the world. I open my eyes in the middle of the night and lie dazzled.'[25] Such pathos, such love of country, came from a writer who had spent parts of his childhood at Voëlfontein and who in later years was persuaded that the whole way of life it represented was coming to an end. There was also the reading Coetzee had done before writing *Dusklands*, on the ethnography of the Khoikhoi and Nama of the northern Cape and their interactions with the Dutch settlement: *Waiting for the Barbarians* empties known colonial discourses of specific ethnic markers but retains the sharp cultural differences and conflicting lifestyles of the eighteenth-century Cape.

∽

The context behind Steve Biko's death was the state's deployment of its security apparatus in a single-minded and ruthless suppression of the Black Consciousness Movement: 1976 had witnessed the Soweto revolt, which the movement had inspired; by mid-1977 the uprising had been suppressed and the campaign against its organizational base began in earnest.

In October 1977 dozens of left-wing organizations were banned, most of them associated with Black Consciousness. Biko had already been arrested, and died in police custody on 12 September, following which there was the inquest, beginning on 14 November. The international media coverage of the events was sufficient to galvanize 128 members of the US Congress to sign a letter to the South African authorities, insisting that an American team be dispatched to examine the laws pertaining to political prisoners and detention without trial.

The role of Biko's death in the novel was central but not straight-forward. 'This may not be entirely honest,' Coetzee writes, 'but I must make the relation of the story to the Biko affair, the inspiration of the story by the Biko affair, clear. End it with a massive trial scene in which the accusers get put in the dock.'[26] A trial scene was never written, but Colonel Joll and his henchmen do look beleaguered towards the end. The fictional translations of the political context are clear enough: the clampdown by the security detail (South Africa's BOSS, the Bureau for State Security, renamed the Third Bureau after Tsarist Russia), the torture chamber, and the effects of these on people of liberal conscience, represented by the magistrate.

But why would Coetzee suggest it 'may not be entirely honest' to admit that these elements derived from the Biko affair? The answer, no doubt, is that, in fact, he absorbed these developments into a structure the essential elements of which had already been worked out: it was important to the novel's taking-off that he should write about desire, or write desire into life, a project requiring an elusive, and female, 'you'. After the introduction and fictionalization of the political events, this 'you' became the barbarian girl: a torture victim, crippled and partially blinded by Colonel Joll, a girl whom the magistrate takes into his rooms, where the previously imagined polymorphous-perverse sexuality of Milis finds a highly charged, and now culturally loaded, application. So the problem of finding the right 'habitation for desire' was solved by the contemporaneous events taking place just at the time that Coetzee most needed them.

The cocktail that Coetzee had invented was immensely powerful: a combination of peculiar sexuality, involving a tortured body, cultural difference and a regime on the brink of collapse. Nevertheless, or perhaps because of this, he continued to be unsure about what he was doing: 'It is difficult to believe in this ridiculous story. My only hope is that some transmutation will occur to me.' His intuitions were that the 'sexual alienation of the man had better be linked to the torture'; that he would convey a sense that there was 'no privileged space' for the body; that the man 'will have to live through what is going on in the torture room more intensely'. He also sensed that the man himself would have to undergo pain: 'Why not let him be wounded in the attack of the barbarians on his party?'[27]

Six years after publication, in an essay entitled 'Into the Dark Chamber', Coetzee wrote, 'In 1980 I published a novel (*Waiting for the Barbarians*) about the impact of the torture chamber on the life of a man of conscience.'[28] His sense of the novel's theme could hardly have been clearer, judging from this statement, but equally, in the writing of it, the *directness* of the events would have to be managed, recontextualized and fictionalized, with appropriate depth and aesthetic consequence. Coetzee's reflections in the essay bear this out: torture has exercised a 'dark fascination' for South African writers, he says, for two reasons, the first being obvious: the relations in the torture room encapsulate the relations generally between authoritarianism and its victims.

The second reason is more novelistic: 'the novelist is a person who, camped before a closed door, facing an insufferable ban, creates, in place of the scene he is forbidden to see, a representation of that scene, and a story of the actors in it and how they came to be there'. In other terms, an atrocity presents novelists with a challenge unique to their craft, which is how to represent the cruelty without repeating it: 'how not to play the game by the rules of the state, how to establish one's own authority, how to imagine torture and death on one's own terms'.[29]

For the next year and a half, Coetzee took these provocations with him as he developed one version after another. In late 1978, having been writing for nearly a year, he embarked on a reading campaign. In his notebook he began to list themes and quotations: on cemeteries and their rituals, on death and despair (Kierkegaard, Henry James, Boris Pasternak on suicide), on art (Flaubert is quoted as saying, 'In days gone by people thought that only sugar cane yielded sugar. Nowadays they get it from practically everything; it's the same way with poetry'), on pleasure (Roland Barthes), on Tantrism (Octavio Paz), on space (Henri Bergson), on sound (Walter Ong), on Madame Bovary (Leo Bersani), on dreams (Freud). Ong is quoted as saying, 'Barbarians turn out rather regularly to be the custodians ... of the culture on which they prey.' He reads Paul Ricoeur on the body, Simone de Beauvoir on what it means for a woman to be 'dressed', George Steiner on fantasies of invasion. Simone Weil's aphorism 'the crime which is latent in us we must inflict on ourselves' finds its way into the manuscripts and into the final text.[30]

By 1 June 1979 he had a typescript, which he continued to revise by hand. The typing and redrafting of much of the later manuscripts were done while he was travelling: he spent January to May 1979 in the linguistics department at Austin, Texas, followed by June, July and August in the linguistics department at Berkeley, California.[31] By his account, it was a lonely but productive period.[32] The declared reason for his travels was academic: he had sabbatical leave from the University of Cape Town and used it to enhance his linguistics scholarship. At Texas he attended seminars run by Lauri Karttunen on syntax, and conducted research that led to three essays: one on 'the rhetoric of the passive', another on 'agentless sentences' and a third on Isaac Newton's efforts at producing 'a transparent scientific language'.

When asked whether there were connections between this linguistic work and the novel he was writing, he demurred, saying, 'We must at least entertain the possibility that some of the writing I do is play, relief, diversion, of no great import outside its own disciplinary field.' The relief he refers to here is the essays, not the novel. He continues: 'Except perhaps that it may be a telling fact about me that I spend some of my time (too much of my time?) in occupations that take me away from the great world and its concerns.'[33] He is being self-critical here for indulging in the essays on syntax as a form of diversion. By common standards, the essays are rather abstruse; the novel in fact continued to develop themes and narrative lines that related to questions of political morality at home.

His travels would certainly have facilitated the detached treatment that *Waiting for the Barbarians* gives to South Africa, since he wasn't confronted by the daily clamour. He continued to write about South African literature: an essay for *Index on Censorship* on *Staffrider* and a review for *Research in African Literatures* of Michael Wade's study of Nadine Gordimer, in which he comes to the conclusion that Gordimer was more resolute than Wade allows for in imagining a dark future for white South Africa – an argument that resonated with the apprehensions that were finding their way into his novel.

Coetzee's personal isolation, too, would almost certainly have influenced his creativity in these months. He was still married to Philippa but he was away from home for nine months, implying that the family unit was no longer what it had been. The children, Nicolas and Gisela, were teenagers and must have weighed on his mind, because the novel is dedicated to them. Already in late 1978, he was weaving his concern for them into his notes: 'Am struck by my concern for my children's future. One would die for them. The behavior strikes me as instinctual. This man [X, who became the magistrate]: will he not break out of his passivity, his contentment at the moment when he sees the girl, as his child, threatened?'[34] The children of the novel's town, who play in the square and build a snowman in the poignant concluding paragraph, did have their counterparts in Coetzee's life.

The magistrate is very much the lonely male, at a loose end, trying to steady himself with archaeological pursuits and historical speculations. Coetzee was living the condition, a state of ennui described in 1978 that would have become stronger during his travels: 'Through a lifetime of heroic repression, enforced and then interiorized, I am now in a state where I desire nothing. That is to say, beyond desiring to desire. "To desire nothing" means you are only interested in death, if "interest" is the word. Apathy.' And then: 'Out of the absence of desire you cannot write a book, not even a book about the absence of desire. The prose only flows as an investigation, a question. "Desire is a question without an answer."'[35] Restless, inconclusive questioning: the mood is intrinsic to *Waiting for the Barbarians*.

When Coetzee discusses the challenge that torture represents to the writer, he alludes to the temptation to succumb to the pornography of violence. This position was discovered *en passant*; it was not declared in advance of his writing *Barbarians*, because at the particular point in the manuscript where he begins to deal with torture, he has the older of two prisoners butchered in front of the younger one, a boy. The torturers' assumption is that the child, in terrified innocence, will blurt out some truth about the barbarians' intentions. The death in this scene is repulsive: the elderly man is run through with a sword and beheaded – explicit violence on a scale we last saw in *Dusklands*.

The question, then, is: when was the lesson of 'Into the Dark Chamber' learned (the lesson being, how to represent torture without repeating the power relations of torturer and victim)? The answer seems to be that it was learned in the course of writing the magistrate: in the final text, events on this scale of brutality are told through the magistrate's growing awareness of what is taking place; in this way, torture is rendered as a moral problem, especially for the powerful but appalled.

The two key elements of the novel as it gets under way are, firstly, the arrival of the security agents from the capital, and, secondly, the magistrate's relationship with the girl. In the arrival of Joll and his team, parallels are unmistakable between the report submitted by Joll to the magistrate on the death of a prisoner and police accounts of Biko's death at the inquest, where the presiding officer eventually found that no one was to blame. The circumlocution is what survives into the published text:

> During the course of the interrogation contradictions became apparent in the prisoner's testimony. Confronted with these contradictions, the prisoner became enraged and attacked the investigating officer. A scuffle ensued during which the prisoner fell heavily against the wall. Efforts to revive him were unsuccessful.[36]

The first draft of this is much more clearly cued by the details that emerged at the Biko inquest, especially the fact that the victim died of brain injuries:

> 'I understand, Colonel, that another of the prisoners died under interrogation. How did that come about?'
>
> 'Ah yes, that happened a few days ago. Yes. We were questioning him. We confronted him with a statement he had made earlier, a statement which contradicted what he was now saying. He went beserk. He attacked us. It took four of us – myself, Colonel B, and our two assistants – to bring him under control. There was a scuffle. In the course of the scuffle ~~his head~~ came into contact with the wall. I understand that was the cause of death. An injury to the brain.'

This was written on 23 December 1977, a month after the inquest; Coetzee was writing at white heat, using details from his newspaper clippings. In later revisions, we find him omitting brain injury while retaining the official evasiveness. A reported incident in which Steve Biko was said to have thrown himself at his attackers is retained but recontextualized: the elderly victim becomes the girl's father; the magistrate imagines that his rage would have been the result of his seeing his daughter witnessing his suffering and humiliation.[37] Coetzee shifts the pathos into the parent–child relationship.

In the relationship between the magistrate and the girl, Coetzee found a vehicle for exploring desire, but the configuration introduced by the Biko material changes the emphasis to an exploration of the effects of violence on intimacy. When the magistrate discovers that true reciprocity is impossible, he decides that he must return the girl to her people. He organizes an expedition. When the journey reaches its destination and she is given the choice, she chooses to free herself from his clutches. On his return to the settlement, despite the flagrantly personal nature of his quest, the magistrate is accused of collaborating with the enemy, tortured and publicly humiliated. Thereafter, the Colonel leaves the settlement, which is now in a state of anxious disorder, expecting to be overrun. Only the children provide a measure of hope for a different future.

Once Coetzee found his milieu and the dramatic potential of torture, his writing focused on the magistrate's attentions to the girl. Initially, we find out about her condition through his misapprehensions: she hobbles, which he surmises is because her feet were bound as a child; she begs with a bowl before her, kneeling, and he wonders why she cannot sit cross-legged; her feet are wrapped in rags and felt because, he assumes, she has no shoes – and so forth. Soon he learns the truth, which is that she has been damaged through the method known as 'the thousand blows', beatings on the ankles. He obsesses about her, has distorted dreams. He brings her into his rooms and gives orders to take her into service rather than have her beg on the streets. Initially, Coetzee uses familiar South African master–servant relations of the 1950s to create the situation: she wears a cotton tunic he provides; she eats the food he gives her with her fingers – but in later revisions, such details are discarded.

At the magistrate's insistence, the girl removes the bandages, thongs and 'shapeless sheepskin slippers' from her feet and he begins to wash her. Two elements of these encounters stand out as sharply different from the published text. The first is that the magistrate communicates with her in the local patois, which allows Coetzee to recast the social possibilities of Afrikaans. Secondly, the sexuality is far more explicit here than it is in the novel. In the final version, the magistrate's exhaustion is unconnected to anything quite so mundane as having orgasms. Instead, the eroticism has a poetic indirection, as if the tiredness was a psychological manifestation of the deficiencies of the relationship, or of metaphysical longings in the magistrate that the girl cannot answer.

> ... in the very act of caressing her I am overcome with sleep as if poleaxed, fall into oblivion sprawled upon her body, and wake an hour or two later dizzy, confused, thirsty. These dreamless spells are like death to me, or enchantment, blank, outside time ...
>
> I touch my lips to her forehead. 'What did they do to you?' I murmur. My tongue is slow, I sway on my feet with exhaustion. 'Why don't you want to tell me?'
>
> She shakes her head. On the edge of oblivion it comes back to me that my fingers, running over her buttocks, have felt a phantom criss-cross of ridges under the skin. 'Nothing is worse than what we can imagine,' I mumble. She gives no sign that she has even heard me. I slump on the couch, drawing her down beside me, yawning. 'Tell me,' I want to say, 'don't make a mystery of it, pain is only pain'; but words elude me. My arm folds around her, my lips are at the hollow of her ear, I struggle to speak; then blackness falls.[38]

The first attempts at such passages are less evocative: he washes her entirely, her genitals, her anus, he lies down with her, rubs her with oil, strips, places her foot against his penis: 'when he feels the faintest arch of the foot, the faintest answering pressure of her toes ... at once he ejaculates.'[39] Desire for reciprocity is paramount in the drafts, and it continues into the published text, but without relying on such explicit details. The literary criticism makes much of the *indirection* of these encounters in the novel, the mystery of non-connection, strangeness, otherness. What the manuscripts reveal is that this quality is a function of editing, of late, tactical omissions: deletion is shown to be central to the process of invention.

Matters change when the magistrate looks into the girl's eyes and finds them 'dead, flat, like the eyes of a dead fish'. A hot iron brought too close to her face has left her blind. The discovery sickens him; his night-time attentions become 'full of nostalgia'. 'He watches her jealously when she comes into his room, when she moves, when she undresses, hoping to capture movements of her body that belong to an earlier free state; ~~before she was blind and~~ but everything she does is crabbed, tentative, defensive, the movement of a trammeled body.'[40] From this moment on, the magistrate knows that things cannot continue as before.

In the published version, the magistrate's efforts to reconfigure the relationship are concentrated on the expedition. In the manuscripts, other possibilities are explored: Coetzee turns X into the commandant of the outpost who has taken on the role of magistrate, not the magistrate himself; when a real magistrate arrives, he lets slip that X is expected back in the capital, a development that encourages X to think of returning the girl. Then X, as commandant, tries to persuade this newly arrived magistrate to devise a quasi-legal ceremony in which he could adopt the girl as his daughter. He refuses. The townspeople are puzzled because while they do not object to X taking a woman to his apartment, turning this into a filial bond is unseemly. X considers a marriage under barbarian law, because, in customary terms, until she is married she remains the daughter of her dead father's brother; he hopes that while the barbarians will see the match as a marriage, he will be free to assume a more paternal role. Coetzee is borrowing from and adapting local African (particularly Nguni) custom.[41] These elements were omitted from the final text, but in exploring a cross-cultural legal arrangement as an alternative to a conventional Western marriage, Coetzee was laying down precedents, once again, for what would develop in *Disgrace*, in Lucy's marriage to the polygamous Petrus.

As for the magistrate and his wandering desires, the eroticism gives way to the need for reparation. 'Somewhere, always, a child is being beaten,' Coetzee writes, again with reference to Freud.[42] 'I think of one who despite her age was still a child; who was brought in here and hurt before her father's eyes; who watched him being humiliated before her, and saw that he knew what she saw.' The magistrate's desire is to take the father's place, but 'I came too late, after she had ceased to believe in fathers. I wanted to do what was right, I wanted to make reparation: I will not deny this decent impulse, however mixed with more questionable motives.' After the father was exposed to her, naked and in pain, and after they hurt her, 'she was no longer fully human, sister to all of us. Certain sympathies died, certain movements of the heart became no longer possible to her.'[43]

Arguably, *the* climactic moment in *Waiting for the Barbarians* is when the magistrate, undergoing torture, imagines that he is on the point of death. He is made to ascend a ladder, blindfolded, with a noose around his neck strung from the branch of a tree. His handler keeps the rope tight as he ascends; at the top, the ladder is pushed over; because there is no free-fall, he survives. In this moment, the image that comes to his mind with remarkable clarity is the image of the barbarian leader. He recalls 'standing in front of the old man, screwing up my eyes against the wind, waiting for him to speak … The girl, with her black hair braided and hanging over her shoulder in barbarian fashion, sits on her horse behind him. Her head is bowed, she too is waiting for him to speak. I sigh. "What a pity," I think. "It is too late now."'[44] His displacement is palpable here; revolution is registered dramatically, in a moment of anticipated speech; desire is rendered futile. In an early version of this, his reflections are more elaborately developed:

> From the moment my eyes lighted on her sitting at the barracks gate
> she was wrapped in a miasma of lies. Carried across the desert, too, by
> a man comically self-deceived. What did I want with the barbarians!
> I thought of marrying into them not because I longed for a pastoral
> existence but to become the owner of the marks on her body, to hear
> her go through a ceremony in which she acknowledged them as mine.

How could I have believed her so stupid? From first to last she listened
to her heart and acted in harmony with it. She knew me for a false
seducer from the very first. Who knows, if she had had the words she
might even have told me the truth, told me what was in my own heart:
'Join your Colonel with the black eyes. Find a fresh body. Let him
show you how to sign it with your mark.'[45]

Coetzee's efforts to imagine a future after apartheid had to focus on the
psychology of transition and on intimacy, if he was to be the person
who would carry off such a narrative. A novel that begins by probing
a psychosexual malaise that accompanies a revolution becomes a
narrative about the effects of violence on intimacy. The invention of
a credible, largely unprecedented fictional universe as the setting for
this narrative was an imaginative feat.

Looking back on South Africa's recent past, since the transition, from
a vantage point after the revolution, such as it was, one is struck by the
fact that the ordinariness of post-revolutionary life did not come into
view when Coetzee was writing. *Disgrace* does not fare much better on
these terms, because it is suffused with a dystopian vision of revolution,
in which the social transformation has no effect on recalcitrant sexual
energies; like the early drafts of *Waiting for the Barbarians*, *Disgrace* is
interested in 'the vitalities thrown up by the last days of the republic'.
Prevented by history from writing a *Vita Nuova*, Dante's story of
youthful love and the poetic imagination, Coetzee discovered that
what he could write, and in some sense must have wanted to write, was
the story of an impasse. A year into writing *Barbarians*, he realized that
the book was about 'waiting for a desire which does not come because
one is waiting for it. *Waiting for Godot* is about waiting for a subject.'[46]

The psychology of waiting is also expressed in the book's tendency
to withhold meaning. As the ending came into view, he noted of the
magistrate: 'the centre of his bafflement must be that his life has never
become clearly emblematic, even at its crisis points. The meeting with
the barbarians was vacuous, no words were exchanged, the police are
not simply evil, the girl refuses to betray her meaning to him, and

finally the barbarians do not come ... <u>This is a novel in which meaning is continually held back</u>.'[47]

Part of the point of these comments is that Coetzee is anxious to reassure himself that the realist novel he has written embodies some degree of textual self-consciousness. At one point he considered introducing a marginal commentary, an idea that was strengthened by a reading of Jacques Derrida's *Glas* (the kind of layered text he had written in *Dusklands* and would write again in *Diary of a Bad Year*). But he adds, 'just another twist of self-consciousness is what I <u>don't</u> want, perhaps a series of quotations. Not sources, just illuminations.'[48] The retrospective paragraphs penned by the magistrate towards the end have just this quality, and they are appropriately inconclusive.

Suspension, withheld meaning, both are essential features of *Waiting for the Barbarians*, and they are also highly relevant to a society in a state of paranoia, seemingly on the edge of dissolution. The topicality of the book was one reason for its success, both in South Africa and abroad, and it enabled Coetzee to draw some of the poison from his homeland during the later years of apartheid.

SUBURBAN BANDIT

Michael K as outlaw

ONE OF THE provocations that lay behind *Life & Times of Michael K* was household burglary – a persistent problem of life in suburban Cape Town. Having spent most of 1979 in the United States, in September Coetzee returned to his home in Rondebosch, near the University of Cape Town, to be reacquainted with this all-too-frequent occurrence. In October, he sketched out a plan for a novel.[1]

A 'man of liberal conscience' returns home one day to find that his house has been broken into and vandalized. He reports the incident to the local police, but his interactions with them reveal that they are more interested in keeping a lid on the anger of the suppressed classes than in dealing with petty crime. Since he has no recourse to the law, the man succumbs to rage. He goes into the black townships to post notices offering rewards, too angry to be moved by the obvious signs of squalor. Matters come to a head when he shoots a night-time intruder. Now inured to violence and out of control, he engages in 'class struggle' (on behalf of the middle class, that is).

As his model for this story, Coetzee chose Heinrich von Kleist's German Romantic novel of 1810, *Michael Kohlhaas* (from which was derived Michael K's name). In Kleist's novel, a sixteenth-century horse dealer is stopped on his way to market and his pass is demanded. When he is unable to produce one, his horses are confiscated. Later we learn

17.x.79.   A man of liberal conscience returns home one day to find his house burgled in a particularly sordid way (random destruction, shit on the floor, etc.) He makes the usual liberal noises to the police as well as to his friends; but the traces of the invasion come to obsess him. Though he has lucid spells in which he sees — with horror — what is happening to him, he moves, in a dogged way, toward an uncovering of the resentful, hate-filled violence of disposition that had for all his adult life been covered over by a liberal ideology — an ideology which (he now recognizes) had only been permitted him because such agencies as the police stood between him and the violence of the suppressed classes.

This "movement" of the book culminates in an act of violence on his part (e.g., a shot he fires at an intruder) which formally marks his renunciation of his charitable liberalism and his engagement in class struggle.

The first movement is carried out at a swift and "relentless" pace. The model is Kleist's Michael Kohlhaas. It constitutes a mere prelude to the body of the work.

Rather than having the house that is burgled be his city residence, it should be a country

Notebook entry with outline of 'Life & Times of Michael K'.

that the officials involved are corrupt; the pass was not required; but in the meantime Kohlhaas becomes an outlaw bent on regaining his property, embarking on a campaign of robbing and killing and leading a rebellion. It is Martin Luther, no less, who persuades him to give himself up and arranges safe passage, but not even Luther can prevent Michael from being tried and convicted. The court acknowledges that he has suffered unjustly, but he is condemned to death for his crimes. *Michael Kohlhaas* is a novel about the failure of law and government, followed by the disintegration and disaffection of the hero, who later comes to represent a pure, post-Enlightenment idea of freedom.

Most readers believe that behind Coetzee's 'K' lie Franz Kafka and his Josef K. The assumption is certainly correct: at one stage in his drafts, Coetzee even mused that he might call the novel 'The Childhood of Josef K'.[2] It is not clear how he planned to get to this point from *Michael Kohlhaas*, but it could have been his knowledge of Kafka that led Coetzee to Kleist, as Kafka himself is known to have admired *Michael Kohlhaas*. But it was the picaresque quality of Kleist's novel that interested Coetzee, as much as its theme. He sought to replicate Kleist's swift pacing as he began drafting *Michael K*, this being another dimension of Coetzee's continuing interest in eighteenth-century prose, an interest that would flower in the next novel, *Foe*. With as much Kleist as Kafka, then, in the original design of *Michael K*, it is not surprising that Coetzee was cagey when asked about the link to Kafka. He said that he had 'no regrets' about using the letter K, over which there was 'no monopoly'.[3]

Michael K began as the story of a vendetta. The idea of the vendetta as the basis for a representative South African fiction appealed to Coetzee: when *Michael K* was well under way, he wrote an outline for a version of Alan Paton's famous novel, *Cry, the Beloved Country*, as a vendetta narrative. Coetzee's grim recasting of Paton's plot would startle readers who are familiar with Paton's liberal Christian vision:

Cry, the Beloved Country and the vendetta. The ancestral crime announced on page 1 – theft of the good land. The black son carries the

vendetta into the city and kills the white son. Entry of (a) Christ, (b) the law as forces to end the vendetta. (Both of them are specifically opposed to the principle of the vendetta.) The expiation by Jarvis that does or does not make reparation. The problem of the generation of the grandchildren.[4]

Coetzee thought of bringing *Michael Kohlhaas* directly into *Michael K* by making his character an academic working on a verse translation into English of Kleist's German prose. The character's rage would be fuelled by the discovery that while vandalizing the house, a burglar used his typescript to wipe his backside. Coetzee's practice of basing his text on a canonical precedent is present here, but it was seldom combined with such deep anxiety about being derided.

By May 1980, after eight months of drafting, the focus had drifted away from Michael as a middle-class intellectual. Instead, a man and a woman enter the frame, ethnically marked as coloured. Almost all of the ethnic tagging would be removed from *Michael K* by the final version, except for one obscure reference to Michael as 'CM', which readers attuned to apartheid-era discourse would recognize as meaning 'coloured male'. The pair are, in the sequence of drafts, first a couple, later a grandmother and grandson, a husband and wife again, and, finally, a mother and son. Initially their names are Albert and Annie, a familial touch on Coetzee's part, for Albert and Annie were his great-uncle and great-aunt on his mother's side of the family. Both had literary inclinations, Albert being an Afrikaans novelist and Annie, of *Boyhood* fame, the translator who rendered her father Balthazar du Biel's German religious writing into Afrikaans.

In a version called 'Monologue of Annie', Coetzee returned to the post-revolutionary situation of the early drafts of 'The Burning of the Books' and *Waiting for the Barbarians*, with Annie speaking her text to a man who spends his days hunched over a table writing a great poem based on Kleist. The 'old times' have gone. The scene is Sea Point in Cape Town ravaged by civil conflict: abandoned cars, unkempt grass verges, dead animals, the streets and seafront promenade deserted, the electricity down, vagrants chopping up furniture to make fires in hand-basins, pawnshops broken into, a street vendor selling tortoises for food.[5]

Annie fusses over Albert, who is ill and coughing, transported by her belief in him and in the transfiguring power of art – a belief acutely at odds with the devastation around her. She worries about Albert's silence, invoking Ezra Pound in describing Albert as 'silent with grief at the spectacle of a wasted life'.[6] While he sleeps, she avidly reads what he has written. She decides to take him to the mission village of Genadendal, where they can live off the earth and he can recover.[7]

How these elements would eventually develop into the outlaw narrative of the original design was still far from clear. In fact, the more Coetzee wrote, the less clear the story became. 'After writing for a few days, I am face to face with the fact that I cannot continue until I clarify my ideas about the historical reality in which this action is supposed to be taking place. All that I have done thus far is to enclose the woman, with a silent partner, in a room in Sea Point in a world in which, it appears, the forms of everyday life have broken down (how? why?).'[8]

Instead of a post-revolutionary historical situation, he decided on something much more indeterminate: 'What one wants is chaos: jeeps roaring through the streets at night, sabotage, executions, fear everywhere, people sheltering behind locked doors, rumors.'[9] Later he imagined that the political context would be the forced '*ontruiming*' (removal) of Africans from the Western Cape, a policy requiring strict control over people's movements. Eventually, the ethnic particularities would be omitted, while the control over movement remained; hence the need for K to have a permit to leave the city.

In addition to these efforts to get the social background right, just as pressing for Coetzee were questions of form: 'But really, for No. 4, there needs to be some inventiveness in form. It can't just be another loony soliloquy, with a corpse rotting in a closed-off bedroom, etc. [referring to *In the Heart of the Country*]'[10] He contemplates including photographs with overdrawn arrows and bogus captions like 'The General Post Office. Plein Street, a few seconds before the explosion'.[11]

He wonders about writing the book as a screenplay, with descriptions of stills. There is still no movement, however: 'I sit in front of this blank page an hour at a time. I am getting nowhere.'[12] He contemplates making Albert and Annie not coloureds but déclassé whites, with Albert still working on his translation but protected by Annie, who wields a pistol, shooting at intruders.[13]

As this doesn't work either, he returns to his original conception, which involves staying closer to Kleist, but now he identifies two problems, one 'spiritual', the other 'technical'. The technical problem is straightforward and evident enough from the avenues he has pursued thus far: it is 'that I cannot interpret <u>MK</u> "into" a recognizable present situation (in fact I don't even know the text [Kleist's] well enough)'.[14] The spiritual problem is more revealing, and more intractable:

> I show no advance in my thinking from the position I take in <u>WfB</u> [*Waiting for the Barbarians*]. I am outraged by tyranny, but only because I am identified with the tyrants, not because I love (or 'am with') their victims. I am incorrigibly an elitist (if not worse); and in the present conflict the material interests of the intellectual elite and the oppressors are the same. There is a fundamental flaw in all my novels: I am unable to move from the side of the oppressors to the side of the oppressed. Is this a consequence of the insulated life I lead? Probably.[15]

The 'spiritual' was, in fact, political. From a position of class privilege, he found it almost impossible to write the story of the underclass K. Coetzee construes this as a 'spiritual' problem because it was about desire, empathy and social belonging. The contradiction he was wrestling with was this: how to attach the outlaw narrative of *Michael Kohlhaas* to the outrage felt by someone like himself: a liberal-minded, middle-class, white victim of crime. Even if this victim were to find himself saying 'a plague on both your houses' (as K does, eventually), and even if he were to become a disaffected internal exile, this would not exactly make him an outcast in the sense of being a fugitive from the law. Coetzee's 'technical' problem of translating

Kleist's novel into contemporary South Africa, and his 'spiritual' problem of feeling that he was too 'elitist' to be able to carry off the story, were actually one and the same thing. Apparently, Coetzee had hit on a contradiction that threatened to capsize the entire project.

A lesser novelist might have buckled under the pressure, but Coetzee's solution was to turn *Michael K* into the book that it became: the story of an outlaw who is so far beyond the reach of the law that even the very idea of the law, its conceptions of the citizen and civic responsibilities, are unable to contain him. Michael K is really the kind of rebel that Coetzee, the author, *could* invent, complete with some of Coetzee's temperament and inclinations: an intense bond with a mother; the farm as an invented place of origin; fondness for a version of pastoralism that privileges self-sufficiency over commerce (K's gardening; we see this too in 'Nietverloren' and in Lucy's market-gardening in *Disgrace*); asceticism around food (K's refusal to take nourishment); and social withdrawal (K's determination to stay out of the camps). As regards K's dietary restraint, Kafka's 'The Hunger Artist' is mentioned at a late stage of drafting, but early on it is Knut Hamsun's novel *Hunger* that appears in the notes.

Michael Kohlhaas is a disaffected member of an emerging middle class. Michael K is not middle-class, but his inclinations are, in some respects, suburban. To turn him into the powerful, prodigious figure that he would become, Coetzee had to make of him a hyper-outlaw whose resistance confounds all attempts to understand him. The terrain on which K's campaign is ultimately conducted is that of society's habits of thought, and indeed of language itself. K had to transcend all social norms, though without being other-worldly, or else his story would become mythic, beyond plausibility and too ideological.

Of the Albert version of the character, working on his translation, Coetzee wrote, 'when asked on the road what he does for a living, he says he is a poet, and sings part of the verse translation of MK. He also discusses it as an aesthetic ideal.'[16] This is mawkish literariness and clearly would not work either; it is excised when K ceases to be an intellectual altogether and becomes a gardener.

While K had to be plausible in realist terms, he could not be a full-blooded, violent rebel, like the Kamieskroon killer who was introduced as a possible model in the manuscripts, and who still survives, though enigmatically, in the published version. The Kamieskroon killer was an actual murderer about whom Coetzee kept a press clipping, who went on a killing spree aimed at whites in the northern Cape town of Kamieskroon. Coetzee was curious about this incident, but he would not be able to inhabit K's consciousness on the model of the underclass Kamieskroon killer with any credibility (a problem Athol Fugard also confronts in his novel *Tsotsi*).

K himself takes a lively interest in the Kamieskroon killer when he reads a news report in the Sea Point flat, but that is as far as it goes. Before including the relevant passage in the manuscript, Coetzee wrote in his notebook, 'Maybe we can drop the idea of K reading MK [*Michael Kohlhaas*] in Sea Point, and instead have him reading a front-page report of the Kamieskroon affair, with a color-picture of the man in chains, bloody but triumphant, a policeman holding a gun.'[17] Allusions to the Kamieskroon killer in *Michael K* have kept critics busy, but he is present largely as a remnant of the novel's original design.

So Coetzee started again, this time with a story that drew on his strengths: realism defamiliarized by means of textual mirrors: paradox, indeterminacy and self-conscious fictionality. Coetzee had to make *these* qualities the grounds of K's resistance. Gradually, the novel became what it was trying to be: a self-reflexive story about Anna K and her son Michael, who live in a room beneath the stairs of an apartment block in Sea Point, behind a door marked DANGER–GEVAAR–INGOZI ('danger' in the three main languages of the region), but the dangers associated with violent rebellion were turning into something more literary and more ambiguous.[18]

Coetzee still felt confined by his material. He writes, 'the only way out would seem to have to do with language itself'.[19] There were two aspects to the feeling of circumscription: the first was the 'technical' problem discussed earlier, of how to translate *Michael Kohlhaas* into South African terms. This was the problem of finding a class position that would render credible the feelings of outrage and alienation that were the novel's point of departure. The shift to materially impoverished coloured characters, rather than a middle-class intellectual, was a partial solution. The second constraint was formal: given the materials he was using, based on Kleist, Coetzee had tied himself to realism.

He found temporary relief by proposing that the book should at the very least be self-conscious about its realism: he envisaged it becoming 'an avid and rigorous *meditation* on realism [my emphasis]'.[20] Minimally, this would involve making explicit the eighteenth-century models, and exploiting the strategies of Defoe and Fielding in faking an authentic record. He pressed on in this vein, feeling uncomfortable – at times nauseated – by the tedium of having to spin out a naturalistic story. He turns Michael into a nine-year-old boy being read to out of *Michael Kohlhaas* by his grandmother, the boy identifying the fictional character as a father figure, in the absence of a real father.

Gradually, the life of the Michael of Coetzee's invention began to resemble Michael Kohlhaas, still his fictional hero. As he takes his grandmother and, later, mother in his cart out to Genadendal (the purpose being to settle her in her childhood home; Albert has disappeared from the drafts by this stage), he becomes more and more the outcast. He steals food and is used as a prostitute, but he still manages to retain an 'analytic directness and intelligence'.[21] To flesh this out, Coetzee made notes about the boy in Chaucer's *The Prioress's Tale*. Wordsworth's Immortality Ode is mentioned, and he speculates about Rudolf Steiner's educational doctrine, remembering the songs used by Waldorf school pupils about angelic children.[22] K speaks of 'God and the angels and his [fictional] hero, Michael'. The influence of Günter Grass is ruled out, although a novel by Grass was on his mind: 'one of his models is not the little boy in *The Tin Drum*'.[23]

Coetzee was still frequently exasperated: 'make him older and simpler (getikt)'. *Getikt* is colloquial Afrikaans for 'crazy'. The point of the plot, he noted, was that Michael was trying 'to extract his mother from the siege of Mafeking' (Cape Town in a civil war), but this was not promising; it felt like the middle of Fielding's *Tom Jones* and a series of petty incidents. Coetzee tried to wrench the plot into yet another shape, using both Kleist and the Kamieskroon case: 'this is just naturalism,' he writes, but 'let us pursue the idea for a while'.[24]

Through this tortuous process Michael gradually became a gardener. He sets off with the grandmother to Genadendal; they are held up; she dies en route; an official obstacle leaves him embittered; he takes to the mountains above nearby Greyton, from where he goes on a rampage in the town, committing an atrocity; because it is a time of war, the authorities will take him seriously only if he is shown to be an enemy of the state rather than a mere criminal; nonetheless, he is tried and convicted.

The novel as we know it had emerged, though still with a resemblance to *Michael Kohlhaas*. A change of setting was to come, from Genadendal to Prince Albert in the Karoo, where Coetzee had deeper roots. The important step was that K would have to cease to resemble Kleist's rebel altogether and become a quietistic gardener by vocation rather than an incendiary. He would also have to become more detached and impervious to the administration of justice. For Coetzee, at this stage, the 'basic problem' was literary; it was 'not how to write this story: it writes itself, that is the trouble. The problem is to introduce consciousness into it.'[25]

To get beyond the conventional realism, Coetzee introduced a new perspective in the form of a second narrator, who would eventually materialize into the medical officer of Part Two of *Michael K*. The development is signalled by this notebook entry:

There are two parts to the text: A and B, labeled thus. A is the story of K and his grandmother. B – which is much longer – is an assemblage of passages which lay out (expose) the basis of A: the kind of narrative on which it is based, both in terms of style and in terms of narrative ordering (*Michael Kohlhaas, An American Tragedy, Native Son, The Chant of Jimmie Blacksmith*). B also contains alternative presentation of A, e.g. K from the 'inside'. Also perhaps <u>materials</u>: evidences of Sea Point, of the road they travel, etc. (? Photography). Finally, perhaps, evidence of me.[26]

The second perspective came out of Coetzee's determination not to lose himself in realist narration (the picaresque story on the model of Kleist), but to find a way of bringing self-consciousness into the text. He wanted to write the epistemological second-guessing which reflected his own wrestling with the story and its form.

The last sentence of this entry – 'Finally, perhaps, evidence of me' – is especially revealing, confirming that for Coetzee metafiction has an autobiographical implication in so far as it is about the book's *being written*. The stakes for this mode of self-conscious narration are much higher than postmodern game-playing and they certainly don't involve self-masking – on the contrary, self-consciousness in the narration marks the place where the need to define oneself is most acute.

The notebook is illuminating here because it shows that Coetzee is frequently anxious about 'attaining consciousness'. He writes, 'The problem that torments K on the mountainside: How am I going to prove my innocence = How am I going to tell my story = How am I going to find a voice = How am I going to attain consciousness in this book.'[27] 'Attaining consciousness' means two things: showing that one properly understands one's materials; and bearing witness to one's existence in the act of writing.

There were several more twists and turns before the narrative of *Michael K* settled into the shape we know. Michael becomes older (including 'a version of Hendrik in <u>ItH</u> who got away'),[28] then a child again, before finally settling into the wise simpleton or idiot-sage or holy fool that we know him to be. At one point, Coetzee was exploring the use of Afrikaans for K's speech.

They approach a house, inquire if the owners know the Adams family. Stony silence. K speaks: 'My ouma was lank laas in Genadendal. Seker al veertig-vyftig jaar. Ons probeer nou om haar ou kennisse op te spoor. Ons is K – ... Die K's het seker lankal vertrek of uitgesterf – my ouma het geskryf – maar daar was geen antwoord nie. Ons loop lang pad, van die Kaap af.'[29]

This was not a solution, however, because the naturalism of Afrikaans would only have *deepened* the formal difficulties that Coetzee was trying to overcome. The move he sought was to move away from realism altogether: 'What I need is a liberation from verisimilitude!'[30] The second narrator was crucial to this, because it is only after he is introduced that K becomes the elusive figure who is able to slip past all attempts to capture and to understand him.

Coetzee spent a good deal of time and effort developing K's voice. The problem of accessing K's consciousness was solved finally by the use of multiple voices, and by having different perspectives being played off against one another. Critics have noticed this subtle feature of the point of view in the novel, the fact that the narration shifts between K himself and an observer, puzzlingly located inside K's consciousness. These ambiguities of perspective were even more pronounced in the drafts, where Coetzee experiments with quotation marks at the beginning of each paragraph, as if he is imagining a voice that is not the voice of a conventional narrator but that of another character who has still to be disclosed. He also tries a mode of narration derived from film, with passages of dialogue and passages of voice-over set alongside one another, recording a sense of liberation in this layered narrative:

Sense of elation yesterday for the first time re this project. New idea: to cast the whole as a screenplay, with the addition of (1) passages from a <u>hypothetical</u> novel behind it (set on the page in quote marks), and (2) voice over spoken by K – from his hospital bed to the narrator: only when we get to the hospital sequence do we understand the vantage point. Also perhaps (3) voice over of the narrator (to be called 'my voice').[31]

These techniques were deployed in almost exactly this fashion in the next novel, *Foe*. The reason the multiple voices were felt to be liberating would seem to be that Coetzee could use them to make K a more elusive figure – more liminal, slipping in and out of view. To the doctor in the Prince Albert hospital who is trying to get to the bottom of his story (the scene of this encounter is later shifted to a rehabilitation camp in Kenilworth, a suburb of Cape Town), K says, 'You can't make a book out of my life. Life has just slid past me.'[32] After this, the meaning of K's life becomes apophatic – which is to say, it is defined not by what it is, but by what it is not.

Eventually, all rationalizations fail to capture the essence of K, even his own. The medical officer's account, which is ultimately un-comprehending, is a proxy for Coetzee's, its failures deliberate, how-ever, because they make possible K's slipperiness. In this very quality Coetzee had found his true theme: Michael Kohlhaas, the insurrectionist, had finally turned into Michael K, the consummate escape artist. The loose-leaved style of narration brought out a version of K that was resistant to being written but, *mutatis mutandis*, a K who was also a more pertinent expression of Coetzee's relationship to his material.

There was trouble ahead, though, because Coetzee still had to tackle the politically sensitive question that the writing of *Michael K* had produced: the matter of K's relation to the guerrillas operating from bases in the mountains. When the novel was published, it won applause abroad, but some critics at home were uneasy. Most memorably, in her review for the *New York Review of Books*, Nadine Gordimer argued that a 'revulsion against all political and revolutionary solutions rises with the insistence of the song of cicadas to the climax of this novel'.

The problem, for Gordimer, was K's indifference to the anti-apartheid struggle, and the fact that Coetzee 'does not recognize what the victims, seeing themselves as victims no longer, have done, are doing, and believe they must do for themselves'.[33]

Two decades later Coetzee still felt the smart of this criticism, as we have seen, noting in the draft of *Diary of a Bad Year* that Gordimer had accused him of lacking political courage.[34] This sad outcome is made sadder, in retrospect, by the fact that Coetzee had anticipated just such a reaction and had tried to head it off as he wrote. The problem was the consequence of the essential contradiction that the novel sought to overcome from its earliest moments: how to turn Kleist's violent rebel into the pacific, internal exile that is Michael K. If he *were* a revolutionary, like Michael Kohlhaas, it would not be difficult for K to make common cause with those who had chosen armed opposition, but Coetzee had been getting further and further away from his model, turning K into something quite different.

In one respect, K and Michael Kohlhaas remain ideological bedfellows: in standing outside the law, both are radically free subjects, citizens of the universe – but while Kohlhaas embraces violence, K does not. In that respect, Coetzee was in danger of setting himself apart from the freedom struggle in South Africa, which arguably was closer to Kleist's model than his own. Coetzee had to make a simple but irrevocable decision in his drafting: would Michael join the guerrillas or not? If he did, it would betray what he had become; if he did not, Coetzee himself would stand accused of being politically spineless. Coetzee writes, as if in self-admonishment, 'The book started with Kleist behind it. Is Michael K– ever going to take to the hills and start shooting?'[35]

Coetzee did feel quite close to his subject, even implicated in his choices. He weighed up different explanations for K's refusal to become a freedom fighter. One explanation, which was quickly rejected, was to have K distance himself after witnessing guerrilla atrocities.[36] Another was to insist that his vocation was to be a gardener, a version of which survives in the published text: 'There

59

is empty, he trots over to fetch the spade, returns, and begins to
turn the earth over, burying the ashes.

    Voice-over (K—): I could have made a grave, and put flowers
                on it, if there had been flowers, if it had
                been the season for flowers; but it seemed
                better that she should make things grow…

[3.vii.80] * The road to Prince Albert. K— walks. He is not
wearing the black coat or carrying the box. He has washed the Red
Cross jacket and wears the beret at a smart angle.

    Voice over (K—): Already I was beginning to feel what my
                mother had called the healing effect of the
                country air. I would not have gone back
                to the town if I had had the choice.

    * The same general dealer's store that K— has already
visited. K— enters watchfully. There are at least a dozen customers
standing around waiting to be served. Those behind the counter are the
proprietor (with whom K— had crossed swords) and a young assistant.

    K— leaves the store and stands outside on the stoep. A child
comes out of the store carrying a parcel wrapped in newspaper. The child
passes him, then turns around and gives him a smile: it is the same
little boy who gave him directions to the farm. K— recognizes him
and smiles back.

    K—: Can you do something for me again? (He comes close
to the boy and takes out his purse.) Can you buy something for me?
I'll give you the money. I want you to buy me some seeds, some
packets of seeds: beetroot, carrot, onions. Can you remember that?
Beetroot, carrot, onions. One packet each. Here, take my purse;
and buy yourself sweets for ten cents too.

    Boy: Are you living on the farm?

    K—: Just for a little while — but you mustn't tell anybody
    K— holds the boy's parcel while the boy goes into the store.

Film techniques used in the drafting of 'Life & Times of Michael K'.

were enough people who thought that one should fight in order that one should be free later to be a gardener. That thought was in no danger of dying out. I wanted there to be at least one gardener throughout. Who did not hoe and plant in order that a war should be won and he should be free to garden but because the earth called to be hoed and planted.'[37] But Coetzee was still unsure. If this is indeed the 'message' of the novel, he wrote, then he needed to qualify it by adding its critique. The solution was for K 'to go to the field to pick food for the men, but when he gets there he finds the horses eating the vines.'[38] With this incident, K's naivety and lack of forethought emerge as an explanation for his political quietism.

But Coetzee seems to have felt that this would be a betrayal of K, because he proposed another solution, in which the problem of K's political nakedness would be flung back at his accusers in a trial scene: 'At the end: the trial of K– for harboring; which turns out to be identical to the interrogation of the novel.'[39] There is no grand finale of this kind, the climax of a trial; instead, K is continually accused and evasive, and the entire weight of the narrative is thrown behind his outlook. Coetzee therefore solves the problem of the novel's political nakedness by turning the accusation on his own potential accusers. The metaphor that enabled him to effect this reversal was that of the host and parasite, which he borrowed from an essay by J. Hillis Miller in *Deconstruction and Criticism*.[40] Accused of being the parasite, K turns out to be the host, not only of the predatory authorities in his own universe, but also of those readers and critics who would accuse his author, Coetzee, of spinelessness. Coetzee was gambling on the dynamics of the story protecting both K and himself.

Coetzee had developed a metafictional turn that would challenge the politicization of fiction itself – this is another of the novel's autobiographical moments. He knew perfectly well that K was in certain respects an extension of himself. He writes, K's 'not going off with the guerrillas is thematized as a lacuna in his story. It is a lacuna in the logic of his political progression, a lacuna in my own position. It is an unbridgeable gap (and must be so with all comfortable liberal whites), and the best one can do is not leave it out but to represent it as a gap.'[41]

But while K did become a means through which Coetzee would answer the demands of the culture, it was also important to him that K become more than a confidence trick. 'In his original inspiration, K– was one of those C18 wandering heroes. He has become a purely reactive character. He must get his own desires again.'[42] He felt the frustration of uncertainty, though: 'So what is it all <u>about</u>? It's just an evasion of social relations, past and future, by past relations dead and refusing future relations. I'm postponing all the justifications to the end, and I don't know how to make them.' As with *Waiting for the Barbarians*, the position of internal exile suggested itself. Perhaps the novel was about damaged people refusing to have to justify themselves: 'private lives, private fates'. The autobiographical–metafictional element was again not far behind: 'Why interview me? Why write a book about me? How does the interview[er]/writer justify himself?'[43]

What Coetzee was certain about was that despite K's attachment to the earth, he would not allow the novel to end up as a justification of pastoralism. K 'is not going to be absorbed into a South African rhetoric of liefde vir die bodem [love of the soil]'. Nor was he going to be 'a mad seer, someone outside and above society'.[44] Coetzee felt that he was between cultures and systems of symbolic value, and that he ought to keep K as an indeterminate figure who had no natural or cultural home. 'K struggles to exist between the Scylla of Representativeness (the Historical Novel) and the Charybdis of Individuality (the Modern Novel). In the background also lurk the lone heroes of the American Romance (Natty Bumppo, Huck Finn, etc.).'[45] He hit on his title soon after coming to this realization.[46] *Life & Times of Michael K* implies that he was anxious to preserve the historical representativeness – 'life and times', with no definite article 'the' – but in a way that set this mode in tension with modernist individuality.

As he had done at a critical stage when writing *Waiting for the Barbarians*, Coetzee went looking for the resources he most needed. He found them in Kafka's ape in *Report to an Academy*, and Kafka's story 'A Hunger Artist', in Dostoevsky's figure of the holy fool, in Pascal's *Pensées*, in Nietzsche's *The Dawn*, in Flaubert's *Un coeur simple*, in Melville's *Bartleby the Scrivener*. He read medical texts on the cleft palate (K's condition), and on nutrition and its disorders. He read Marshall Sahlins on scarcity economics. Intriguingly, with more absorption than for any of these other sources, he read the German existentialist theologian Rudolf Bultmann: *History and Eschatology*, *Theology of the New Testament* and his commentary on the Gospel of John. Bultmann argued that Jesus' meaning inheres in his historical specificity and humanity. Coetzee observes of Bultmann's position, 'The kairos of Jesus does not mean, "not now, but later," but asserts that the time (the "now") of the revelation cannot be determined at all from the world's point of view.'[47] Influenced by Heidegger, Bultmann argued that the purpose of the Gospels was to teach theology *as story*, to give an experiential rendering of the sacred.[48]

Coetzee found Bultmann helpful, but K's transcendence is provisional and secular rather than religious – he stands outside ordinary language, this being the literary implication of his harelip. Coetzee steadily transformed K into a figure whose meaning is neither obvious nor immanent, but who nonetheless gestures towards a meaning that cannot be understood by the world in which he lives. K's apparent lack of meaning (or his absenting himself from meaning) is his very strength. Friday, in his silence, would have similar capacities in the next novel, *Foe*.

The medical officer in *Michael K* is correct in discerning what K stands for: 'Your stay in the camp was merely an allegory, if you know that word. It was an allegory – speaking at the highest level – of how scandalously, how outrageously a meaning can take up residence within a system without becoming a term in it.'[49] Since K also escapes from the medical officer's benevolent clutches, he evades even this perfectly respectable conclusion, and so we are left with a K who escapes, ad infinitum.

Coetzee triumphed over his own earlier difficulties by creating a powerful anomaly – one which, when read back into the culture from which it springs, stands as an affirmation of artistic and intellectual freedom (even if such a declaration, in its finality, traduces what the novel itself argues). But Coetzee doesn't leave matters there: the novel's last gesture, as reflected in the notes, is to invoke the spokesperson of the servant class, Dilsey, in Faulkner's *The Sound and the Fury*: 'They endured.'[50] *Michael K* ends with an image of K's endurance: he imagines returning to the farm, where, in order to extract water from the well that the soldiers have blown up, he would lower a teaspoon on the end of a string. Implausible in naturalistic terms, it is a memorable image of survival. To acquire its full rhetorical effect, the teaspoon has to be deliteralized. Much of Coetzee's fiction works this way: beginning with the ordinary, it involves a determined process of deliteralization.

8

CRUSOE, DEFOE, FRIDAY

Foe

What is the whole thing all about? I have no interest in this woman,
there is no potential in her as there was in the Magistrate or
Michael K. The only figure I can generate anything but
puppetry out of is <u>myself</u>. When am I going to enter?[1]

BEFORE READING 'He and His Man,' the story that was his Nobel
Lecture on 7 December 2003, in the reception room of the Swedish
Academy in Stockholm, Coetzee introduced it by recounting a
childhood encounter with Daniel Defoe's *Robinson Crusoe*. In 1948
or 1949, when he was eight or nine years old, he read the book in
what would have been an abridged version based on the first of the
Crusoe stories. A few months later, he came across an entry in *The
Children's Encyclopaedia* (it would have been the work by Arthur Mee
mentioned in *Boyhood*) to the effect that *Robinson Crusoe* was written
by a man called Daniel Defoe who wore a wig and lived in London.
'The Encyclopedia referred to this man as the author of *Robinson
Crusoe*,' Coetzee said, 'but this made no sense, because it said on the
very first page of *Robinson Crusoe* that Robinson Crusoe told the story
himself.' So who was Daniel Defoe? Was the name perhaps an alias
that Crusoe adopted when he returned from the island?[2]

The lecture followed – a tightly composed allegory of the relations between an author and his creations. 'He' is Crusoe, 'His Man' is Defoe. Already in his introduction, Coetzee had begun to conflate these figures by saying, archly, that he could never remember the title of his story, whether it was 'He and His Man' or 'His Man and He'. (Behind the story lies Jorge Luis Borges's 'Borges and I', a story about a man's relationship with his authorial name.) In calling Crusoe and Defoe He and His Man respectively, Coetzee was specifically occluding Friday, because in Defoe 'His Man' is always Friday – the possessive pronoun implying servanthood and possibly slavery. Friday's exclusion from Coetzee's allegory is unexplained but perfectly deliberate, for reasons that will become clearer later on.

Coetzee's pre-lecture anecdote to the Swedish Academy shows how far back his relationship with Crusoe/Defoe goes. The island story would have struck a chord in a child who felt socially and culturally isolated. In the drafts of *Summertime*, he writes,

> He asks his mother (somewhat accusingly) why she impressed it on him that the world was hostile, that his education should be devoted to making a nest for himself where he would be invulnerable. It strikes him that the children's books that had most enthralled him had revolved around stockades and fortresses: *Treasure Island, Robinson Crusoe*.[3]

It is an evolving, lifelong interest which, by the time he wrote *Foe*, was as much about eighteenth-century prose – its faux reportage, its epistolary forms – as about Defoe's ideas. The Nobel Lecture also condenses a wide-ranging familiarity with Defoe's writing, not only the three episodes of *Robinson Crusoe* (*The Life and Strange Surprizing Adventures*, *The Farther Adventures*, and *Serious Reflections during the Life and Surprizing Adventures*), but also *A Journal of the Plague Year* and *A Tour Through the Whole Island of Great Britain*.

Foe tells the story of Susan Barton, who during a sea voyage in search of a lost daughter, finds herself stranded on an island off the coast of Bahia, where she meets the characters of Defoe's famous novel: Cruso (Coetzee spells the name without an 'e') and Friday. In its early drafts, *Foe* was the story not of the mother, but of the daughter figure in another major work of fiction by Defoe, namely *Roxana: The Fortunate Mistress*. The daughter's name is also Susan Barton, and she is looking for her mother, who has repudiated her while climbing the social ladder as an exotic courtesan. It was only well into the writing of *Foe* that Coetzee switched the characters around, making Susan the mother. At one point, her daughter is the product of a relationship she once had with Cruso; later, the daughter's origins become more obscure and she becomes the focus of a struggle between Susan and the author, Foe, over the details and the meaning of her narrative. In the end, we never find out what the true story of Susan's daughter is in *Foe*. She is there simply as the point of contention in the argument between Susan and Foe. Coetzee had had the idea of a novel based on Roxana's daughter for some years and began writing it on 1 June 1983, although notebook entries in which he sketched out possible plot-lines go back still earlier, to 1982, when *Life & Times of Michael K* was in press.

The appeal of Defoe and the Crusoe tradition seems always to have been linked in Coetzee's mind to questions of authorship – to the autobiographical investments that are hidden in realist stories, and to the possibility of an author's inventing a double life. *Foe* was certainly going to explore this terrain: 'Foe sleeps with Susan to get to know her side of the story. Susan sleeps with Foe to get closer to her mother. He is old, she is young. (There is a Mrs Foe in the background? Perhaps not.) Their eyes are both on someone else: Roxana.'[4] Susan becomes a servant in Foe's household, secretly reading his manuscript of *Robinson Crusoe* and wondering when he is going to get down to writing *Roxana*. Another discarded backstory gives a different account of how Susan came into Foe's service: she has read *Robinson Crusoe*, thinking it was written by Crusoe himself; she leaves copious letters with a bookseller, offering to go into his (Crusoe's) service; thus she discovers the identity of Defoe and becomes his servant instead.

These storylines are all abandoned, needless to say; instead, in the final version Susan begins an account of how, in her wanderings in search of her daughter, she finds herself on Cruso's island, and at this point the novel begins to take shape as the story of the woman that Defoe himself declined to tell. Gradually, the narrative on which *Foe* is based, Susan's 'The Female Castaway', is written.

By comparison with previous novels, the manuscripts of *Foe* seem remarkably fluent, as if Defoe's world, and the pastiche of eighteenth-century prose, were congenial to Coetzee. 'Where is this voice from that speaks in me, that I speak in?' he writes in the notebook. 'It comes through the clean, firm flesh of my throat, it utters itself through clean lips and tongue. It is as if I am born out of the sky, a woman of twenty with the flesh of a baby, so new and clean that one might be forgiven for wanting to eat me …' He adopts the tactile simplicity of the style but not without self-parody, as the cannibalistic hint suggests. 'I feel as if I am a cherub flying down from high, but full of words already, piping them.'[5] Susan leads Coetzee to William Blake's *Songs of Innocence*, which is the source and derivation of the cherub, but this is all far too good to be true and he begins to worry about how he will do justice to the story's shadows – to the cruelty that haunts the Atlantic trade, and to the self-consciousness that is brought on by the very simplicity of the style:

> The <u>cleanliness</u> of Defoe's world, the world of the early eighteenth century. This woman needs no passport to pass between Bristol and Bahia, she does not suffer from migraines during the passage, there is a fresh breeze on her face every day, there is cordage to lean against as she scans the horizon, there is the oak of the bulwarks, that someone scoured and planed with his own two hands. By entering this world I pretend not to know any longer what it means for a merchantman to be plying between Bristol and the New World, or what this gentleman is up to who has set up his trading house in Brazil. The language I

am writing (the language of Defoe I am imitating) is incapable of knowing itself, of knowing that these merchantmen and factors are engaged in an enterprise of mapping the world. To Defoe's language, the merchantman is merely a sturdy sailing-ship; by giving myself up to that language I am giving up any capacity to reflect on the meaning of my story. The cleanliness and simplicity of the language is also an obtuseness, a lack of edges. I am yielding myself up to that obtuseness, like an old woman rocking back and forth, telling a story that she barely hears the meaning of, so deeply is she lost (once again) in the feeling of the familiar syllables in her throat, on her tongue, through her lips. I am going to struggle every now and again in this text to come to the surface and breathe again, look around me, know where I am; but the language that looks so clean and simple is in fact as turgid and heavy as the sea; this is going to be a story about drowning, a continual drowning without a death (it is on the left-hand page that the meanings can release themselves, that I draw breath, that I can think).[6]

So a layered text begins to emerge, involving a raw narrative of experience embedded in epistolary frames, the structure we are familiar with in *Foe*. 'So who is Daniel Defoe, author of this language? On the one hand (the right hand) a man who lives in his world, in his language like a fish in water, who I chose to follow; on the other (the left) a figure whom I see as an inexhaustible source of meanings, that I hope to release.'[7]

The empirical directness of the eighteenth-century style appeals to Coetzee, but it also represents an irrevocable innocence, a mode of nostalgia even, that is best avoided. Something like this tension came into Coetzee's earliest autobiographical efforts. He began writing *Boyhood* in 1987, and by 1993 he had developed the controlled, ironic, third-person perspective that rules over the whole trilogy; but there was a period from 1993 when he shelved the project for a full year. The reason for the postponement leaps from the page in the manuscripts: it is the feeling that he is too detached. He writes:

Who is this he who will not speak his name?

Why will he not bring the story to life? What puritanism keeps him from evoking those wet winter mornings, wind-still, droplets on every leaf, mist over the roads, the glow of headlights and the soft swish of approaching tyres, and the boy on his bicycle breathing, breathing in mist and breathing out mist; the velvety softness of the mist? Why not live with this living boy?[8]

Coetzee's inclination is usually to resist abandonment to a dense, richly textured, empirical language, but occasionally, as here, there is a taste for it, and it seems that imagining an eighteenth-century world enabled him to lose himself in it for brief periods. When an island off the coast of Bahia became too challenging, he imagined setting the novel on a rocky island off the coast of Namibia; then he cajoled himself into imagining the island as the Cape Point Nature Reserve, just south of Cape Town.[9] These settings would have freed him to write a known landscape, an indulgence of sorts.

But 'losing himself' to a language of empirical richness was clearly what Coetzee also did *not* want from this text. 'The only hope for this book is if it moves to a climax. That is to say, it will have to justify itself at the end (*Michael K* justified itself somewhere in the middle). Which will entail a stripping away of all disguises, down to ME.'[10] Putting himself in the story despite, or perhaps because of, the remoteness of the context was important: 'What is the whole thing all about? I have no interest in this woman, there is no potential in her as there was in the Magistrate or Michael K. The only figure I can generate anything but puppetry out of is myself. When am I going to enter?'[11]

The answer to that question – as it was in *Michael K* – was tied up with introducing greater self-consciousness into the project. The language 'that looks so clean and simple' is actually 'as turgid and heavy as the sea'; so, if this was not going to be 'a story about drowning, a continual drowning without a death', then his self-conscious being would have to be in it somehow, but 'without disguises', as 'ME'. He writes in his notebook:

With every book I have written, the temptation has been to extend (to get length) by adding planes of consciousness. Every time this stratagem has been (rightly) avoided. Insofar as the books have achieved anything, it has been that they have reduced the planes to (projected the planes onto) a single plane.

Now once again I sit trying to add planes to a story. When I think of 'breaking out', of writing a less traditional kind of book, it is always in these terms in which I think. That isn't the way I ought to be thinking.

On the other hand, I can't see a way to get back from this tedious London to the present day except via the consciousness of the writer.[12]

To which he adds, 'Dostoevsky shows that consciousness is no solution.' Nevertheless, it was consciousness, specifically the consciousness of the *writer*, that he wanted to represent and that, in due course, shaped the structure of *Foe* as a series of narrative frames. It begins with Susan's account of her time on the island; it proceeds with her letters to Foe; then it moves on to her narrative about Foe; and finally, it ends with an enigmatic final section in which an unnamed narrator explores a shipwreck that represents the Crusoe tradition, only to find at its centre Friday, still mysteriously alive under the water, with a strange language of silence issuing from his mouth.

The conclusion to be drawn from this narrative structure, which is very much a story of Coetzee's search for himself among his materials, is that it was in Friday that the search was going to reach its conclusion. The edginess and volatility of the whole project, the site where Coetzee's self-conciousness as a writer would be most exposed and most in evidence, would be Friday. It is not surprising, then, that one of the titles Coetzee considered was, simply, *Friday*.[13] Of course, it is not remotely the case that Friday represents Coetzee's image of himself; it is rather that in Friday, in a willed, almost fatalistic way, Coetzee would confront his own limitations.

Friday is a dynamic, changing presence in the early drafts of *Foe*. Early on, he is far from the enigmatic, sexually ambiguous, silent figure that we know from the published text. Susan has no doubts about his sexual potency, and she and Friday teach each other their respective languages, with Friday teaching her to speak 'cannibal'. Her efforts are so poor, though, that Friday tells her to desist:

> he said to me, 'Ni-wa mu-a paku-wa!' which is to say, 'Do not speak the cannibal's tongue!' Fire seemed to flash from his eyes; I have never before seen him so cross. He grasped two of the gourds we used for water and held them to himself like breasts and in a falsetto voice, mimicking a woman, began to recite in a tongue that I knew to be cannibal, though I could not make out the words until it dawned on me that he was repeating everything I had said, the names of all the things about us, but in a mangled, twisted form that I cannot reproduce here, in order to deride me.[14]

Friday resists her, clearly, as an active, articulate subject, through mimicry. This is certainly an improvement on the situation in Defoe, where Friday is given a debased form of English, but Coetzee became suspicious of the version of Friday that he was creating in these exchanges. He told himself that the voice and identity of Friday – meaning, of all the world's Fridays – had already been spoken and represented many times before in the literature of the twentieth century, in the literature of decolonization specifically, and that this was not the story that he felt especially qualified or motivated to tell. He did not want the novel to become 'a vindication of Friday, with a simplistic moral ... There has to be a stronger passion than for Friday merely to "win a round" against Cruso/Defoe.'[15]

If he was not the writer who would give Friday speech and a redemptive history, then what would he do with him? Out of this quandary developed the idea of Friday being unable to speak because he has been mutilated, his tongue severed – in the earliest version of this, by cannibals, and later by whom we don't know, although it is hinted that it might have been by Cruso himself.

Friday's mutilation is undoubtedly the enigmatic heart of the novel. His speechlessness puts all of Susan's efforts at self-articulation under

(20)

For answer Crusoe motioned Friday close and motioned to him to open his mouth. ~~Friday gaped~~ Friday opened his mouth. 'Look,' said Crusoe to me: 'look in there'. But I could see nothing save a black hole and some very white teeth. 'La-la-la,' said Crusoe — 'Go on, Friday, say la-la-la'. 'Ha-ha-ha' said Friday from the back of his throat. 'Do you see now?' said Crusoe to me — 'He has no tongue'. And gripping Friday by his woolly hair he pushed his face forward and held his jaws open. 'Say la-la-la', he said. 'Ha-ha-ha' gasped Friday. 'Take him away,' I said to Crusoe. Crusoe released the black man. 'They cut out his tongue,' he said to me. 'That is why he ~~cannot can~~ can no longer utter the words of his heart. They cut out his tongue because the tongue is a delicacy among them, and because they wished to spare themselves his screams. I saved his life, but I did not come early enough to save his tongue.' He turned to Friday. ~~Bed,~~ 'Wash ~~sleep,~~ Friday,' he said; and Friday ~~stuck took~~ took up our utensils and slunk off to the little rock-basin where we did our washing.

'Nor is Friday a slave,' said Crusoe. 'I did not bring him here, I do not own him. He remains because he wishes to, and because he cannot leave, as you cannot and I cannot.' 'Nevertheless he is not free', I said. 'You are his master, whom he must obey, ~~and~~ whom he cannot leave. His condition is that of slavery.' 'Friday is free to leave my service whenever he wishes,' said Crusoe. 'But does he know that?' I replied. 'Does he understand he has that freedom? And of what use is such freedom to him, the mere freedom to leave your service? What can he do on your island but starve? He cannot plant unless you give him corn. He cannot hunt unless you give him a musket

Susan Barton learns that Friday's tongue has been severed.

a cloud, because she is unable to account properly for the time she has spent with him, both on the island and after their return to England. It is not as if the novel provides an alternative perspective to Susan's from which we can glimpse the inner Friday, either. The novel's perspective is in fact no different from Susan's, except at the end. Most critics who have commented on this aspect of *Foe* settle for the idea that Friday's silence represents colonialism's negation of the black and colonized voice and identity, a reading that vindicates Coetzee by turning the text into an allegory of colonial brutality. But Coetzee's thinking was actually far more conflicted than this. He writes:

> Friday is always there as the other inhabitant of the island. But what Friday threatens to be or do (to murder Cruso, to rape Susan, to be revealed as tyrant of the island and king of the cannibals; or alternatively to become the mute victim of colonialism) never happens. His dark presence never disappears from the background, his presence comes to carry with it an atrocious history; but further than that, further than as a jog to the conscience, he never emerges into meaning.
>
> Friday is at the centre of this story; but I seem incapable of conceiving for him any role in the story. How much interest do I really have in Friday? By robbing him of his tongue (and hinting that it is Cruso, not I, who cut it out) I deny him a chance to speak for himself: because I cannot imagine how anything that Friday might say would have a place in my text. Defoe's text is full of Friday's Yes; now it is impossible to fantasize that Yes; all the ways in which Friday can say No seem not only stereotyped (i.e. rehearsed over and over again in the texts of our times) but so destructive (murder, rape, bloodthirsty tyranny). What is lacking to me is what is lacking to Africa since the death of Negritude: a vision of a future for Africa that is not a debased version of life in the West.[16]

Friday's silence is therefore not simply Coetzee's judgement of colonialism; it is his judgement about the failure of post-colonial nationalism. Moreover, this failure disables Coetzee as writer, both because it *is* a history of failure, as he sees it, and because he has neither the inclination nor the authority to supply the vision that is missing. This is how he expresses the predicament in *Doubling the Point*:

> Let me put it baldly: in South Africa it is not possible to deny the authority of suffering and therefore of the body. It is not possible, not for logical reasons, not for ethical reasons … but for political reasons, for reasons of power. And let me again be unambiguous: it is not that one *grants* the authority of the suffering body: the suffering body *takes* this authority: that is its power. To use other words: its power is undeniable.[17]

The problem is that Friday represents suffering, *is* suffering, pure and simple, and victimhood too; he is the great wound whose presence represents a categorical demand. For a writer of Coetzee's social position and background, there is simply no uncompromised position from which to express it, denounce it or assume responsibility for its amelioration. The sense of disablement of the (white) writer that Coetzee expresses here, through the mutilated figure of Friday, would later drive him towards a different kind of encounter with woundedness, namely the suffering of animals, in *Disgrace* and some of the stories in *Elizabeth Costello*.

The remoteness of *Foe*'s fictional milieu from South Africa's pressing demands was certainly not lost on Coetzee:

> They ('they') want me to be a realist. They want my books to be about, specifically, to be about South Africa, about social relations in that country. They check my text against what they have picked up in the popular media about SA, and where there is correspondence they say it is 'true'. The rest they cannot, will not read.

To which he adds, 'I have always written best from an adversary position.'[18]

He felt accused writing the previous book, *Michael K*, as we have

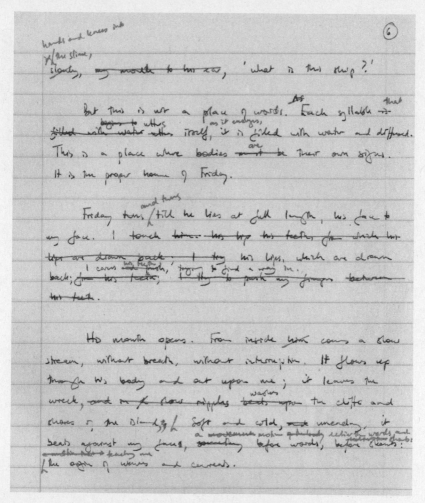

Draft of the final page of 'Foe'.

seen, and the problem was not eased by *Foe*. He writes a passage of dialogue in which Foe accuses Susan of being secretly pleased that Friday has no tongue, because it enables her to say that what Friday wants nobody knows, whereas it is obvious that if Friday could speak, he would almost certainly say, 'I want my freedom.' She replies, 'You say that I rob Friday of his tongue in order not to hear him,' and then demands the right to answer the charge: 'if the slaveowner's words are never to be heard, then he too is condemned to be without a tongue'.

Her rather desperate self-defence is the following:

> What Friday wants is more than freedom. Or what Friday calls
> freedom is more than the word freedom can ever hold. If Friday had
> his tongue, if he truly had his tongue, if he had the tongue of an angel,
> if Friday sat among the angels by the throne of God, he would say
> what the word <u>freedom</u> truly meant. ~~But for man to tell what Friday's~~
> ~~true desire is~~ But though this is a terrible thing to say, though I wish
> with all my heart that Friday had his tongue back, Friday with his
> tongue would be no better equipped than Friday without his tongue
> to tell the truth of Friday's desire.[19]

So Friday's desire, and indeed his freedom, are beyond not just Susan's
speech, but beyond speech itself, beyond comprehension altogether,
including Friday's own. This was to be the last conversation between
Susan and Foe. 'Therewith, I think, is resolved the problem of the
book,' Coetzee writes.[20] To sum up the resolution he had arrived at:
Friday's desire is real and palpable but language cannot grasp it. The
novel must therefore end by representing a quest for understanding
that is beyond language's reach.

And so we have the extraordinary final section of *Foe*, in which a
narrator – *the* narrator and, clearly now, Coetzee's sense of his own
presence in the book, the 'ME' he wrote of earlier – descends into a
wreck on the seabed only to find Friday, from whose mouth issues 'a
slow stream, without breath, without interruption' that 'washing the
cliffs and shores of the island … runs northward and southward to
the ends of the earth.'[21] Having begun as Susan's story, the story of a
woman adrift in Defoe's world who achieves notoriety by surviving to
tell the tale, *Foe* ends with a revelation about its author, who in seeking
to represent Friday discovers that Friday's story is not his to tell. The
ending dramatically illustrates the limits of representation that have
been imposed on Coetzee by history.

Coetzee had, once again, come face to face with time – face to face,
that is, with the times that his authorship had to live through.

9

MOTHER

Age of Iron

YOUR MAJESTIES, *Your Royal Highnesses, Ladies and Gentlemen, Distinguished Guests, Friends,*

The other day, suddenly, out of the blue, while we were talking about something completely different, my partner Dorothy burst out as follows: 'On the other hand,' she said, 'on the other hand, how proud your mother would have been! What a pity she isn't still alive! And your father too! How proud they would have been of you!'

'Even prouder than of my son the doctor?' I said. 'Even prouder than of my son the professor?'

'Even prouder.'

'If my mother were still alive,' I said, 'she would be ninety-nine and a half. She would probably have senile dementia. She would not know what was going on around her.'

But of course I missed the point. Dorothy was right. My mother would have been bursting with pride. My son the Nobel Prize winner. And for whom, anyway, do we do the things that lead to Nobel Prizes if not for our mothers?

'Mommy, Mommy, I won a prize!'

'That's wonderful, my dear. Now eat your carrots before they get cold.'

Why must our mothers be ninety-nine and long in the grave before we can come running home with the prize that will make up for all the trouble we have been to them?

To Alfred Nobel, 107 years in the grave, and to the Foundation that so faithfully administers his will and that has created this magnificent evening for us, my heartfelt gratitude. To my parents, how sorry I am that you cannot be here.

Thank you.[1]

Coetzee's after-dinner speech at the banquet in the Stockholm City Hall on 10 December 2003, following the Nobel Prize award ceremony, amazed the twelve hundred guests. There was a conspicuous reaching for tissues. Ten years later, it was still among the first points of conversation in Stockholm when Coetzee's name came up. It seemed so uncharacteristic: his rather recondite Nobel Lecture a few days earlier had done little to mend a reputation for reserve and severity. While the banqueting hall and television audience braced themselves for more *gravitas*, Coetzee surprised them with a disarming tribute to his mother.

To those who had read *Boyhood*, the pleasure of hearing this speech would have been mixed with recognition. For *Boyhood* places much emphasis on John's relationship with his mother, beginning with a tender sequence about one of the difficult phases in the life of Vera Coetzee. When his father, Jack, lost his job in Cape Town in 1948 and the family moved from the comfortable suburb of Rosebank to rural Worcester, Vera would have felt diminished. One day, not long after moving to the drab environs of Worcester's Reunion Park, Vera came out saying that she wished she had a horse. She had grown up on a farm, Oude Wolwekraal, near the town of Uniondale. Instead, she bought a bicycle which she had yet to learn to ride.

The men in the family, Jack and the two boys, mock her efforts to learn, but John is sufficiently aware of what is at stake for her. While he is at school, Vera wobbles into the town centre: 'Only once does he catch a glimpse of her on her bicycle. She is wearing a white blouse and a dark skirt. She is coming down Poplar Avenue toward the house. Her hair streams in the wind. She looks young, like a girl, young and fresh and mysterious.' Later, the 'memory of his mother on her bicycle

John's mother, Vera Coetzee.

does not leave him. She pedals away up Poplar Avenue, escaping from him, escaping towards her own desire.'[2]

Vera Hildred Marie Wehmeyer was born on 2 September 1904. Assuming that the bicycle episode of Coetzee's memory bears some relation to fact, she would have been forty-four, old enough for her dignity to be in jeopardy when learning to ride, but young enough to carry the air of having lived under different horizons.

John would scarcely have known his father until the age of five, when Jack returned at the end of World War II. In the years when he was away, Vera and her sons lived in a state close to penury: according to *Boyhood*, £6 a month from Jack's lance-corporal's pay and a further £2 from the Governor-General's Distress Fund. Between John's birth on 9 February 1940 and Jack's return, Vera moved house ten times: from Victoria West to Warrenton; then to Mowbray in Cape Town for a few months, to live with Vera's eldest sister, Winnie; from Mowbray

Vera with John and David, c.1944.

to Prince Albert, where she rented a room for a few months, before moving to Johannesburg and a succession of flats. When Jack joined up, she was pregnant with David. John remembers being sent to a crèche while his mother went out to work. In 1944 she moved to within range of her in-laws, first living on Voëlfontein for three months, then in Prince Albert, then back to Voëlfontein, then Plettenberg Bay, where she rented a holiday cottage for the better part of a year: off season, such rentals were cheap. When Jack came back they returned to Voëlfontein, then to Skipperskloof, a farm near Williston owned by Jack's sister Girlie's husband. Finally, they moved to Pollsmoor in Cape Town.

In the first five years of John's life, then, his father was either largely absent or rather feckless, while Vera came close to living the life of a refugee, nurturing a toddler and a newborn. It was obviously in this period that the intense bond between mother and son developed. The account in *Boyhood* is that Vera's relationship with her in-laws was strained, which would explain her being unable to settle on or near the farm. The summer in Prince Albert, especially, which was sandwiched between periods on Voëlfontein, is recalled with bitterness:

> Of Prince Albert he remembers only the whine of mosquitoes in the long hot nights, and his mother walking to and fro in her petticoat, sweat standing out on her skin, her heavy, fleshy legs crisscrossed with varicose veins, trying to soothe his baby brother, forever crying; and days of terrible boredom spent behind closed shutters sheltering from the sun. That was how they lived, stuck, too poor to move, waiting for the invitation that did not come.[3]

John therefore becomes 'her son, not his [Jack's] son'.[4] This account reflects the power of the relationship in the telling of it. It was essentially Vera's view of the situation, because Coetzee's Aunt Sylvia (née Smith, who was married to Uncle Son, at the time the custodian of Voëlfontein) speaks warmly of Vera and mentions how affectionate John was as a child towards his uncle and aunt. She remembers Vera being protective: when John went wandering in the veld, she would follow closely behind, something Karoo people saw as over-protective.[5]

In Coetzee's teenage years, after the family moved back to Cape Town, little changed in the intensity of the relationship with Vera. In fact it was confirmed, because Jack's practice failed again and it was left to Vera to pay John's school fees at St Joseph's College from her teacher's salary.

The separations from both parents that came in John's late teenage years and early adulthood, as they are recalled in *Boyhood* and *Youth*, are tangled and painful. Washing dishes over the kitchen sink as he moons about the house complaining, Vera casts a look at him that reveals that she 'was not brought into the world for the sole purpose of loving him and protecting him and taking care of his wants. On the contrary, she had a life before he came into being, a life in which there was no requirement upon her to give him the slightest thought.'[6] He leaves home and makes a bid for financial independence as soon as he can. Looking back on his student days, Coetzee said later, 'He pays his own way through university doing odd jobs, if only because he is too squeamish to witness his mother's sacrifices.'[7]

∞

Vera's influence on Coetzee's authorship is profound but by no means straightforward. To begin with, she was responsible for creating his particular relationship with the English language. It was also through her and her reflections on education that John's reading developed, from Arthur Mee's *Children's Encyclopaedia* to Paul Gallico's *The Snow Goose* to *Treasure Island* to *The Swiss Family Robinson* to P.C. Wren and on to *The Adventures of Robinson Crusoe*.[8] Unlike most parents of the day, she encouraged the reading of comics, believing that if the child was reading both the image and text, the benefits were doubled.[9]

Her intelligence, the struggles in her marriage, her limited financial means, the strength of her relationships with her sons, all left their mark on Coetzee's writing. Many of his leading characters are women, articulate heroines who struggle against trying circumstances, often contesting patriarchal authority: Magda in *In the Heart of the Country*, Susan Barton in *Foe*, Mrs Curren in *Age of Iron*, Elizabeth Costello. There are other influences on Coetzee's female fictional authors too, including the example of Nadine Gordimer. And without having to refer to either Vera or Gordimer, there is Coetzee's own shrewd sense that the female narrator is a strategic way of positioning oneself on the margins of authoritative traditions. The assertively feminine position in Coetzee's writing is at times a proxy for a self-staging that has little to do with gender. Nevertheless, Vera's perseverance would have shown the way.

∞

First notebook entry for 'Age of Iron'.

Vera Coetzee died on 6 March 1985. In June of the following year, Coetzee began work on the novel that would become *Age of Iron*. Here, too, the point of departure was conflicted. He wrote in his notebook:

Who shall guard the Guardians? Who shall censor the censors? The question is unanswerable without a theory of absolution. It is not answerable in a secular framework. There must be a class or caste of people outside society who are shunned or kept at a physical distance because they touch pollution …[10]

The opening phrase is from Juvenal's *Satires* (6, 347–8), 'Quis custodiet ipsos custodes?' where it refers to those who stand in judgement of adultery, but it has since been widely used in political philosophy. The argument is that if the lawmakers are corrupt, the only cure is a general cleansing of souls. Coetzee refers to this as a problem particularly for secular societies, which have no means of achieving absolution and therefore have to rely on a class or caste of 'othered' souls who carry the pollution away.

The origin of the mysterious Vercueil in *Age of Iron* lies here then, in Juvenal, as well as in Tolstoy's story 'What Men Live By', about an angel who visits an elderly, poor couple in the guise of a stranger. Coetzee's major essay on confession ('Confession and Double Thoughts: Tolstoy, Rousseau, Dostoevsky') is also in evidence.[11] While he may have been drawn to these themes in their own right, the notebook shows that he was wrestling with them in a more personal way.

Vera's death revived the problem of historical guilt. How was it possible, he was asking, for someone who was a quintessential bearer of love to be the bearer of the crimes of her generation? He writes, 'It [the novel] must be about innocence. Historical innocence. How my mother, belonging to her generation in SA, was nevertheless innocent.' The first entry seems to have had little to do with bereavement, but this is explained in part by his writing, 'Which means tackling the abstract question, and taking a "difficult" position on it.'[12] The personal dimension was in fact very clear: 'Write the story of my life for Gisela, and the story of my mother's life. Because we are all going to die in Africa.'[13]

Thus began a novel called 'The House on Toll Road', which was Coetzee's address in Cape Town, written in the third person and the perfect tense, a formally conventional work about the impending death of a woman who in all respects resembles Vera Coetzee. Initially called 'No. 6', 'The House on Toll Road' went through other titles: 'Rule of Iron', 'Winter' and, eventually, *Age of Iron*.

Coetzee found it difficult to locate the voice in this work. At one point he wrote, 'In the other books – particularly the last two – I had a conception of the prose to begin with (Kleist, Defoe) from which the text generated itself. Here --?'[14] The solution was to recast everything as 'letters to the departed', at which point 'all becomes possible'.[15]

The letters were from a son, addressed to a departed mother. Some of the letters were also addressed to a sister named Ellen, who had absented herself to another country, with the son informing her of the arrangements he was making: 'I have hired a nurse, for the days. Nurse Africa: a young woman, very beautiful.'[16] So we have an ageing, ailing body with a history – 'a body where a certain history played itself out', a history 'that will never again find utterance' – and a grieving son.[17]

In choosing to begin 'No. 6' this way, Coetzee was making himself as vulnerable as possible, writing a text in which all the intensity of his relationship with Vera was on the surface. The drafts are filled with grief. At the same time, the writing agonizes over the fact that the mother's views on South Africa and her place in its history were plainly unacceptable. It circles back repeatedly to the contradiction between love and ethical misgiving, as if Coetzee understood that the novel would have to be a family row in some sense. He would also have known that to transform this material into something less personal would be a struggle.

To access the mother's inner life, Coetzee told stories from Vera's childhood. A version of the following exquisite passage survives in the published novel, and is also used in the drafts of *Boyhood*:

> It is the year 1910. It is a summer's night, in Africa. It is a summer's night, and the sky is full of stars. There is a chill in the air, for we are high, on the very crest of the pass, Prince Alfred's Pass, named after the young prince Victoria's son, who has never seen it and never will. We are at the crest of the pass, where the road widens to a stopping-place, an <u>uitspanplek</u>. If we listen carefully we can hear the peaceful oxen chewing. The last embers of the fire glow dully. Beside the fire the

servants lie sleeping. In the wagon, asleep, lie your parents. Beneath the bed of the wagon, beneath the sleeping parents, on two horsehair mattresses, crosswise, you and your sisters sleep. That is, your sisters sleep: you lie awake.

The same person who breathes now in the night, in the old house, breathed then on that night. The same person. You.

The wheels of the wagon are blocked with great stones. ~~If the stones are removed You imagine taking away the stones~~ If someone were to take away the stones, now, the wagon would creak and lurch and then begin to roll; faster and faster it would roll, down the pass, down the valley; through the one street of Plettenberg Bay it would roll, past the shops, past the amazed people; ~~past the~~ chased by barking dogs it would thunder across the sand, into the sea. One could imagine all this, from beginning to end, and you do imagine it, as a game. Under the warm eiderdown, with the ~~sleeping~~ breathing bodies of parents and sisters and servants ~~all~~ around you, ~~protecting~~ guarding you from the night, with ~~the~~ crickets singing ~~and the oxen~~ in the bushes, you lie awake, staring ~~unwinkingly~~ through the spokes at the stars. You imagine the first creak, the first lurch; the wheels gather themselves and begin to roll. A shiver runs through you; you ~~continue to~~ stare unwinkingly at the stars, waiting for ~~the stars~~ them to move, waiting for a shooting star. This is ~~the~~ a game I play with myself, you say; in all the world it is only I who play the game. You keep your eyes open, trying not to blink. But you blink, and ~~then~~ at once you are asleep.

This is the game you used to play in 1910, under the wagon at the top of the pass on the way to Plettenberg Bay; it is your game, and only I am left to remember it; I and you.[18]

In the novel, this story is told by Mrs Curren about *her* mother. She tells it to Vercueil while they are driving down the Cape Peninsula in her ancient Hillman along Boyes Drive, to admire the view over Muizenberg.[19] She tells it to reach out to Vercueil, but he remains stony-faced and silent.[20] The connection to Vera is dropped, but what remains is the inner life of a girl, part-remembered, part-imagined by *her* child, then passed on by means of a letter to a third generation.

In the drafts, the Boyes Drive sequence explores the gulf in political morality between the mother and the son. The focus is on the politics of landscape. The son is driving and stops the car so that she can look out over the bay and, before she dies, have an 'intimation of what it is like to live in Florence's [her domestic worker's] country',

> where the spray that leaps is the same spray as before, but subtly different, in ways that cannot be explained to strangers or recorded by a camera, where the stone clock-tower over the station is no longer a little bit of the old country regenerated in Africa but an allusion (but how fanciful too! How poignant!) to a ~~remote architectural style~~ bygone architecture, where the very air (if you ~~open~~ roll down the windows) is not the same air that once bore upon you like a weight pressed down from above, but promises to circulate for ever and ever, washed clean each time by the rains, a gift, a breathing in our lungs, breathing all of us, man and beast, impersonally, kindly.[21]

The passage is about the pleasure to be found in the beauty of the scene, unalloyed by social anxiety. The son wants the mother to imagine that specific pleasure, but this entails a moral leap that she is not capable of taking. He hopes that the splendour of the prospect before her will release from his mother an outpouring of goodwill, in which she will acknowledge Florence's claim to the country:

> 'Let her have it back,' I want to hear you say. 'Let her have it back, not because I am dying and no longer care, but because it was a mistake, from beginning to end. A mistake – let us leave it at that, let us not go into explanations and least of all clarifications. Let the heart's good impulse come forth and stand there naked in all its obscurity. And if doubts remain in you whether Florence will appreciate the view from Boyes Drive any better once she is its owner, or whether she will endeavor to maintain Table Mountain in a pristine state (that is to say,

in its state as of 1652), so much the better, so much more generous will the heart's impulse have been.[22]

In the novel, these efforts by the son to manipulate the mother's desires are not narrated; instead, we have Mrs Curren simply admiring the long breakers, a distant surfer and the blue Hottentots Holland Mountains in the distance. The impulse that comes from her is neither confessional nor politically accommodating: 'These seas, these mountains: I want to burn them upon my sight so deeply that, no matter where I go, they will always be before me. I am hungry with love of this world.'[23] She sobs inexplicably: 'I am sorry, I don't know what has come over me.'[24] The rush of feeling here is existential, and unrelated to unresolved questions of political morality. The politicization has burned off and what remains is her encounter with this beauty in the context of her own mortality.

Age of Iron attends to generational differences between Mrs Curren and her daughter (the one who will not return until the current rulers are swinging from the lampposts), and between Mrs Curren and the young black militants who are mounting an insurrection from the townships. Florence's son Bheki is a key presence, as is his steely friend who goes by the name 'John' (a *nom de guerre*, as it parodies the European names colonials forced on their gardeners and houseboys). The crisis of the plot involves John being shot dead in an outbuilding of Mrs Curren's house because he is suspected of harbouring weapons brought in by liberation forces from outside the country.

Mrs Curren suffers through this episode in a state of utter dismay. Her relationship with the boys is permeated by distress at the fact that they are surrendering their childhoods to a heartless code of masculinity and the slogan 'Freedom or death!' She argues with Florence and the ex-teacher, Thabane, about their willingness to accept that the children have taken charge; to her, this attitude exemplifies the coming of the 'age of iron', a phrase borrowed from Hesiod and Ovid, where it refers to a succession of ages in which life gets harder, after the ease of the golden age. In these reactions to the conduct of the

The clock tower on Muizenberg station, from Boyes Drive, Cape Town.

struggle, Mrs Curren takes a position of outraged liberalism, informed by her age, her respect for individual life, her code of decency and her learning as a retired professor of classics.

In the manuscripts, by contrast, the generational differences are intra-familial, with the son accusing the mother and her generation of undermining the children's future and destroying the country. Parents have cut their children off by taking all they could, without regard to the consequences for subsequent generations:

The corruption of colonialism: is this how I am to understand you? That from ~~centuries of~~ your colonial experience ~~in the colonies~~ you had learned how to gut a place and leave it, mine it and abandon it; that you were in truth not farmers but predators, regressed from culture to hunting: freebooters, exploiters; that when you looked around the South Africa you had inherited you saw forty or fifty years of easy living, meat three times a day, and when the herds were shot out, when the time came to reap the whirlwind, you could be gone, sucked into the next world, leaving only the echo of your laughter hanging in the air?[25]

This portrait is far from the representation of Mrs Curren, needless to say. It is the outpouring of a politically sensitive son feeling betrayed, venting anger and anguish. The same tone continues in a passage in which the son recalls his mother going off to the Rondebosch Town Hall to vote in the election of 1984 (the era of P.W. Botha), struggling to make her way there on foot, with a weak heart, then coming back with the news that she has voted for the National Party candidate: 'When I saw you that evening … you told me the story, and told me too who you had voted for: told me with a certain smile, in which there was defiance, I know, but also, I think, malevolence, the malevolence of the dying for the living.'[26] Coetzee still had some distance to travel, to work through this bitterness and refashion the mother into what she would become.

Some of the emotive detail from these passages does remain consistent from draft to novel, though its contextual uses are different. At the end of the passage just quoted, where the son reacts to what he sees as the mother's malevolence towards the young, we find Coetzee writing, 'The reason I do not let go of you is that malevolence, that ill wish aimed like a shaft at me, a Partisan shaft, I think the expression is.'[27] Then, in a sentence written as a paragraph on its own: 'That is why it is important for me not to let go of you.'[28] Love, then, even when it seems impossible.

In a similar way, Mrs Curren's views about Bheki and his friend John develop into strong imaginative sympathy,[29] and she also learns to trust Vercueil, even if he has not earned it, leaving him to post her last words to the daughter. The novel invests in the idea of trust, therefore, and it is difficult to escape the implication that the root of this investment lies in the familial bonds beneath the surface of the final text. There is a trace of feeling there that was strong enough to survive the book's many revisions.

∞

A major development in the writing of *Age of Iron* was a shift in point of view, from the son to the mother. A progressive fictionalization occurs, beginning with a son who is not quite Coetzee; he is at various stages a sculptor, a teacher of photography, a book designer. He loses his grip on things, resigns his post at an art college, stops paying insurance on the house because he refuses to install the mandatory alarm system, and settles into writing diatribes about the failures of colonial history and his mother's role in them. He would take her books to the charity shop were it not for the fact that she has annotated the poems in her copy of *Palgrave's Golden Treasury*. His ex-wife is concerned about his state of mind; he buys a pistol. Before it turns into a series of letters, his text is a book about trying to create a life on his own terms, 'the project of living in South Africa, in these times'.[30]

Then we have his letters, but a step change occurs when the perspective switches from the son to the mother. At this point, the moral calculus is turned over: instead of a son alternately grieving and accusing, the mother ('evidently her name is Evelyn Curren', the name appearing for the first time) takes up her own narrative, and the child becomes detached and estranged by being politically judgemental. These developments came during an especially productive period of writing between January and March 1988. A further major development is that Coetzee was now able to write himself into the voice of Mrs Curren. No longer the grieving son but the intellectual and fellow humanist, Coetzee was able to develop Mrs Curren's classicism. She becomes a retired professor, enabling Coetzee to borrow, among other things, from Virgil's *Aeneid* as a way of giving cultural weight to her approaching death.[31] The intertextual work of fleshing out Mrs Curren's classical learning proceeds quickly from this point. The text is personal but in a different way: it has gone beyond mourning and has become a vessel that can carry Coetzee's own cultural freight.

∞

In one of the interviews in *Doubling the Point*, Coetzee uses a puzzling phrase when discussing *Age of Iron*. In response to a question about Mrs Curren's death and the suggestion that it represents a form of political absolution, he says,

> So a contest is staged, not only in the dramatic construction of the novel but also within Elizabeth's – what shall I say – soul, a contest about having a say. To me as a writer, as *the* writer in this case, the outcome of this contest – what is to count as classic in South Africa – is irrelevant. What matters is that the contest is staged, that the dead have their say, even those who speak from a totally untenable historical position. So: even in an age of iron, pity is not silenced.[32]

He uses a powerful phrase here: 'totally untenable'. Why would Mrs Curren's liberalism, the highest expression of which is her humane classical learning, receive this degree of opprobrium? In the critical literature this has been taken to mean that at the height of the political conflict in the late 1980s, when the state and the township youth were locked in a death struggle, liberal humanism had little purchase and was even derided. But totally untenable? This seems like an exaggeration. The 'dead' do refer to the classics and their part in the conflict taking place in Mrs Curren's soul, but it is hard not to see the presence of Vera Coetzee in the remark, the woman whose views were totally untenable to the Coetzee who began writing the novel by writing about her. The grief overpowered the political misgivings in the end, both in the writing of the novel and in the self-reflection afterwards, and with Vera in the background of *Age of Iron*, it is easier to understand why 'pity is not silenced'.

10

FATHER

Summertime

THE THIRD OF Coetzee's autobiographies, *Summertime*, ends on a troubling note in which John's elderly father returns from hospital, where he has had a laryngectomy for throat cancer. One of the ambulancemen hands John a sheet of instructions for the care of his patient, to which he responds incredulously, 'I can't do this.' The orderly shrugs off the objection as if to say it is not his problem, at which point John realizes that he has reached a tipping point. Responsibility for his father has devolved on him; either he will have to become a nurse, or 'he must announce to his father: *I cannot face the prospect of ministering to you day and night. I am going to abandon you. Goodbye.* One or the other: there is no third way.'[1]

It seems a callous conclusion, but in fact John has been caring for his father for several years already. The point is that the incident is pivotal, signalling the end of John's being the child. The drafts of *Summertime* present the problem more candidly: after his return to the country, John realizes that his parents' meagre earnings have been eroded by inflation and they have no pensions, so he is going to have to look after them. 'Yet psychically he still feels that he is the child, that they owe him a duty of care. This becomes the central conflict of Book 3.'[2]

The father's death is therefore less important to the story than the son's maturation, which is the theme confirmed by the title, and indeed the whole trilogy is organized around the emergence of the writer, ending with the publication of his first novel. The episode of the father's return from hospital to face death brings to an end the story that began in *Boyhood*, of intense Oedipal conflict in which Jack is rejected, to the point that the teenage John imagines, even hopes, that his father is suicidal. The conclusion to *Summertime* overturns this outcome and places an ethical burden on John that the child of *Boyhood* could not comprehend. The phase of blaming the father is at an end.

∽

Zacharias (Jack) Coetzee was born on 29 September 1912 in Prince Albert, and died at the Arcadia nursing home in Observatory in Cape Town on 30 June 1988. The family's movements during John's childhood were the result of vicissitudes in Jack's career. His law practice in Victoria West was already under a cloud when John was born. In May that year, when John was three months old, he moved the family to Warrenton, an even smaller Karoo town further north on the western Transvaal border, where he tried again, but the new practice also failed. Jack was mishandling trust funds and was struck off the roll of attorneys.

A year after setting up home in Warrenton, the Coetzees moved to a flat in Johannesburg, where Jack worked as a bookkeeper, first for a motor spares firm and then for the appliance manufacturer Electrolux. In July 1942 he joined the Sixth South African Armoured Division and went to North Africa, the Middle East and Italy, where he remained until the end of World War II.

When Jack returned, the Coetzees settled into a military camp in Pollsmoor, Cape Town, consisting of prefabricated houses established for returning servicemen. Jack soon found a job with the Controller of Letting, an office of the provincial administration that arranged ex-servicemen's residential lets, and the family was able to move to a more comfortable home in Liesbeek Road, Rosebank. However, in 1948

Father and son, c.1942.

Jack was made redundant and accepted another position as an accounting clerk, this time with the fruit-packaging company Standard Canners. It was this move that took the family to Worcester, a few hours' drive north-east of Cape Town over the Du Toit's Kloof Pass.

During the Worcester years, Jack worked successfully to persuade the Law Society to readmit him as an attorney, which meant the family could eventually move back to Cape Town. Jack's practice was this time in Goodwood, a lower-middle-class suburb of Cape Town, and the family lived in a succession of houses in Plumstead. John was enrolled at St Joseph's College, an independent Catholic school in Rondebosch, almost certainly because, despite excellent school reports, the boy with the Afrikaans surname from rural Worcester was rejected by the prestigious English-language state schools of the Cape Town suburbs.

John (right) with brother David in Reunion Park, Worcester, c.1949.

But in these years, Jack's old habits returned. With Vera earning the money for John's fees from teaching, he mishandled his attorney's funds again and descended into alcoholism. This is the last we see of Jack in *Boyhood*.

Jack died two years after Vera's death. In the three years between 1986 and 1988, Coetzee lost both parents and his son, Nicolas. *Age of Iron* is dedicated to them. There was a fourth bereavement in this phase of Coetzee's life, too, because his former wife Philippa died on 13 July 1990, soon after *Age of Iron* was completed.[3]

Coetzee chose to emphasize these years when reconstructing the events of his life in *Summertime*. The narrative collapses two quite distinct periods: his return from the United States in 1971, and the years between the deaths of his parents. There are other manipulations of fact too, such as his giving extra lessons, something he did while a student in the late 1950s rather than in 1971, but these details are less consequential. The effect of the contraction of the two periods is that Coetzee's immediate family life, the life he shared with Philippa and

The story untold in 'Summertime': Nicolas, John, Philippa, Gisela, in Buffalo, NY, c.1970.

the children, is excluded altogether. In the early 1970s, far from being the lonely, sexually awkward *schlemiel* (the word the text uses) that he portrays himself to be in *Summertime*, he was living a suburban life with his family in Cape Town, where they are remembered by friends and former colleagues as unconventional, a family whose routines and protocols had been shaped by 1960s America.

Philippa appears briefly in the early drafts of *Summertime*, at one stage fictionalized as Marcia, but once Coetzee changed the time frame, she disappears from the narrative altogether. Presumably, Coetzee felt that if Philippa's story were to be told, it would be best not to tell it in the context of an account of the development of his own writerly persona. The story of his marriage is one that Coetzee has not broached in any of his autobiographical pursuits. One assumes that his highly developed and unconventional views on autobiography, which include the notion that 'facts' get in the way of deeper truths, would meet their limit in Philippa. The facts that are left out of *Summertime* are those that relate specifically to her, the person to whose memory he would no doubt owe a strong residual loyalty.

∽

Summertime begins and ends with Jack in lightly fictionalized extracts taken from Coetzee's notebooks. In between, the biographer, Vincent, interviews former lovers, friends and colleagues, but the organizing frame is provided by Jack in the final months of his life. Perhaps the most enigmatic statement attributed to Jack in the entire narrative comes in a conversation with the fictional Julia. She sees him waiting at a bus stop and gives him a lift, and in the course of conversation Jack mentions that John is not an only child. There is a younger brother who has quit South Africa for England and shows no sign of returning. 'You must miss him,' says Julia. Gazing into the distance, after a long pause Jack whispers, 'Well, one misses so much.'[4]

The text does not explain what Jack might mean. The answer can only be extracted from the context of the whole work: the South Africa in which Jack was formed is inexorably passing into history. The fact that the remark is unexplained gives it general force; it reveals that Coetzee *himself* feels the passing of that world. This is a moment in a larger pattern in which it becomes clear, as we will see, that John has overcome most of his resentment towards his father.

The first extract from the notebook, in which John tries to engage Jack in a political conversation about the atrocities being committed by South African security forces against ANC bases in Botswana, ends with John writing, '*To be expanded upon: his father's response to the times as compared to his own; their differences, their (overriding) similarities.*'[5] John is reflecting on the history they share: reading his father, he reads himself.

In the drafts of *Summertime*, before he contracted the time frame, Coetzee had Jack moving into his house in Toll Road, Rondebosch, where he was living on his own, though intermittently with the children following the divorce, in the early to mid-1980s. This period was the phase that Coetzee puts into the fictionalized text set in the early 1970s. According to the notes, John and his father shared sporting interests, watched rugby and cricket together, looked over old photograph albums, and embarked on gardening projects. In the evenings, John would read while Jack did the crossword in the *Argus*, the afternoon newspaper.

The professional misdemeanours and alcoholism of Jack's middle years as recounted in *Boyhood* recede from view in *Summertime*; instead, writing in a voice that is now indistinguishable from his own, Coetzee reflects on the 'fatality' that drew Jack into law as a vocation.[6] The idea of the law as an amoral practice, as trickery, as a matter of 'getting people off', seems to have rubbed off on Jack, robbing him of a deeper sense of vocation. Add to this the social withdrawal brought on by his social position – directly as a result of his failures, but indirectly too, as a consequence of his anglicization and the social drift that came with being an Afrikaans-speaker who had turned his back on his people's political aspirations – and Jack became a lost sheep. All the bitterness of *Boyhood* has now gone, in this version of the story. Bitterness it certainly was:

> He steps closer. His eyes are growing accustomed to the light. His father is wearing pyjama pants and a cotton singlet. He has not shaved. There is a red V at his throat where sunburn gives way to the pallor of his chest. Beside the bed is a chamber-pot in which cigarette-stubs float in brownish urine. He has not seen anything uglier in his life.
>
> There are no pills. The man is not dying, merely sleeping. He does not have the courage to take sleeping-pills, just as he does not have the courage to go out and look for a job.[7]

The drafts of *Boyhood* throw out an even more bizarre moment of repudiation, when the teenage John complains to his mother that he doesn't like to see Jack hanging around the boundary of the cricket field at St Joseph's watching him play because the other boys think he is coloured. He knows how shameful it is to say this, but in his declaration of war against them, he is flinging his parents' racial outlook back at them.[8]

All of the disadvantage in John's childhood could indeed be construed as the consequence of Jack's misdemeanours and misfortunes: the shortages, the nomadism, the social descent from Rosebank to Worcester, the weakening of the connection with Voëlfontein. Coetzee may have found his mother's sacrifices unbearable, but his early decision to strike out and become financially independent as soon as possible came down to Jack. Despite their anglophile highcultural aspirations, the Coetzees were becoming déclassé, thanks to Jack's mismanagement of their lives. If Coetzee had come to feel, when writing *Boyhood*, that he had been malformed by South Africa, then in part it is because Jack provided no protection and no entrée as his son made his way in the world.

But there is another way of looking at this. Coetzee says that Jack was temperamentally unsuited to law, a sapling unable to bear its moral challenges. As a young man, he had wanted to go to sea. He fell into an early marriage with a woman eight years his senior, who was intellectually and culturally in authority. Outside the home, he had little cachet, which is the reason he used his trust funds to buy himself friends. It is no wonder that the child in *Boyhood* is directionless, fearing Afrikanerdom, not knowing whether he is a Jew, a Catholic or even a Christian, choosing the wrong side in the Cold War.

In the mature John, the poignancy of Jack's life overwhelms the earlier bitterness. Among other things, *Summertime* is an act of reparation. *In extremis*, father and son learn to accept one another. The passages in which this is most memorably achieved are those in which the father's inner life comes sharply into view: in relation to sport (his enjoyment of the steadily dying tradition of club rugby at Newlands), opera (the son's guilty reflections when he remembers his impatience with Jack's love of opera, after his return from war-time Italy), his war memorabilia, and the son's discovery of his father's melancholy over the fact that love has passed him by.

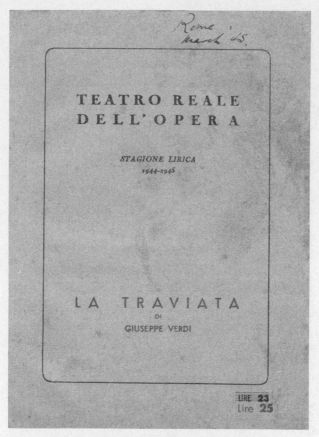

*Opera programme kept by Jack Coetzee,
Rome, March 1945.*

It is curious that Coetzee should rearrange the time periods in which these phases of his life occurred, creating the impression that his emergence as a writer coincided with, and even depended on, a rapprochement with his father. *Dusklands*, we might remember, has a fictional father, a historian who is an apologist for the National Party version of history. The fictional father who makes his appearance in *Dusklands* is a far cry from the father who appears in *Summertime*, and yet the autobiography supposedly covers the period when the novel was being written.

By looking back and composing a restoration of the father–son relationship in *Summertime*, Coetzee was acknowledging that a condition of his authorship coming into its own was that he had to learn to deal with history on his own terms, not Jack's.

THE SHOT TOWER

The Master of Petersburg

THERE IS NO shot tower in St Petersburg, nor has there ever been one, judging by historical maps, descriptions, engravings, drawings and photographs of the city, starting in the 1860s. There are domes, spires, bell towers and chimneys of various heights and shapes, but no shot tower. A feature of the urban landscape of nineteenth-century industrial British and American cities, shot towers are conical structures up to seventy metres tall, designed for the manufacture of ammunition. Molten lead was dropped through a giant sieve and, by the time it hit a pool of water at the bottom of the tower, it was sufficiently rounded to insert into a shotgun cartridge.

Coetzee puts a shot tower in St Petersburg (on Stolyarny Quay, to be precise) in *The Master of Petersburg*.[1] An Internet search for 'shot tower' and 'Stolyarny Quay' will take you straight to Coetzee's book. It is a brilliant insertion, looming organically out of the world of the novel, which is full of perverted fantasy, obscure motives and dark threats. The period in which the novel is set, around 1869–70, is perfect for a shot tower. While the cultural geography makes the tower incongruous, assuming you know about shot towers and the cities that housed them, the novelistic situation it facilitates is so compelling that it seems entirely intrinsic.

The chapter called 'The Shot Tower' falls precisely in the middle of the book, chapter ten of twenty. The scene involves the great novelist Fyodor Dostoevsky being led up the stairs at night to be shown the point from where his stepson, Pavel Alexandrovich Isaev, fell to his death. The guide, who is deeply untrustworthy, is Sergei Gennadevich Nechaev, the leader of a revolutionary movement called the People's Vengeance, whose creed is social leveling, to be achieved by any means possible.

According to Nechaev, whose purpose is to intimidate Dostoevsky into being useful, Pavel was assassinated by the police for his involvement in the movement; Dostoevsky, for his part, suspects it was Nechaev himself who murdered him after he fell out with his comrades over instructions to begin a campaign of killing. (Pavel's papers, which are in the police's possession, include a hit list, not written in his own hand.) Such is the confrontation in the tower: manipulation of the older man's grief and reputation, answered by disbelief and counter-accusation.

To exacerbate matters, Dostoevsky suffers from epilepsy; the possibility of his following Pavel into the abyss is real: 'He grips the railing, stares down *there* into the plummeting darkness. Between *here* and *there* an eternity of time, so much time that it is impossible for the mind to grasp it.'[2]

The guidance typically given to students of *The Master of Petersburg* by Dostoevsky scholars can be illustrated by the annotation that accompanies Coetzee's name in *Dostoevsky's 'The Devils': A Critical Companion*, edited by W.J. Leatherbarrow: 'Interesting, if historically unreliable, fictional account of the period in Dostoevsky's life when he was working on *The Devils*.'[3]

Joseph Frank, Dostoevsky's distinguished biographer, gives *The Master of Petersburg* sustained attention but his conclusion is not much different. Frank reviewed the novel in the *New Republic* within a year of its publication.[4] Coetzee was more than aware of the pertinence of Frank's biography to his fiction: he reviewed the fourth volume of Frank's *Dostoevsky: The Miraculous Years, 1865–1871*, in the *New York Review of Books* in the same year, 1995.[5]

In fact, from Coetzee's notes for *The Master of Petersburg*, which begin in February 1991, it is clear that he had been reading Frank's opus for several years, along with other writers on Dostoevsky. It is curious that Frank was unable to detect any of Coetzee's indebtedness to him; it may be that Frank was too exercised by the liberties Coetzee takes with the historical record to notice. He acknowledges Coetzee's right to fictionalize, but continues, 'Still, it is regrettable that he did not include a warning to his readers, many of whom will be unfamiliar with the details of Dostoevsky's biography, not to take his fiction as fact. Many will no doubt do so, for the same reason that, as Dostoevsky complained, people thought he had murdered his wife because this was the crime imputed to the narrator of *House of the Dead*.'[6] Frank is so reluctant to accept Coetzee's 'playing fast and loose' with the facts that he refers to Coetzee's character Pavel as Pasha, a familial name from the sources that Coetzee himself never actually uses.

Among the invented details that Frank points to is that during 1869, when Dostoevsky was living in Dresden to avoid being thrown in prison for debt, Coetzee has him return to St Petersburg on hearing that his stepson has died, using a false passport in the name of Isaev (thus pretending to be Pavel's biological father). His purpose is to establish what has happened because the circumstances are mysterious, and to collect Pavel's personal effects. The historical Pavel lived on unexceptionally, doing various clerical jobs until his death in 1900. This is the most consequential of Coetzee's alterations of the record, because it enables him to focus the events of the novel entirely on the relationship between the stepfather and stepson and on the fictional Dostoevsky's grief.

In Frank's reading, this alteration is never convincingly explained: 'The theme that dominates Coetzee's early chapters – Dostoevsky's desire somehow to keep Pavel alive in memory and his guilty despair at his failure as a father – becomes quite tedious after a while, and less and less artistically persuasive.'[7] This judgement is of a piece with Frank's sense that Coetzee 'makes no attempt to provide any realistic psychological motivation for his figures and their actions'.[8]

Before drawing his conclusions, which link the novel to Coetzee's South African background, with its resonances of the revolutionary ferment of mid-nineteenth-century Russia, Frank reaches this assessment: 'This is an enigmatic and rather puzzling book whose aim is difficult to unravel … [Coetzee] prefers to make use of his writer's liberties and to invent his own details. He makes only a very perfunctory stab at filling in the St Petersburg background, and the effect that he creates is more somnambulistic than realistic.'[9]

Coetzee had not been to St Petersburg, but the novel is by no means lacking in naturalistic detail, much of it taken from Dostoevsky himself, notably *Crime and Punishment*'s depiction of the run-down neighbourhoods near Haymarket Square, and some of it from Frank and other scholars. The list of Dostoevsky's works to which Coetzee alludes includes *Poor Folk*, *The Double*, *A Raw Youth*, *The Brothers Karamazov*, *Crime and Punishment*, *A Writer's Diary*, and shorter fictions and published notes.

In fairness to Frank, there are numerous details that are never quite resolved. How *does* Pavel die? We assume Dostoevsky is right in blaming the People's Vengeance, but this is not conclusively proved. How, if at all, does Dostoevsky manage to leave St Petersburg and return to Dresden, having become entangled with the Nechaev conspirators and the police? What are the consequences of the affair with Pavel's St Petersburg landlady, Anna Sergeyevna? What is the child Matryona's reaction on seeing Pavel's diary, in the obscenely falsified state in which Dostoevsky leaves it for her?

By leaving such questions hanging, Coetzee was following Dostoevsky's penchant for deliberate inconclusivity. But more pressingly, and Frank is right to observe this, Coetzee's treatment of

John's son, Nicolas Coetzee.

the relationship between Dostoevsky and Pavel is burdened to an extent that is never fully explained. The novel asks us to take the hero's condition of unbounded grief on trust, though neither the historical background nor the terms of the relationship with Pavel are really sufficient to explain it to us. The inconsolable Dostoevsky of Coetzee's creation is not in a world of credible motivations; on the contrary, he arrives in his droshky at 63 Svechnoi Street from another world altogether.

Nicolas Coetzee died shortly before midnight on 21 April 1989, two months before his twenty-third birthday. From Coetzee's notes we learn that in the early months of drafting, his fictional Dostoevsky was mourning not the stepson but indeed a son by his first marriage, Nikolai Fyodorovich Stavrogin (named after his mother).[10] 'What kept him calm at the funeral service, what gave him an air almost of equanimity, was the vow he had made: that he would write his son into immortality.'[11] Is this Coetzee writing about himself, remembering

Nicolas's funeral, or is he writing about his character, Dostoevsky? The answer is best thought of as an amalgam of both. Coetzee is writing about the fictional Dostoevsky in himself. The idea that comes to this writer after a lengthy period of waiting after the son's death – a single 'visit from the dove' – is that 'the son could be resurrected as Stavrogin.'[12]

Nikolai Stavrogin is the lead character in the historical Dostoevsky's novel *The Possessed*, also translated as *The Devils* and *Demons*. The action is driven by Pyotr Verkhovensky, who is the fictional counterpart of the actual Sergey Nechaev, the author of a notorious pamphlet, *Catechism of a Revolutionary*, and the murderer of a student, Ivanov, at the Agricultural Academy in Moscow, the event which Dostoevsky uses as the basis of his plot. The leading figure in the revolutionary circle that Verkhovensky draws around himself is Stavrogin.

Initially referred to as the Prince in Dostoevsky's drafts, Stavrogin was to be the anti-hero of a work called 'The Life of a Great Sinner'. As *The Possessed* developed from this work in progress, Stavrogin's stature grew. With his nobility, hauteur and indifference, Stavrogin became a continuation of Dostoevsky's critique of the revolutionary tradition that went back to Mikhail Bakunin in the 1840s. In *Notes from the Underground* and *Crime and Punishment* – through Raskolnikov – Dostoevsky showed his distrust of the irreligious rationalism of this tradition, its spiritual vacuity, which represented the worst of liberal Western influence. 'Nihilism' was the term given to it in its time, not because it lacked principle, but because it eschewed religious morality.

Dostoevsky's Orthodox beliefs were hard-won. He had been a fellow traveller with the socialists as a member of the Petrashevsky circle in the 1840s, and when they showed signs of becoming more than a discussion group they were arrested and convicted of subversion. Tsar Nicholas orchestrated a sadistic punishment in which they were lined up before a firing squad before having their sentences commuted at the last minute. Dostoevsky spent the next ten years in Siberia, at first in the Omsk prison and later in a labour camp. During his confinement, as he records in *The House of the Dead*, his views underwent a complete reformation, and he became convinced that rational schemes to transform society would never succeed while humanity was in need of salvation.

The Orthodoxy brought with it Slavophilism, partly because, in Dostoevsky's view, the Roman Catholic Church was too close to political power and Western materialism. By contrast, the *narod*, the people, the Russian soul, had integrity, so much so that they had a special destiny that would save the world. The anti-rationalist critique from the time of *Notes from the Underground* onwards in Dostoevsky's oeuvre was underpinned by this personal and intellectual history.

Stavrogin, in the nihilist tradition, is opaque in *The Possessed*, his evil matched by his mysteriousness. He was meant to achieve greater definition in the chapter called 'Stavrogin's Confession' (also translated as 'At Tikhon's') in which he confesses his sins to the monk Tikhon, including the previously unknown facts that he had raped a child and failed to intervene in her suicide. The attempt to achieve a clean breast fails and he hangs himself.

'Stavrogin's Confession' was considered too shocking by the editor, Mikhail Katkov, who refused to publish it in the *Russian Herald*, where the novel was being serialized. This put Dostoevsky in the awkward position of having to make retrospective alterations to his drafts before they could be published, removing the foreshadowing of the encounter with Tikhon.[13] When the novel was collected and published in 1873, the censored chapter was still excluded. It was only in 1922, when it was found in Dostoevsky's archive on the death of Anna Dostoevsky, that, through the influence of Virginia Woolf, it was translated and published by the Hogarth Press.

Presumably, Dostoevsky scholars would have been more content if Coetzee had restricted himself to a factually reliable historical novel that recreated the conditions under which *The Possessed* was drafted and eventually published. They might even have been happier with a novel that worked out of Dostoevsky's notes, to recreate the conjuring

of Stavrogin and his place at the diabolic heart of the book. These
elements are relevant to Coetzee's purposes, but to understand Coetzee
we need to be willing to entertain the idea of a prequel to *The Possessed*.

The autobiographical move in *The Master of Petersburg* is to pro-
pose that at the centre of Dostoevsky's creativity in *The Possessed* was
an episode of disorienting grief. Coetzee has remarked that he found
the record of the relevant period in Dostoevsky's career 'absorbing and
very humbling to follow' because it speaks of Dostoevsky's struggle
with indirection and uncertainty.[14] The sense of affinity Coetzee
speaks from here includes another empathic leap: imagining his own
grief as Dostoevsky's.

To appreciate the implications fully we need to assemble the
biographical details.[15] Nicolas was found in the morning after his
death, having fallen from the balcony of his eleventh-floor flat in
Hillbrow, Johannesburg. He was taken to the mortuary and identified
by a family friend. The cause of death was noted as 'multiple injuries'.
Two days later an autopsy was performed, the report of which has
been lost. The autopsy would not have been able to clarify why Nicolas
had fallen, but it might have established whether alcohol or substance
abuse was relevant. In the 'Register of Deaths', the word 'Jumped' was
entered, but, as John Kannemeyer observes, this was a hasty suppo-
sition on the part of a police clerk.

Coetzee, who had a visiting appointment at Johns Hopkins
University at the time, flew from Baltimore to Johannesburg on 28
April and the funeral was held on 2 May. An inquest took place on 23
October in a magistrate's court, but this report has also disappeared.
The loss of these official records probably signifies incompetence
rather than anything sinister.

Accident, suicide, murder: each of these suppositions would have
fuelled the anguish among everyone who had been close to Nicolas.
From fragments of evidence that gradually came to light, murder and

suicide have since been ruled out. Far from the scene and from the family, the question being asked in Cape Town was whether Nicolas was being hounded by the security police. Rumours to this effect were revived after the appearance of the novel four years later, but in fact Nicolas was not politically involved. If anyone was with him on the night he died, there was no trace in the flat.

Later a witness in a neighbouring block of flats came forward to say that he had heard Nicolas calling from the balcony, 'I can't hold on, can you help me?' Scratch marks were visible on the balcony wall. In the absence of a diagnosed depressive condition or suicide note, the circumstantial details suggest an accident.

This conclusion was strengthened by the knowledge that Nicolas was reckless. Kannemeyer informs us of his rebelliousness and an estranged relationship with his father. He was intelligent but dropped out of school to complete his matriculation at a cram college. As an American citizen, he left for California to avoid conscription into the South African military, living in San Francisco doing odd jobs while depending on his father's support. When he found it impossible to register at an American university with his South African school-leaving certificate, he returned to do a BA degree at the University of Cape Town, while also taking courses by correspondence.

Throughout his high school years, Nicolas had lived with John, while Philippa lived in Johannesburg. As a teenager there were bouts of truancy, binge drinking, pot smoking, and housebreaking. On one occasion, John had to bail him out of the local police station. After his sojourn in America he refused support from John, who had to go to increasingly absurd lengths to give him money. 'I have to create elaborate chains of fictional benefactors,' Coetzee wrote to a friend, Howard Wolf, in Buffalo, 'usually involving his mother', 'money without which he would either starve or drop out of college. So that in the end he can maintain his stance of independence from his father. The day he comes to me to play out the reconciliation scene, I'll really have some truths to tell him.'[16]

But it was not to be.

Certain passages in *The Master of Petersburg* are written straight out of a father's grief:

> What he cannot bear is the thought that, for the last fraction of the last instant of his fall, Pavel knew that nothing could save him, that he was dead. He wants to believe Pavel was protected from that certainty, more terrible than annihilation itself, by the hurry and confusion of the fall, by the mind's way of etherizing itself against whatever is too enormous to be borne. With all his heart he wants to believe this.
>
> *

> He unfolds the receipt and passes it across the counter. Depending on whether Pavel gave up the ghost before or after midnight, it is dated the day after or the day of Pavel's death …
>
> *

> Maximov takes the letter from his slack grasp and peruses it again. It is the last letter he wrote from Dresden, a letter in which he chides Pavel for spending too much money. Mortifying to sit here while a stranger reads it!
>
> *

> 'Let me ask you: Why do you think he took his life?'
>
> The room swims before his eyes. The investigator's face looms like a huge pink balloon.
>
> 'He did not take his life,' he whispers. 'You understand nothing about him.'
>
> *

> Upon him bursts the thought of Pavel's last moment, of the body of a hot-blooded young man in the pride of life striking the earth, of the rush of breath from the lungs, the crack of bones, the surprise, above all the surprise, that the end should be real, that there should be no second chance. Under the table he wrings his hands in agony.[17]

This anguish cuts right through the knots of the novel's complexity. As readers, knowing about Nicolas's death, we are torn between sympathy brought out by raw feeling and an intellectual responsibility to the fictionalization. But with this knowledge of the background, there is no turning back. Let us look at the process of composition as a way of finding a path through the quandary.

On Christmas Day 1992, when the work's gestation had been under way for nearly two years, Coetzee recorded in his notes, 'Christmas Day and Nicolas is not here. The project: to recover the truth of his relation to the dead boy. That truth: not to bring the dead boy back into this world but to go into the world of death without fear. In this his conductress will be A.S. [Anna Sergeyevna]'[18]

The project was not strictly, therefore, to recreate the conditions under which *The Possessed* was written – the scale of that undertaking would have been impossible, as Dostoevsky's own voluminous notes reveal.[19] He did indeed begin on 21 February 1991 by writing the suppressed episode in *The Possessed*, that is to say, Nikolai Stavrogin's abuse of the girl. But on the evidence of the notes, of their most impassioned entries, the intention was to use the fictional material as a mode of entry into writing that would transmute the son into life on the page:

A turn of the head, the line of an eyebrow, a figure disappearing around the corner – in all of these I mistake you, and my heart lifts for a moment. Lifts as a wave does, and then goes down again. Mistaken, taken by the wrong thing, taken in. Like an abandoned lover catching glimpses everywhere of the lip, the eye of the woman who abandoned him.

What was one has become distributed. The beloved is everywhere, scattered: fragments of the beloved body, torn up like the body of Osiris, of Orpheus: young men who had too much, glowing, doré, chrysos, golden-bodied.

Now a matter of gathering together the golden hoard, putting together the scattered parts, assembling the broken body in its perfection again. Poetry: listing the parts so that the eye, leaving the page, will for an instant have before it the image of the whole body, resurrected.[20]

Much more is at stake in this exquisite writing than would be the case if it were straightforward historical fiction. The genre is autobiographical historical fiction, if that is imaginable. If the intentions had been milder, they would have involved reinventing the conditions under which Stavrogin came to occupy centre stage in *The Possessed*.

How this came about in Dostoevsky's work is indeed a puzzle, even after the publication of his notes. For most of *The Possessed*'s composition, Stavrogin was a benign figure, the Prince, who had not fully emerged from the earlier conception of him in 'The Life of a Great Sinner'. Moreover, this Prince in Dostoevsky spends a good deal of time expounding all the virtues that Dostoevsky himself believed in: Orthodoxy, national feeling, anti-nihilism, anti-liberalism. Only in the completed work does it emerge that Stavrogin does not have the psychological and moral backbone to live out these virtues. He abandons them in cynicism and despair, having drawn his fellow conspirators into a state of moral ennui. How this transformation comes about is a mystery in Dostoevsky's sources, but that is precisely where Coetzee's novel intervenes.

Edward Wasiolek, who has edited Dostoevsky's notebooks, says, 'Dostoevsky comes to Stavrogin's character at the pace of a tortoise. He resists the real Stavrogin by evasions, twists, and wrong turns. He gives the Prince the wrong words, the wrong actions, the wrong loves, and the wrong feelings.'[21] In this relentless self-questioning lies Dostoevsky's genius, Wasiolek continues; it lies 'in his ability to recognise what is wrong' and in his knowing that he has 'to sacrifice what he wants for what must be'.[22] Into this opacity Coetzee inserts his own compulsions, imagining that the indirection of Dostoevsky's writing was the result of grief; that if there had been the death of a son, a boy from whom he had been estranged, it might have driven the urge to create Stavrogin.

This puts Coetzee squarely into a relation to Dostoevsky that Harold Bloom describes in *The Anxiety of Influence*, in which the point is to absorb the influence of a powerful forebear and then get beyond it.[23] Coetzee places his own anguish in the vessel of Dostoevsky's writing, and quietly watches the master's ship tack a different course. Coetzee was more than conscious of the struggle he had entered into:

> The idea was: Stavrogin. The idea was that his son could be resurrected in Stavrogin, if Stavrogin could be resurrected from the death to which Stavrogin's maker had consigned him. It was an audacious idea, since Stavrogin's maker was Fyodor Dostoevsky and the death to which Stavrogin has been consigned by his maker a powerful death. But the idea could not be forgotten, which is to say (he thought) he must have faith in it. What he thought was: There must be life in the idea, or else it would die. It is a matter of finding the life. It is a matter of bringing Stavrogin back and finding why it is that a voice says: In Stavrogin he can live. And then it is a matter of making Stavrogin live again. That is, in the first a matter of taking him, Stavrogin, away from that powerful dark old man who had wanted him to die.[24]

Coetzee's creative process was extremely peripatetic, and, in that respect, it followed the example of the 'powerful dark old man' himself. He proceeded by inventing and revising plot situations, changing them frequently in order to create different perspectives, ideas and outcomes. First, Dostoevsky is in Switzerland when he hears that his son has been arrested. The son is still called Nicolas/Nikolai Stavrogin, not yet Pavel, the stepson. He is angry and delays his return; later it emerges that the son has committed suicide, and thus begins the father's quest to discover the truth. This structure is then abandoned, prompting him to comment,

> I used to be able to write stories quite easily. I would write down one or two people on the page, and they would get talking, and pretty soon there would be the beginnings of a story between them. Then all I would have to do would be to pursue them like a faithful dog till the story worked itself out … Now it is all changed, or seems to be. Now I am like a dog without a bone: I dig here, I dig there, I dig up the whole garden, but nowhere do I find it.[25]

He tries out a situation in which Matryona commits suicide, recalling the events of 'Stavrogin's Confession'. The fictional Dostoevsky attends the inquest and meets the mother there for the first time. It soon appears that Stavrogin has confessed everything under interrogation and those who knew him are disgusted. Stavrogin also commits suicide, whereupon the mother and father begin a relationship, during which Dostoevsky discovers that the mother had a hand in her daughter's death.

Seven months into the writing, Coetzee crosses out 'Nikolai Fyodorovich' and enters 'Pavel Aleksandrovich' – a crucial development, signalling the switch from son to stepson. In the same phase, he begins recording naturalistic detail from Dostoevsky's letters, and also from Joseph Frank. The political aspect of the novel begins to emerge, with Pavel being associated with the revolutionaries, although his role in the circle is still unclear: he could be any combination of Verkhovensky, Kirillov (who commits suicide) and Stavrogin. He records details of the Dostoevskys' life in Dresden, with Fyodor travelling to Wiesbaden and Hamburg to gamble. He wonders if something could be made of the gambling. He invents Dostoevsky's paedophilic eye for Matryona and the possibility of transferring this venality to the son.

Once Nicolas/Nikolai becomes Pavel, the manner of his death is settled with remarkable pragmatism:

> Drop the notion that Pavel dies falling from the fourth floor of No. 63. No. 63 only has three storeys. The third floor, D thinks, is not enough to die from. Instead, Pavel is said to have died by falling from the shot tower on the banks of the canal. His body is brought to the apartment the morning after. The police surgeon arrives, decides he died from falling, not the result of an assault.[26]

Thus enters the shot tower, and the chapter called 'The Shot Tower' could be written.

As with previous novels, much of the intertextuality enters Coetzee's writing only once the text has found its feet. He works into his revisions of *The Master of Petersburg* ideas drawn from mythology (Orpheus and Eurydice); biblical literature (the story of Abraham and Isaac – 'see Kierkegaard'[27] – and later, the notion of *kairos*,[28] which is revelation through crisis). He reads Emmanuel Lévinas ('The Greek tradition is scopic. In the Hebrew tradition, to have regard for someone is not to look at him/her with the gaze of desire').[29] He reads Saul Bellow on ageing, and Franz Kafka's letter to his father. *The Possessed* is prefaced by the parable of the Gadarene swine from St Luke's Gospel, but Coetzee's notes make no mention of this story; instead, he refers to a passage in St Mark (9, 17–27), in which Christ exorcises a demon from a boy. It was the boy that interested him.

As might be expected, Mikhail Bakhtin, the Russian scholar of Dostoevsky, features prominently in Coetzee's note-taking. Bakhtin coined a number of critical terms that are commonplace in modern criticism: polyphony, heteroglossia, dialogism, carnival. Coetzee reflects on these terms, absorbing them into his writing. He works with 'carnival', for example, using it as another strategy to circumvent dull forms of verisimilitude. He goes to certain lengths to ensure that his characters are not 'frozen in their social types', introducing Pavel as a 'shape-changer'. Dostoevsky himself becomes a shape-changer by wearing Pavel's white suit.[30]

The white suit is an important device in *The Master of Petersburg*. It implies dandyism, suggesting that Pavel was not entirely straightforward in his dealings with women. The story Dostoevsky tells Matryona, of Pavel visiting Maria Lebyatkin, a simpleton, dressed in the suit in order to give her fantasy of being courted for marriage a certain validity, is a story about Pavel's generosity and chivalry.[31] But at the end of the novel, Dostoevsky writes into Pavel's diary, for Matryona to read, a very different version, in which Pavel marries Maria as a joke.[32] In this story, which is invented to upset Matryona, Pavel is a cynic who is well on the way to becoming Stavrogin.

The possibilities in dressing up are further developed in Nechaev, who spends much of the novel in disguise dressed as a woman. Coetzee is again drawing on Bakhtin and playing with unstable representations, as a way of deepening the pervasive mood of insecurity.

By December 1992, Coetzee had developed the plot much as we know it and he began to force matters to a head: 'it occurs to me that I have more analytical/descriptive notes on Nechaev (as well as others) than I can ever incorporate by naturalistic means'. The prospect he faces is

> of FMD sitting at the table in his son's room creating Stavrogin (or finding Stavrogin within himself or expelling the devil by identifying the devil as Stavrogin), in the process of negotiating and withstanding the siege of everything that comes with the room – (1) whatever he wants to do with Matryona, (2) his desire for her mother, (3) his love and mourning for Pavel. Because – yes – these three figures besiege him.[33]

The novel ends with the chapter called 'Stavrogin', in which Dostoevsky writes a stream of obscenity into Pavel's diary in the knowledge that Matryona will read it. How this episode comes to acquire the power it has, and how it serves as the point of closure to Dostoevsky's quest, requires some explanation. The turning point comes a little earlier, in the chapter called 'Poison'.

Dostoevsky and Matryona are alone in the room. The conversation is perilously intimate, but he manages to retain her confidence, to the point that she asks him questions about what it is like to die. She wants to know, among other things, whether it hurts. He is flooded with relief at this, imagining that she is speaking in sympathy with Pavel, but it soon emerges that she has been used as a courier and has handed over to Katri, the Finnish girl, and one of Nechaev's closest aides, a vial of poison which she has used to commit suicide after being taken into custody. With gentle probing Dostoevsky then elicits from Matryona a canvas-wrapped bundle containing a pistol, leaflets and more poison, which he undertakes to dispose of.

Emboldened by Matryona's confidences, and by the fact that she has conveniently lost her innocence already, thanks to this corrupting by the nihilists, Dostoevsky touches her face, brushing the hair from her cheek. She responds, to his astonishment, with a coquettish look, then the moment passes: "'No!" he says. The smile she wears is taunting, provocative. Then the spell passes and she is a child as before, confused, ashamed.'[34]

Dostoevsky reflects, 'what he has seen comes not from the world he knows but from another existence'. It is comparable to a seizure – one of his epileptic fits – except that this is more profound. It is *possession*, he thinks: 'everything that for the past twenty years has gone under the name of seizure has been a mere presentiment of what is now happening, the quaking and dancing of the body a long-drawn-out prelude to a quaking of the soul'.[35]

The descent into obscenity and an ethical malaise from here on is represented as epileptic fitting, falling, flying and madness. 'Falling' was proposed as a title for the novel in the notes, before being abandoned, because it was already in use by another writer. At several points, Coetzee wondered how to achieve a state of madness in his writing, through which an ending could be found. 'D thinks: Perhaps I must go mad. Not in order to be cured of grief but in order that the locked stasis of self-control can be shifted/unlocked. So that I can follow Pavel.'[36] He asks, 'is there an abandon that is beyond all calculation of pleasure … beyond the body, that uses the body as a vehicle only, as an embodiment because it cannot live disembodied, as souls do when they elect their residence on earth? Is there a way of falling that is a way of flying?'[37] In sentences such as the following from the published text, it seems that the answer to these questions was yes:

> If to anyone it is prescribed to live through the madness of our times, he told Anna Sergeyevna, it is to him. Not to emerge from the fall unscathed, but to achieve what his son did not: to wrestle with the whistling darkness, to absorb it, to make it his medium; to turn the falling into a flying, even if a flying as slow and old and clumsy as a turtle's. To live where Pavel died. To live in Russia and hear the voices

of Russia murmuring within him. To hold it all within him: Russia, Pavel, death.[38]

The writing of the madness is double-edged: it betrays Pavel by corrupting his diary and legacy; it corrupts Matryona for whom it is written. This is the passage in which 'Stavrogin' appears, when Pavel is transformed into Stavrogin.

It begins with a bedroom scene in which a child is sexually violated. It continues with a passage called 'The Apartment', in which a dissipated student who is a member of a *kruzhok*, a 'circle whose members experiment with free love', has sex in the presence of a young girl, leaving the evidence on display, with the purpose of grooming her. Reflecting on why he does this, the student articulates the view which the historical Dostoevsky found abhorrent, and embodied in a number of his characters, including Raskolnikov, Verkhovensky and Stavrogin: 'History is coming to an end; the old account-books will soon be thrown in the fire; in this dead time between old and new, all things are permitted.'[39]

The final passage of 'Stavrogin', called 'The Child', contains the story of Pavel's white suit and his mockery of Maria Lebyatkin. As he writes all this, Dostoevsky is shaken out of himself. 'He is writing for eternity. He is writing for the dead.'[40] It is a metaphysical experiment: throw down the gauntlet to God to see if He responds. As JC says in *Diary of a Bad Year*, Ivan Karamazov does something similar by handing in his ticket to heaven and mounting 'a tirade against forgiveness'.[41]

As the culmination of the fictional Dostoevsky's intentions, Coetzee's chapter achieves what he wants it to achieve: Pavel emerges as the prototype of Stavrogin. He has been transformed into the morally malevolent force that will dominate Dostoevsky's great work, remaining immortalized there for as long as it is read. There is of course no permanent immortality in the universe Coetzee builds around this novel; the best we can hope for is a 'limited' immortality, which is all that is possible 'on an earth spinning towards its death'.[42] In the face of the brute facts Dostoevsky has become a spiritual megalomaniac:

'Somewhere he stands and watches while he and God circle each other. And time stands still and watches too. Time is suspended, everything is suspended before the fall.'[43]

∞

Naturally, readers tend to look for signs of redemption in this strange story, but Coetzee provides no comforting conclusions. 'He has betrayed everyone,' says Dostoevsky, musing about his own actions, 'nor does he see that his betrayals could go deeper. If he ever wanted to know whether betrayal tastes more like vinegar or gall, now is the time.' The novel then ends with the line 'Now he begins to taste it. It tastes like gall.'[44] Gall is bile, an Old English word. In the derivation 'galling', it implies bitterness that has to be endured. Its medieval usage was pharmacological, but that meaning seems remote from Coetzee's purposes.

Who has been betrayed? Pavel has been betrayed because he has been transformed into the diabolical Stavrogin. His life has also been turned into currency, a commodity: '*They pay him lots of money for writing books*, said the child, repeating the dead child' (original emphasis).[45] Can one conclude from this that Coetzee is troubled by the possibility that Nicolas, too, has been betrayed, because his life has been written into a book and sold by J.M. Coetzee, and perhaps also because, in the minds of those who make the connection, Nicolas's memory will always be associated with this disturbing story?

The book prompts the questions, but answering them seems callous. The task the novel undertakes is inherently conflicted, even contradictory. A grieving father, a writer, Coetzee/Dostoevsky, writes a dead son, Nicolas/Nikolai, back into existence. By definition, the son can only emerge from the father's shadow by becoming other to the father, by assuming his own being. The father, who is of course no ordinary novelist, knows this only too well, so he has to invent a situation in which he can lose himself, become other to himself, in which the son can begin to emerge from the darkness of death.

It is all tangled: if the father wins, he loses; if he sets out to lose, he might win. To solve the problem, he invents a bizarre solution in which the paradox is dissolved in an act of moral hubris. It works, but only up to a point: the son is written into the great book, but this does not feel like victory. On that note, the novel ends.

Mikhail Bakhtin famously argued in *Problems of Dostoevsky's Poetics* that Dostoevsky was a master of the 'dialogic' novel, which is a novel in which the author's voice does not dominate, but is distributed across the range of voices of the characters. For Bakhtin this kind of novel was not just interesting; it was ethical. The author or creator, he said, had to cut 'the umbilical cord uniting the hero to his creator'; if this was not done, 'then what we have is not a work of art but a personal document'.[46]

As a follower of Bakhtin, and the author of a riskily personal novel, is Coetzee's *The Master of Petersburg* a personal document, in this sense? The answer to that question would seem to be that Coetzee pushes himself as far as any author could be expected to go, by writing a novel in which the umbilical cord simply *cannot* be cut. There is some protection in the creation of a fictional surrogate, but not enough to contain the emotional spillage.

It is difficult to imagine any author who had recently lost a son devising a resolutely impersonal story about an author writing a son back into life. The novel is a personal document seeking to become impersonal, and only partly succeeding. If this were not so, its strangely burdened narration would remain a mystery, as it did for Joseph Frank. If we insist on reading *The Master of Petersburg* without acknowledging the sorrow of its author, it will have at its centre an unaccommodated grief, the artistic equivalent of the shot tower in Petersburg: incongruous and out of place in the surrounding landscape.[47]

∞

To live in Russia and hear the voices of Russia murmuring within him.
We have seen that Coetzee writes himself as he reinvents Dostoevsky.
If so, then in writing about late-nineteenth-century Russia, Coetzee is
also writing about South Africa. Not every invented fictional milieu
is an occasion for coded national allegory, but this novel raises the
question.

Dostoevsky saw the political, cultural and spiritual condition of
Russia in the 1870s as irredeemable except by a general turning of
hearts. It was possessed by malevolent souls, a situation in which *The
Possessed* intervenes by imagining a moral catharsis. Disentangling
Coetzee's judgements about the South Africa of the early 1990s from
his representations of Dostoevsky's Russia cannot be straightforward,
but, as it happens, he made the connection explicitly:

> I have been left behind by South Africa as it enters Africa. Horror of
> irrational violence, of a vision I can all too easily believe in but can't
> afford to believe in because my self-culture rests on a denial. FMD
> in the same position. Pavel-Nechaev call up a vision of casual and
> even serial? killing to which he has a twofold reaction: (a) denial,
> abhorrence, wish that the offenders should be locked up, (b) retreat
> into the past, into old age, as he sees that this is what the new world
> is and wants.[48]

The note is a tinderbox that needs delicate handling. It toys with
some alarming notions, such as that, as South Africa becomes more
recognizably part of the African continent, it is drifting into a state of
endemic violence. Coetzee's response to this possibility is complex: he
asks whether he can entertain this Dostoevskian vision, and answers
that he can, but that there is another part of him that wants to deny
it. For 'self-culture', read liberal decency: it is indecent to regard
Africa as inherently violent, but he is also saying that to deny this is
untrue and psychologically unhealthy. At their deepest level Coetzee's

reflections amount to an acceptance of whatever it is that Dostoevsky might represent *in himself*: Dostoevsky feared the violence of nihilism; Coetzee follows the master's beckoning finger.

There are other moments when the connection to South Africa is explicit. Edward Wasiolek, the editor of Dostoevsky's notes, attributes the development of the character of Stavrogin to his failure to negotiate successfully the distance between Russian Orthodoxy and secular nihilism; this failure, Wasiolek says, leads to a cynical abandonment of all principle. Reading Wasiolek, Coetzee wonders whether this condition is comparable to 'the children in SA who want no one to excel so that all shall be equal'.[49]

The militant 'children of South Africa' make another, incongruous appearance in Coetzee's notes. He records watching a film of the stage production of *Sarafina!* (amusingly, he misspells it 'Seraphina') and is struck by the 'relentlessness of dancing, gesture, physical being of children (actors playing children)'. *Sarafina!* was a commercially successful musical and later a film based on the Soweto student uprising of 1976, starring Whoopi Goldberg. In the same paragraph of the manuscript in which he records watching the film, Coetzee writes: 'Nechaev does not come. Instead an agent of his comes, a girl even more relentless than he. Short, almost squat in her muscularity. She seems 12, is in fact 21. A Finn.'[50] Thus emerges Nechaev's accomplice in *The Master of Petersburg*, the hapless Finnish girl, Katri, to whom Matryona gives the poison so that when she is captured, instead of gaily going back to Karelia, the pleasant holiday countryside on the Russo-Finnish border whence she comes, she will kill herself.

The dancers of *Sarafina!* are clearly the prototype of Katri; perhaps not all the dancers, perhaps specifically the star, Leleti Khumalo. It is not difficult to imagine Coetzee enduring *Sarafina!* and then penning the following words on behalf of his long-suffering Fyodor: 'I am not here to live a life free of pain. I am required to live – what shall I call it? – a Russian life: a life inside Russia, or with Russia inside me, and whatever Russia means. It is not a fate I can evade.'[51]

The connection between Dostoevsky's Russia and Coetzee's South

Africa is also intrinsic to some of the set-piece encounters in the novel. One example will suffice. Nechaev devises a scheme to trap Dostoevsky into being useful to the revolutionaries. He has read *Crime and Punishment* and, like his incendiary counterparts, he has been inspired by Raskolnikov. So he takes Dostoevsky into the basement of a slum building in the Haymarket district, which is populated by the poorest of the underclass, where there is a printing press. There he offers the famous writer an opportunity to address the masses in a leaflet. Dostoevsky tries to wriggle out of the situation, tries even to subvert the rivalry by giving Nechaev a firm embrace, but then hastily he composes a piece of text that accuses the People's Vengeance of murdering his son. Nechaev is surprisingly gleeful at this – '*Truth? What is Truth?*' he cries (echoing an essay by Francis Bacon, which in turn recalls Pontius Pilate). It is a complex interaction: the point is that Nechaev is in love with chaos; he doesn't actually care what position Dostoevsky takes; it is good enough that he has contributed to the confusion. Dostoevsky realizes that he has been outmanoeuvred and the pamphlet goes out to the streets.

The debate between Dostoevsky and Nechaev in this episode can be profitably read with South Africa in mind. Nechaev: 'You see how the poorest of our black poor of Petersburg have to live. But that is not seeing, that is only detail! You fail to recognize the *forces* that determine the lives to which these people are condemned! *Forces*: that is what you are blind to.'[52] Nechaev's emphasis on forces makes him sound like a literary critic of the left in the South Africa of the 1980s. His discourse, which also speaks of 'lines of force' that 'begin in the ministries and the exchequers and the stock exchanges and the merchant banks ... the chancelleries of Europe', is in fact anachronistic in its context, because the revolutionary movement that Nechaev represents had still to be influenced by the materialism of Marx and Engels. The historical Nechaev grasped bits of Jean-Jacques Rousseau and Charles Fourier and Jeremy Bentham and melded them together – Marx came later. *The Communist Manifesto* was translated into Russian after Dostoevsky's major period. The fictional Nechaev of Coetzee's novel therefore speaks a materialist language of the late twentieth century, a rhetoric that had more purchase in the Cape Town of his own time than the St Petersburg of the 1870s.

The force of the exchange between Nechaev and Dostoevsky comes from a raw nerve being touched in Coetzee himself. 'They will let you write stories of the mute sufferings of the poor to your heart's content, and applaud you for them, but as for the real truth, they would never let you publish it! That is why I am offering you the press. Make a start!'[53] This is again the voice of the left in the 1980s. Dostoevsky's response is as follows: 'And the lines. He is still not sure what Nechaev means by lines ...'; he understands that 'covetousness makes the heart shrivel', but, as for the lines, are they 'Strings of numbers passing through the window-paper and striking these children in their empty bellies?'[54] The riposte undoes the metaphor, but it is facetious. Coetzee would be the first to admit that *possession*, as a contagion of anger, accusation and counter-accusation in apartheid-era South Africa, left few people unscathed, including himself.

12

MIGRATIONS

Irreconcilable lives – *Elizabeth Costello, Disgrace*

Something in the South African material that drives one toward dull realism? A respect for this material that is essentially fearful?[1]

IN THE LATE 1990s, as his sixtieth year approached, John Coetzee renegotiated his relationship to academic life. In 1994 he had been appointed to the Arderne Chair of English Literature at the University of Cape Town, an honour that had in effect been thrust upon him – he accepted so as to avoid the chair being abolished – but by 1997 he was reconsidering his position. The reason he gave for resigning from the chair was that he felt unable to provide the day-to-day leadership it required, and in fact prior to the appointment he had already secured a contract on a reduced salary to make more time for his writing.[2] He was given a distinguished professorship in the Arts Faculty, unaffiliated to any department, and most of his teaching was in creative writing. In hindsight, it appears that the partial disengagement heralded more permanent changes that were to follow, namely retirement and emigration.

By this stage, Coetzee had ceased to be an academic who was also a novelist. He had become a novelist who was a part-time academic – something of an anomaly and, in some ways, a burden. He continued to teach with André Brink in Cape Town and in visiting positions in the United States, such as at the Michener Center for Writers at the University of Texas at Austin, an appointment that further strengthened his ties with the university. Aside from creative writing, the teaching that he found most engaging was the term he spent each year at the Committee on Social Thought (CST) at the University of Chicago, where with Jonathan Lear he taught comparative literature on congenial terms – an entire semester on autobiography, or Tolstoy, or Proust; in these examples, themes and authors that were relevant to the writing he was pursuing at the time, especially the autobiographies. Later, he would refer to the CST as having provided him with an intellectual home.[3]

There was more to this, however, than simply the question of affiliation either to academia or to the life of a full-time writer. It was also a matter of what kind of novelist he had become. The academy had provided security in the early stages of his career, but as his work developed, it did not become less important – if anything, it became more so. It gave him resources, ideas, fields of inquiry and conversation, and a generally appreciative readership for forms of writing that the general book market could not easily accommodate. The academy became an essential part of his artistic practice; so it was not a matter of leaving the room and shutting the door. He later reflected on this situation rather ruefully, stating that when his ambitions to become a writer were still inchoate,

> I calculated that I could use the academy to support me while I surreptitiously followed a writing career. But, as is so often the case, I miscalculated. First I became an academic who did a little writing on the side; later I turned into a writer marked deeply (too deeply?) by involvement with the academy. I would have been better off being just (just!) a writer. But in order to be just a writer, I would have had to be someone other than myself.[4]

These reflections are in notes for *Diary of a Bad Year*. In the published text, 'JC' responds to critics who say about his recent work that he is clearly 'not a novelist at all' but 'a pedant who dabbles in fiction', by commenting that he has 'reached a stage in my life when I begin to wonder whether they are not right – whether, all the time I thought I was going about in disguise, I was in fact naked'.[5]

Whether or not it is true that Coetzee turned out to be as much a professor of literature as he is an artist, it is certainly the case that the academy itself was changing, especially in the 1990s, and that what Chicago offered him had become atypical. 'Now, all over the western world,' he told a University of Cape Town audience, the 'old model of the university finds itself under attack as an increasingly economistic interrogation of social institutions is carried out'.[6] The process referred to in *Disgrace* as 'the great rationalization' was under way.[7]

The Elizabeth Costello stories were partly an outcome of this conundrum. He might have been a reluctant employee of a fast-changing academy, but without the academy he could not be the writer he was. A fair amount of Costello's irritability arises from the fact that, like her author, she is a square peg in a round hole. The Costello stories developed incrementally throughout the late 1990s as a solution to the problem Coetzee regularly faced of being called upon to give academic lectures. He appreciated the audiences but he disliked the form, partly on principle. Frequently, he would preface his readings of the stories by explaining that instead of giving the lecture for which he had been invited, he was going to read a piece of fiction. Before reading 'The Humanities in Africa' at Stanford's Humanities Center, for example, he said that he 'dislikes the conventional lecture form' with its 'pretensions to authority'. 'For some years I have preferred to compose, instead of the lecture, something more like a philosophical dialogue, in which I have devoted considerable energy to fleshing out the narrative, so that the piece doesn't simply emerge as an argument between disembodied voices.'[8]

It says much for Coetzee's ingenuity that as these stories flowed, he was able to develop Costello into the powerful fiction that she became, a vehicle for trenchant thinking about the life of a writer, and the life of literature, in the post-Cold War global marketplace. Once Costello was launched, Coetzee invested as much of himself in her as he had done with any of his creations. Her peregrinations around the United States and Europe, not to mention Antarctica and even the afterlife (in 'At the Gate'), enabled him to bring to the fore questions that had always troubled the furthest reaches of his life as a novelist.

The stories deal with essential questions: his relationship to realism, the bewildering challenges of representing cruelty and evil, the fortunes of the humanities in Africa. They test the ways in which historical guilt impinges on a writer's freedom. In the postscript to *Elizabeth Costello*, entitled 'The Letter of Lady Chandos', the narrator delivers a *cri de coeur* that any serious writer would want to utter at some point: loss of faith in language itself. With their range and intensity, the Costello stories brought Coetzee new readers, including philosophers interested in how literature deals with issues in ethics and phenomenology.

But the provenance of the stories was their author's global mobility, a mobility that had another, inevitable consequence: his life and career were becoming unmoored from South Africa. Seen in this light, the circumstances in which *Disgrace* was written become more obvious and more significant. The situation is redolent of Thomas Hardy's poem about the sinking of the *Titanic*, 'The Convergence of the Twain', in which the 'Spinner of the Years' brings the ship and its 'sinister mate', the iceberg, together in an instant when the 'consummation comes, and jars two hemispheres'.[9] The ecology in which *Disgrace* was created was also a confluence of irreconcilable forces. The first was Coetzee's disengagement from South Africa: he was travelling to visiting appointments, festivals and readings, receiving awards, and spending regular periods vacationing and writing at his daughter Gisela's house in France. Several times in the 1990s, with his partner, Dorothy Driver, he visited Australia, where she had appointments and he gave readings, until the prospect settled into place of their moving permanently to Adelaide. Costello's Australian origins were beginning to take on a new significance.[10]

The opposing force was the history that was taking place in South Africa. For having undergone the euphoric period culminating in the first democratic elections of 1994, the political transition was beginning to work its way into the fabric of everyday life – into public institutions, including the universities, often with ambiguous results that privileged short-term political gains over academic interests. In public institutions, transformation ceased to be the consensual vision it had been in the first half of the decade and became the name of politics, a shift in the balance of power between elites. In the universities, Africanization and neo-liberalism became interchangeable agendas, with transformation often being justified on economic grounds, and rationalization being justified on grounds that served current political interests.

Disgrace confronted these changes, particularly in relation to the universities, but also in the wider society where the deep-psychology of colonial history lingered on. The novel wrestles with South African problems that were untouched by the halo of the rainbow nation, and that the country's impeccably democratic new constitution could not address. Indeed, the novel entirely ignored the successes that had been achieved in the public sphere. Readers unfamiliar with South Africa in the 1990s would not guess from reading *Disgrace* that for a blessed period, the country was a beacon of racial tolerance. Coetzee was more interested in the social and psychic toxicity that he must have felt could manifest itself at any point.

In a public forum in which the rationalization of the universities was being discussed, Coetzee cautioned his university audience against a breezy use of the verb 'confront' as a description of what academics were capable of achieving in this situation. 'Confront derives from Latin *frons*, forehead, brow, and it means to stand brow to brow, face to face, with someone or something.'[11] The force behind the corporatization of the universities was global in scale, he said, and therefore impossible to confront in this sense.

To say that Coetzee himself confronted the times does not seem like exaggeration when we discover that *Disgrace*'s point of departure was the South African Truth and Reconciliation Commission, which, very much against the grain, he read as an exercise of power in the hands of those in authority.

If a jarring of two hemispheres and the metaphor of the *Titanic* meeting the iceberg seem hyperbolic as a description of *Disgrace*'s point of origin, it is worth noting that the novel has received more media and scholarly attention than any other work of fiction in all of South Africa's literary history, eclipsing its forerunner in the top position, Alan Paton's *Cry, the Beloved Country*.[12] It is a painful fact that the most discussed novel in all of South Africa's literature emerged from such contradictory energies.

From December 1994 to March 1997, a period of two years and four months, Coetzee was engaged on an astonishingly wide range of creative projects, apart from continuing his regular work as critic and reviewer. His notebook entries show him switching from one day to the next between autobiography (*Boyhood* at first, later *Youth*), to the Costello story 'What is Realism', followed by *The Lives of Animals* (the two Costello stories written for the Tanner Lectures on Human Values at Princeton),[13] a funny piece on vegetarianism called 'Meat Country' (which starts with a description of the meat department at Central Market in Austin)[14] and *Disgrace*.[15] That he was writing *The Lives of Animals* and *Disgrace* simultaneously is telling, as we will see.

One implication of the simultaneity with which these projects were carried out might be that the formal experimentalism that was always a feature of his writing could be parcelled out to various discrete contexts. In every novel until this point, the formal self-scrutiny, which is often tortuous, as we have seen, leads to generic innovation, whether in the use of numbered paragraphs, multiple narrators, epistolary texts or framed narratives. In the notebooks and manuscripts of *Disgrace*, however, there is comparatively little self-consciousness about the formal basis of the project. Instead, most of the revisions and the note-taking are related to the plot.

The relative absence of formal self-consciousness in the writing of *Disgrace* was a source of concern to Coetzee himself, as the epigraph to this chapter shows, and this may have strengthened what I can only call the novel's valedictory mood. He wondered whether the realism he was writing was a result of insidious intimidation inherent in the South African material, making him (and other South African writers, by implication) 'essentially fearful'.[16] It is a bitter reflection, confirmed by similar frank expressions of resentment in the novel's preparatory papers. Even if it is the case, which it is, that the published novel manages to transform its raw material into an aesthetically detached achievement ('sentence by chiselled sentence', in Derek Attridge's apt description),[17] the resentments are not far beneath the surface.

By contrast, the corresponding notes on *The Lives of Animals* show a Coetzee who is less angry, more engaged, more responsive to the possibilities he was seeing in his project. He borrowed copiously from other writers, scientists and philosophers working on animal rights and ethics. He began planning the Tanner Lectures for Princeton with reflections on vegetarianism: 'Not eating meat is not like not eating pork to a Jew,' he writes. Lacking the prestige of religion, vegetarianism is 'irremediably cranky'.[18]

He refers to two famously sadistic scenes of animal cruelty in fiction: the horse-beating in *Crime and Punishment* (where a mare is beaten to death by its owner when it is unable to pull a heavy cart) and the donkey-beating in Nadine Gordimer's *Burger's Daughter* (where a drunken black man flails a donkey pulling a cart across a stretch of wasteland, meting out on the donkey the frustration of his oppression). In both scenes, Coetzee is interested in the bewilderment of the onlookers, including writers and readers. The cruelty is so extreme, and in Gordimer's passage the context so morally complex, that all judgement fails and the psychic defence mechanisms are quickly engaged.[19] This gives Coetzee the thesis for the Princeton lectures: 'Scenes of sadistic violence (the above, or in an abattoir) can be borne only in a cushioned (aestheticized) environment. Against whoever brings them naked into the open, mechanisms of exclusion come into play.'[20]

Part of the preparation for *The Lives of Animals* involved paying a visit to the Lilly Library at Indiana University, Bloomington, where he read Nadine Gordimer's notebooks from the 1950s. The notebooks record her reflections on reading Sartre, Camus, Merleau-Ponty and others on violence, on 'ends and means'. He records an excerpt that Gordimer takes from Camus ('We must refuse to make violence

First notebook entry for 'Disgrace',
13 December 1994.

legitimate … Violence is both inevitable and unjustifiable'), and makes a note to the effect that he will apply this position to animals and have Costello take it up on the platform.[21] (Confirmation that Gordimer came to mind at least some of the time when he was creating Costello.)

In her notebook reflections of the period, Gordimer would have been adjusting to the climate in which the ANC and other oppositional movements were contemplating revolutionary violence. Forty years later, in an era when violence had become an extension of politics, as Clausewitz would have it, Coetzee was trying to work out a new point of entry into the debate, reorienting it towards animals and emphasizing the dilemmas inherent in representing suffering of any kind.

There are several possible answers to the question why Coetzee would want to reprise the subject of violence by looking at it from the perspective of animals. Obviously, it mattered enough to him to find expression in his daily lifestyle choice, his vegetarianism, but the more salient reason is that what he was looking for was a basis for discussing the representation of suffering that was in itself not already political. He was interested essentially in the *spectacle* of cruelty, and in how cultures manage their witnesses to suffering, whether they hear them or exclude them.

In *Age of Iron*, the essay 'Into the Dark Chamber' and elsewhere, he had explored what it means for certain judgements to lack authority, and what it feels like for certain kinds of people to be made to feel that their judgements are of no consequence. Coetzee has never been persuaded that he inhabits a public sphere where judgements circulate freely among equals. Gordimer was less constrained in this respect: she may have moved left-of-liberal in her political affiliations, and even in her attitudes to violence, but she never showed signs of shedding the belief that she was entitled to judge, publicly. Not so Coetzee, whose work has always implied that the divisions inherent in colonial relations are both fixed and disabling, no matter how impeccable one's intentions may be. For Coetzee, initially at least, focusing on the animal was a way of getting behind the irredeemable politics, and a way of freeing up the debate about representing cruelty.

From this point of view, it is unsurprising that David Lurie's ethical progress in *Disgrace* is measured mainly in terms of his involvement with animals and their dignity at an animal welfare clinic, rather than in terms of his relationships with other people. In both *The Lives of Animals* and *Disgrace*, debates about animals are used as touchstones for debates about cruelty in general. Costello scandalizes her audience by claiming that the treatment of cattle in the stockyards of Chicago provided a model for the planners of the European gas chambers.

In *Disgrace*, some of the most interesting dialogue between David and his daughter, Lucy, is on the subject of animals. For example, Coetzee considered having Lucy take the following view.

Animals are not more like us than we credit them with being, therefore we ought not to kill them. They are, on the contrary, utterly different, incapable of communion, and therefore not part of the polity of rights. The decision on their fate is one in which they can have no part. So, whatever secret communion she feels for them she would conceal it. There will be nothing to see.[22]

The interest taken here, at draft stage, in Lucy's observation that the animal victim's voicelessness puts pressure on the observer is carried over, in the published novel, into the account of Lucy herself after she is raped. In the notebook, Coetzee also writes of Lucy, 'She cares for animals, in a double sense. "I find that there is no way I can declare this. I am estranged by what happens to animals; but by declaring this, in this place, in this time, I place myself outside discourse. I become an animal myself. Very well: I do not mind being an animal. That is who I am, what I am."'[23]

Much of this language is used in the published text, but in the context of Lucy's efforts to explain her withdrawal and adjustment after the rape. She tells David not to raise the subject again, saying it is 'a purely private matter. In another time, in another place it might be held to be a public matter. But in this place, at this time, it is not. It is my business, mine alone.' She adds, 'This place being South Africa.'[24] She also talks about starting again with nothing, 'No cards, no weapons, no property, no rights, no dignity.' 'Like a dog,' David offers, to which she replies, 'Yes, like a dog,' a conclusion that critics have noticed repeats the ending of Kafka's *The Trial*.

South Africa's Truth and Reconciliation Commission (TRC) provided the seed from which *Disgrace* germinated. A truth commission had been floated at an early stage of the negotiations towards South Africa's political settlement. A key outcome envisaged for such a commission was that it should provide a mechanism for securing amnesty for human rights violators, without which it was believed that the country would be dogged by perpetual cycles of retribution and vengeance.

By the time the interim constitution was promulgated in 1993, the need for providing amnesty had been written into its final clause. Once the new parliament was elected, the legislation was prepared and the TRC signed into law, through the Promotion of National Unity and Reconciliation Act No. 34 of 1995. In the intervening period, that is to say, when the TRC had been mooted but before it began holding hearings, Coetzee conceived a novel about a distinguished writer who is invited onto a truth commission but baulks at the prospect because he is about to be publicly exposed for sexual harassment. He fears that he will stand judged not only by the public, but by his daughter, with her 'clear eyes'.

So when the mood in South Africa was buoyant and the TRC under negotiation, Coetzee was registering misgivings about whether ordinary people were capable of living up to the spirit of moral triumph that was taking hold of the nation. In the gap that was opening up between aspiration and reality, he saw the potential for a novel – a Dostoevskian observation, and of course he had been deep inside a Dostoevskian universe, with *The Master of Petersburg* published in the same year.

For some time, as it happens, Coetzee had imagined a novel based on the drama of a man's public humiliation (it was an idea for which his father Jack's misfortunes prepared him), but now the righteousness of the prevailing discourse brought exactly the right moment for the project. An early draft refers to the Book of Job, but Coetzee soon abandoned that allusion, no doubt because Job is tested by God rather than by history. At the end of Job's journey lie redemption and prosperity, not the outcome Coetzee was imagining. For much of the writing of *Disgrace*, the character who became David Lurie was going to commit suicide.

On the evidence of the notebooks, Coetzee was distinctly unimpressed by the moral climate in South Africa. He feared that it was anti-intellectual and potentially tyrannous. For example, his notes include an extract from an account of Mao's Cultural Revolution in which an intellectual is made to wear a dunce cap. In the drafts and final text of *Disgrace*, Mao is edited out, but a female activist carrying a camera confronts David Lurie and takes a photo for the student newspaper, while a male accomplice positions an inverted waste-paper basket strategically in conical fashion over his head. It appears above the caption 'Who's the Dunce Now?'[25]

Roland Barthes's 'Inaugural Lecture' makes a surprising appearance in the notes in this context, at a point in his argument at which Barthes says that the performance of any language system involves setting up rules that define what may and what may not be said. From this Barthes derives the conclusion (it seems excessive now, but this was 1960s optimism) that language is neither reactionary nor progressive, but 'fascist'. Apropos of this remark Coetzee writes, 'Fascism does not prevent speech, it compels speech ... They want to demand a certain speech (confession) of him.'[26] 'They' here refers to the disciplinary committee of the novel's fictional Cape Technical University, which is convened to inquire into allegations of David Lurie's sexual mis-conduct towards the student Melanie Isaacs.

As previously mentioned, Coetzee did begin writing the novel before the TRC fully assumed the character that it did. More useful to him than the TRC itself was the University of Cape Town's booklet on 'Academic Staff Disciplinary Procedure', which he retained in his files and which includes the following clause: 'If the misconduct warrants dismissal and the COI [Committee of Inquiry] decides upon dismissal but considers an alternative to dismissal acceptable, the COI may offer an alternative. If the offer is accepted by the staff member it shall apply.' Coetzee's novel uses these procedures to the letter. As an alternative to dismissal, Lurie is asked to make a public confession; when he refuses to do so, matters take their course and he is asked to resign.

That the TRC provided only a remote sense of context is clear from the points of contention that arise in Lurie's disciplinary hearing. Lurie resists making a public display of contrition. The theoretical argument informing this position is Barthesian, as we have seen, or, equally possibly, it shows the hand of Michel Foucault, who had been influential in Coetzee's collection of essays on South African literature, *White Writing*. The argument is that the politics of power has contributed to our very definition as subjects – or, in an older language, to which the novel is hospitable, politics is invading the inner life. 'These are puritanical times,' says Lurie. 'Private life is public business.'[27] Lucy takes much the same view after being raped.

There is some confusion about this in the criticism, because, contrary to widely held assumptions, it is very unlikely that Coetzee would have applied this analysis in a direct critique of the TRC. If he had, it would have been a misapplication, because demonstrations of remorse on the part of human rights violators were not a requirement for amnesty from the TRC. 'Full disclosure' was, but of events and political affiliations, not of matters of the heart. Lurie's disciplinary hearing has just the opposite goal in mind, to achieve a display of contrition that would lead to a convenient pardon, rather than an even more embarrassing public furore.

Coetzee certainly took the TRC into account, but only as an indicator of the political climate. His attention was elsewhere. In notebook entries made after the TRC had begun conducting its hearings, he goes as far as to link Lurie's resistance to the disciplinary committee's offer of psychological counselling, to 're-education', another nod to Mao, and to the 'victor's-justice (Nuremberg) aspect of the Truth and Reconciliation Committee [sic], with its demand that newspaper editors confess their complicity with "apartheid".'[28] Even if some of the TRC's commissioners made demands from the platform for public apologies, in their personal capacity or under the influence of the role the commission played as a form of national theatre, its legally constituted position was the direct opposite of the view adopted at Nuremberg. The TRC eschewed retributive justice in the interests of restorative justice, of peace and reconciliation.

In the novel, 'victor's justice' is embodied in the steely Farodia Rassool, who alludes to the racial overtones of the case and 'the long history of exploitation of which this is part'. It is Rassool who demands sincerity from Lurie, and so she is the one who embodies most clearly Barthes's notion of linguistic fascism.[29] The novel's perspective on these events has it that social redress is a function of power, no more and no less – this was not the ethos of the TRC. In the vision of *Disgrace*, victor's justice might well prevail because the history being played out was not a transition to a new enlightened order, but the arrival of colonialism's end-game.

The preparatory work for *Disgrace* undoubtedly reveals disaffection on Coetzee's part, but his disquiet actually lay deeper than his scepticism about this or that aspect of the prevailing discourse. It had more to do with anxieties about the future. The problem of how to imagine South Africa's future, as it had been articulated in *Waiting for the Barbarians* and *Life & Times of Michael K*, resurfaces in *Disgrace* but, if anything, in politically more challenging ways because the transition was well under way. The anxieties were also personal as much as they were political, because they had to do with being an ageing parent and imagining one's children and *their* future.

In the novel, David feels bereft when he realizes that with Lucy's pregnancy from rape, his own line will 'run out, like water dribbling into the earth'. The thought paralyses him momentarily, leaving him supporting himself against the wall of the kitchen, hiding his face in his hands and heaving until he cries.[30] It is, of course, only his patronymic line that will run out, not the biological one, which is present in Lucy and her child. Coetzee's own circumstances were entirely different, but they, too, would have challenged his sense of continuity with future generations. Nicolas had died. If he was to remain sanguine, his hopes would rest on his daughter, Gisela. The comfort that a daughter provides for an ageing father was in fact central to the conception of *Disgrace*, as the notebook reveals in referring to a daughter's 'clear eyes', but Coetzee had also planned that the novel's 'moral centre' was to be the following: 'He', that is, the one who would become David Lurie,

> consistently takes the line, Nothing matters, soon I will be dead anyway. In other words, he cannot see beyond his death. Somehow he (I too!) must get beyond that. Hence, of course, the daughter, the only

way in which he (I too!) can conceive of the future. (Think of James Joyce on the girls in Shakespeare's late plays.)[31]

The final parenthesis in this note refers to the Scylla and Charybdis episode of James Joyce's *Ulysses*, which takes the form of a conversation in the National Library of Ireland in Dublin, in which Stephen Dedalus, Lyster (the librarian) and friends discuss Shakespeare. Stephen offers a brilliant if slightly implausible theory about the autobiographical basis of *Hamlet*, and then argues that Shakespeare was able to pass from the darker tragedies like *Hamlet*, *King Lear* and *Othello* to the later romances by focusing on daughters: Marina in *Pericles*, Perdita in *The Winter's Tale* and Miranda in *The Tempest*.[32]

The Master of Petersburg's preoccupation with a father and a son transmutes into *Disgrace's* reflections on a father and his daughter. The daughter figure develops into Lucy, who by the end of the story is pregnant, and David is beginning to learn what Joyce refers to in the same passage as *l'art d'être grandpère*, the art of being a grandfather, a phrase derived from a book of children's poems by Victor Hugo.[33] Coetzee kept notes of Hugo's poems in his files.

In one version of the relationship between David and Lucy, he was to be a fully fledged writer, not just a literary critic and part-time librettist, and he would say to her, 'You are my best critic,' and 'I depend on you to tell me when to stop when my powers begin to leave me.' She reads his work, realizing that it is 'surreptitiously confessional'. When it becomes clear to her that certain episodes could not possibly belong to his 'real' life, she continues to read them allegorically anyway, as if they *were* about him. She reflects, 'He may think that he is being driven by the fiction, but he cannot escape the expressive function.'[34]

In the published text, the intellectual tussle between father and daughter takes different forms, but the consistent thread is that Lucy is the answer to David's problem of feeling that the future is not worth living. He ruminates on verb-tense constructions that he calls 'the perfective', constructions in which the pastness of the past is emphasized ('Burned – burnt – burnt up').[35] When he tries to reassure himself, following the attack on the farm in which his face and hair are burnt, that he will feel better about the world when his wounds heal, he thinks, 'the truth, he knows, is otherwise. His pleasure in living has been snuffed out. Like a leaf on a stream, like a puffball on a breeze, he has begun to float toward his end.'[36] At various stages in the manuscripts David either commits suicide or considers ways of committing suicide, including with Lucy's help, and both in the drafts and the published text she plays a central role in David's recovery by steering him towards an appreciation of the life he shares with animals.

The realism to which Coetzee was committed meant that he had to make the relationships between David and Melanie Isaacs, and David and Lucy, as socially credible as possible. The David–Melanie affair went through several iterations: she is a student of psychology, working on the history of mental health institutions in the Western Cape. He arranges a panel at a conference in Johannesburg on colonial historiography and sees to it that her paper is accepted so that they can spend time together. He then turns Lurie, who is still known as X at this stage of drafting, into an academic lawyer who has been appointed to an investigative tribunal, working in a warehouse, poring over police files and preparing indictments.

X no longer gives lectures but continues with supervisions, and agrees reluctantly to supervise Melanie, who is a psychology postgraduate working on the rights of the insane. The student later becomes a student of literature, writing an MA thesis on 'Landscape and Gender in [Early] South African Settler Writing', with Thomas Pringle as 'colonial conqueror'. It is only at a late stage that she becomes Melanie the drama student of the novel.[37]

If David was to be a member of a TRC-like tribunal, then a realist novel would require his social life and especially his political connections to be fleshed out. This created difficulties for Coetzee:

> Stalled over the question of his political identity. If one makes him belong to the ANC, the question of the texture of his social life arises.

The whole enterprise slides into Gordimer territory. Wouldn't it be better not to make it the story of a man of high station brought down, but rather to make him a lowly toiler in the academy, five years short of retirement? After the event, pressure is brought on him to retire early. He accepts retirement, finds the package includes exclusion from the campus and the library (he was hoping for a researcher's cubicle). This hits him particularly hard. He haunts the SAPL [South African Public Library], spends more and more time with his daughter.

The Lurie we know begins to take shape here, together with some of his intellectual interests. Lurie was to be busy on 'a major work' in keeping with the protagonists of earlier books, and initially this took the form of a study of 'the landscape tradition in the generation before Collins and Thomson, i.e. in Pope, with Virgil and Horace behind him. The mediatedness of landscape.' He would reflect on 'the shantytown landscape of the N2 [a highway east of Cape Town]', making 'the tone of the book lighter, more ironic'.[38]

While the subject would have brought the scholar and his student together, and while it resonated with Coetzee's earlier writing, the ironic touch implies that Coetzee was reluctant to return to landscape as the subject of fiction. Lucy's farm in the Eastern Cape enables Coetzee to rework the tradition of the farm novel, but Lurie's artistic interests took a different course.

The switch from landscape studies to a minor opera on Byron and his lover Teresa was a late development, for which, among other things, Coetzee read Byron's letters and journals and Peter Quennell's *Byron in Italy*. He considered having Lurie write a book on Giacomo Leopardi and toyed with titles derived from Arrigo Boito. He used Leopardi's *Operette Morali* when writing Teresa's lines for the libretto. Lurie's Byron project works much better than the landscape studies might have done, both because it enabled Coetzee to develop Lurie as a properly post-Romantic intellectual, and because Byron is sufficiently removed from contemporary South Africa to bring out Lurie's cultural isolation.

The realism also demanded incident, action. Coetzee recorded the first version of the attack on the farm, the novel's pivotal event, on 20 April 1996. Following his resignation from the Cape Technical University, Lurie removes himself to the countryside and Lucy's house:

> He finds a more or less happy existence living with his daughter, working at the SPCA, looking after the garden. He makes friends with one of the workers at the SPCA. One afternoon this worker and an associate attack him, beat him over the head, try to strangle him, pour motor oil over him and set him alight, and run his car over him, before making off with the car.
>
> His daughter looks after him. He mends, but scarred. He returns to his job, demands to teach.[39]

By this stage, Coetzee had begun to look for ways of making the text more edgy and violent. Soon after imagining the attack he writes, 'What is missing, what makes the whole project so lukewarm is an element of savagery, of anti-social-ism. As it stands it is a plea for ageing men to be allowed to have affairs with their students. The relationship with Melanie is too polite, Melanie herself is too nice (or too blank).'[40] He revises the meeting with Melanie in the university rose garden, making her more sexually precocious. Thereafter, he often sought to roughen the edges of the narrative, making it more menacing, as in the following entry (which did not survive editing): 'In the middle of the night the bulldog growls. He peers out. In the moonlight, a man waits. He thinks: Africa; I'm in a novel by Doris Lessing. He goes out. The man wanders away. Later, sound of talk from Petrus's house. Lucy joins him: "What is it?"'[41]

The realism also demanded that Lucy's inner life be represented. This is a source of much discussion in the criticism because Lucy is, indeed, undeveloped as a character. We see her predominantly through David's eyes, and after she is attacked she becomes defensive and inscrutable. Critics have read this as deliberate on Coetzee's part, as if he was emphasizing that the novel's perspectives are limited, that the subjectivity at the centre is strictly David's.

This interpretation of the published text is undoubtedly correct, but if we look back over the drafts at how the restricted perspective came about, the situation is more conflicted. For what emerges from the novel's development is that while Coetzee realized that the realist portrayal of Lucy would require him to develop her inner life, especially in relation to the violence she suffers, he simply did not have the means, or even the desire, to do so. 'The problem is Lucy. Whatever she is going through, I can't feel it from the inside. Try the following. After the rape she spends long periods with Dot Shaw, getting "support". At the same time she loses interest in the dogs, in the farm. He (and Petrus) have to look after things. Lucy becomes slordig, unkempt.'[42]

The problem was intractable, even threatening to derail the entire novel, or turn it into something different. He writes: 'This is not a novel. Not possible to keep the emphasis from shifting to Lucy's inner world, thus splitting the work in two.' The solution was to 'Speed up the narration, make the control of the narrator more formal, denaturalize it, emphasize symmetries.'[43] It was a phase of crisis that forced Coetzee to look back and recompose the changing narrative structure:

> Thus: (1) his placid concupiscence; (2) the disruption caused by the student, and the fall into disgrace; (3) retreat to his daughter; (4) the daughter's crisis and her attempt to illuminate him; (5) his return to face the hearing. Closes with scene of him making his way through contemptuous crowd. 'They revile him.'
>
> 30,000 words. One of a series of 'exemplary tales'.[44]

He began to think in terms of a 'synopsized novel', as if 'there were a fully written realistic novel in the background which is retold in synopsis. One gets an example in *Don Quixote*, when Q tells the story of a stereotypical romance. Impression of pace. Not being sure whether you are in the base novel or in the summary of it.'[45] Needless to say, the synopsized novel was not the novel he ended up writing.

In earlier projects, like *Waiting for the Barbarians* and *Life & Times of Michael K*, difficulties on this scale led to thoroughgoing revisions, often with metafictional outcomes. On this occasion he pressed on, albeit tempted by the idea of giving a synopsis while hinting at a larger work in the background: 'So: how to give it in summary without moving into a half-baked postmodernist mode.'[46] The crisis passed with Coetzee keeping to the story. Lurie's work with animals, the Byron material and David's relationship with Lucy provided the areas of intensity that were needed to keep the writing responsive, buoyant and forward-looking.

While Coetzee took the view that he could not represent Lucy's interior life or the specific character of her suffering, the historical meaning of her being raped was a subject that he was able to turn into fiction. Moving swiftly towards the most contentious of possibilities in this theme, he writes, 'Rape should be seen as part of project to drive whites off the land and out of the country …'[47] The note is ambiguous: should be seen by whom: Coetzee, the narrator, Lurie, the white community around Salem, the reader? It is too cryptic to be clear.

Less ambiguous is the entry immediately following, in which he develops the difference of opinion between Lucy and David, as follows:

> the problem, as she sees it, is that no amount of individual reparation will suffice to save the individual. There is no way to acquire the mark on the door (cf story of the plagues in Egypt) that will spare one. Only when the white community as a whole is recognized as having made reparation will it cease to be victimized. This is a prospect Lucy does not foresee.
>
> OR: She believes that only in the countryside where people are not anonymous, can salvation be secured at an individual level.
>
> In Lucy's eyes, David Lurie is preoccupied with irrelevant matters. Hence, in part, her indifference to him.
>
> DL sees something that Lucy will not adjust to herself: that she is laying herself open to rape upon rape. How many rapes before one is made clean?[48]

It is more obvious here that it is Lurie's views that are in play. He would argue that Lucy is wrong to imagine that individual reparation will save her. In the novel, David asks Lucy whether by refusing to lay charges against her rapists, she imagines that she will be treated differently in future, whether she thinks that her progressive outlook will be 'a sign to paint on a door-lintel that will make the plague pass you by'.[49] Later, he puts it to her that the rape did not involve personal hatred – it was a matter of 'history speaking through them', that 'it came down from the ancestors'.[50]

From the point of view of the challenges that he was facing, Coetzee pursued what seemed to lend itself to fictional representation, and the issue he turned to was alive and well in the culture of liberal whites: whether or not it was possible, through goodwill or through their actions, for individuals to earn immunity from historical guilt and from the suffering that might come with reparation. The rest of the plot of *Disgrace* answers that question: it is not possible for Lucy to escape reverse-colonial 'subjugation',[51] as she calls it; and, in fact, to have a future at all she must embrace the humiliation fully by submitting to a polygamous arrangement with Petrus.

David, too, would have to own his disgrace in order to progress beyond it. Coetzee even toyed with the idea – though it was not a serious proposition – of having David return to Cape Town and lock himself in the empty lion cage of the zoo on the Rhodes Estate, the problem being that no one would come to look.[52] Coetzee had read David Garnett's *A Man in the Zoo* (1924). The suicidal impulse never leaves Lurie: Lear-like, he is full of empathy as he watches the corpses of dogs roll down the conveyor into the hospital's incinerator.

The novel's final scene, in which David puts down the dog he has befriended, is a residue and displacement of his own suicide, a self-sacrificial gesture in keeping with the self-destructive tendency that was present all along in his surrendering to Eros and the erotic fire ignited by Melanie, but that has now become more dire.

The care with which the final scene is written turns it into a moment of literary sublimity that is mysterious and profound, though behind it lie more ordinary feelings of bitterness and anger. Before the dog was given the touching name Driepoot ('Three Paws'), it was to be called Byron, or George Gordon. If David was to play God in sending the dogs to their deaths, he should learn to do so impartially: 'Pass one, pass all,' Coetzee wrote, using the phrase coined by militant students campaigning against high failure rates.[53]

Coetzee thought of putting together a volume of short acerbic essays on South Africa at this point, including one that would reply to the new education policy of 'affirming the child' (whose feminist roots he saw in eighteenth-century sentimental literature), with a Nietzschean injunction that children should be taught to repress the demonic in themselves.[54]

It is somewhat miraculous that Coetzee was able to burn off much of this palpable bitterness in the incendiary artistic language developed out of David Lurie's wayward desires. Coetzee's standing face to face with time in *Disgrace* included facing down the times he was living through. His reading in the late stages of writing the novel included Milan Kundera's *Testaments Betrayed*, an account of twentieth-century artistic investments betrayed by the history in which they reside. Anticipating the betrayal of art, of *his* art, by a corrosive alliance of market instrumentalism and postcolonial nationalism, Coetzee was handing the culture a story that was proud in its very shamefulness, triumphant in defeat. It was also a resolute reclaiming of the space of art from time's, and the time's, degradation.

THE THIRD STAGE

Australia – *Slow Man, Diary of a Bad Year,*
The Childhood of Jesus

One can think of a life in art, schematically, in two or perhaps three stages.
In the first you find, or pose for yourself, a great question. In the second
you labor away at answering it. And then, if you live long enough, you
come to the third stage, when the aforesaid great question
begins to bore you, and you need to look elsewhere.[1]

And if a better, more peaceable life is not to be found in Australia,
where is it to be found?[2]

THE LETTERS BETWEEN Coetzee and the Brooklyn-based novelist
Paul Auster are written in a spirit of intelligent bonhomie, which
sometimes makes it difficult to gauge their seriousness. In the first of
the epigraphs to this chapter, Coetzee is generalizing from his own
experience but without engaging all the gears of autobiography. It is
also in the nature of all schemas that they simplify. It would therefore
be risky to squeeze Coetzee's career into the three stages he identifies,
but they are pertinent.

The 'great question' is not too difficult to name: on the evidence
of his first two novels it would be something like, *What script has my*
history written for me, and how can I rewrite it? But as for what he calls
the second phase, there is too much variation, too many different kinds

of toil and adventure – as I hope my previous chapters have shown – to be able to say that it comes down to a single answer. Nevertheless, there is little doubt that *Disgrace* marks the end of a phase that would have begun with *Waiting for the Barbarians*, a phase that would be better described as a long and agonistic passage. The third stage is clearer: it is what comes after *Disgrace*.

Coetzee's reflection encapsulates, for Auster's benefit, a more serious line of thought that finds expression in *Diary of a Bad Year* (2007). When he reads the work of accomplished writers of realism, writes the JC of that novel, 'my heart sinks'. He explains, 'I was never much good at evocation of the real, and have even less stomach for the task now.'[3] If a process of attenuation is under way, he continues, it is arguably a common phenomenon among writers who reach a ripe age, the age of growing 'cooler or colder', when the 'texture of their prose becomes thinner, their treatment of character and action more schematic'.[4] There are two ways of looking at this process, he says: from the outside it appears as if the author is losing his powers, but from the inside it can be felt as 'a liberation, a clearing of the mind to take on more important tasks'.[5]

The example JC gives is that of Tolstoy, who every reader would acknowledge was 'alive to the real' when he was young, but who underwent (in the standard account) 'a long decline into didacticism that culminated in the aridity of the late short fiction'. Such is the view from the outside. From the inside, Tolstoy would have felt that 'he was ridding himself of the shackles that had enslaved him to appearances, enabling him to face directly the one question that truly engaged his soul: how to live'.[6] In his letter Coetzee adds a 'loftier' example: at the time of his death Bach was working on *The Art of Fugue*, 'pure music in the sense that it is not tied to any particular instrument'.[7]

Diary of a Bad Year, in which these reflections appear, is a schematic book, so Coetzee was in fact undergoing the process he describes. The novel began as a fictionalized diary in which he, Coetzee, wrote reflections on a range of unconnected topics, both public and personal. Then, while detaching himself from the voice by calling the protagonist JC (although JC is still acknowledged as sharing much of Coetzee's own history), he added two layers of fictional framing involving the secretary, Anya, whom JC engages to help him produce a typescript. (An intertextual allusion is in the background here, because the secretary in question is the near-namesake of the woman Dostoevsky engaged for a similar purpose and eventually married, the stenographer Anna Snitkina.)

The main formal innovation in *Diary of a Bad Year* is to lay out this fictional framing in such a way that we have three bands of text on the same page: the diary entries (which are supposedly destined for a collection to be called *Strong Opinions*), then JC's narrative centred on Anya, then Anya's own narrative. The result is that the diary entries are embedded in fiction – a gesture we would expect from the author of *Elizabeth Costello* – but in reality the fictional narratives are thin. They do not give the reader an experience of the real, or of fiction as realism. That is not their purpose, of course. Their purpose is to give the reader an experience of *fictionality*. The text does so, principally, by inviting us to choose between reading the frames vertically (that is, 'simultaneously'), which would mean experiencing the text as a Chinese box, or reading them horizontally, by following a single narrative line over several pages before returning to pick up the next one, and so on. Coetzee had often been tempted by the idea of adding a layer of commentary to the narrative he was composing, and *Diary of a Bad Year* is a version of this, except that instead of the narrative being embedded within commentary, we have commentary embedded within narrative.

On the evidence of *Diary*, it would seem that Coetzee had reached the stage at which he felt he could give up the obligation to see out the often nauseating business of producing verisimilitude. Instead, he settled for giving his reader a taste of it, on the assumption (in the hope) that the reader would play along. Actually, the opening of *Elizabeth Costello* expects this of the reader too. When introducing the subject of realism, the narrator talks about 'knocking together a bridge' instead of actually knocking the bridge together, which would mean laying out the whole *mise en scène* in careful detail. 'Let us assume that, however it may have been done, it is done.'[8] Some of the most volatile moments in Coetzee's notebooks, as we have seen, are those in which he rebels against the realism he feels bound to produce if the book is to be written. In *Diary*, clearly, he had reached a point of no longer feeling so bound.

In the drafts of *Diary*, before the fictional frames were added, the reflections on the attenuation of a writer's powers and the example of Tolstoy are developed in much more personalized terms. Coetzee writes that while his own evolution is nothing like Tolstoy's (in the sense, one assumes, that he has not reached an equivalent stage of spiritual clarity), he has 'certainly lost for ever the simple urge to represent'. When representation, in this sense, has been unavoidable in recent work, 'there is a perfunctoriness to the result that the reader does not fail to detect ... Readers who come to my recent books looking for the kind of pleasure that one can legitimately expect from the novel, and that one perhaps gets from a book like *Michael K*, find them thin and artificial, and who can blame them?'[9] Coetzee is speaking here about those readers (reviewers?) who have shown that they are *not* willing to substitute the game of realism for the real thing.

Elleke Boehmer makes a related point when she observes of Coetzee's Australian writing that the realism is perfunctory: it has about it, she says, 'a certain sense of correctness and obligation, the politeness of the naturalized citizen'.[10] A 'civil' realism, to develop this observation, would be a realism that does just enough to prove that one belongs, but without being utterly convincing. In *Slow Man*, for instance, Coetzee uses the street names of Adelaide, but it is not a novel of Adelaide in the sense that *Age of Iron* is a novel of Cape Town. Boehmer's conclusion is that this limited realism expresses something about Coetzee's relation to his new country. This is a valid point, but another aspect of the question has to do with Coetzee's relation to realism itself.

Instead of 'the simple urge to represent', Coetzee says that what engages him more is the 'second-order' questions. Examples would be,

'What am I doing when I represent? What is the difference between living in the real world and living in a world of representations?'[11] From inside the process of thinning-out, Coetzee clarifies here what is most important for him: the self-reflection on one's practice. There is no sense of his being embattled when he makes these remarks. It is not as if he is defending himself against the tide of popular culture. If anything, the spirit in which these remarks are made is one of acceptance, even renunciation: I may have done this sort of thing once, but I simply don't have the strength or conviction to do it any more.

In *Diary*, JC says, 'I was never much good at evocation of the real, and have even less stomach for the task now. The truth is, I have never taken much pleasure in the visible world, don't feel with much conviction the urge to recreate it in words.'[12] The draft of this is more plaintive: 'As a real novelist,' Coetzee writes, 'I have never been up to much. I don't live with enough intensity in the real world, don't care enough about it, don't feel with enough force the demiurge to recreate it.'[13] A passage from García Márquez's *The Fragrance of Guava* helps him to define the feeling more precisely. Márquez writes,

> I don't see [inspiration] as a state of grace nor as a breath from heaven but as the moment when, by tenacity and control, you are at one with your theme. When you want to write something, a kind of reciprocal tension is established between you and your theme, so you spur the theme on and the theme spurs you on too. There comes a moment when all obstacles fade away, all conflict disappears, things you never dreamt of occur to you and, at that moment, there is absolutely nothing in the world better than writing.[14]

Coetzee comments, 'Once or twice in a lifetime I have known the flight of the soul that García Márquez describes.' In the draft, he says, 'Perhaps it was the reward for the tenacity of which he speaks.' In the novel: 'Perhaps such flights do indeed come as a reward for tenacity, though I think *steady fire* better describes the needed quality. But however we name it, I no longer have it.'[15]

In the drafts of earlier novels, we have seen Coetzee giving himself the military order, figuratively speaking, 'steady fire'. The metaphor is odd but it is right for a stylist who is this steely and determined. There were moments of quite severe self-doubt in *Waiting for the Barbarians* and *Life & Times of Michael K*, and even in novels where less verisimilitude was required, like *Foe* and *The Master of Petersburg*. But when the business of sustaining realism's illusions felt like a gargantuan chore, his response in each case was to tough it out, see it through and keep firing, or, failing that, to fold the metafictional impulse back into the texture of the illusory world itself.

Thus, in *Waiting for the Barbarians* the magistrate's fascination with the illegible ancient script in the slips of poplar wood, or the second-order narrators in *Michael K* and *Foe*, or the debates about reading and the writer's authority in *The Master of Petersburg*, are all occasions when Coetzee's presence makes itself felt in his material, enabling him to create an existential connection with the project. One of the surprises that come with reading the drafts and notebooks for these projects is discovering the extent to which Coetzee acknowledges that the hyper-awareness of the writer at work in these projects is indeed his own. 'Steady fire' may have meant resisting the urge to add another layer of commentary in place of doing the dirty work of representation.

The third stage, then, is the stage at which that self-control is no longer desirable or necessary. To extend Coetzee's metaphor of the battlefield, when 'steady fire' no longer serves the purpose and the enemy is getting nearer, the next order would be 'fire at will'. That would not be the most judicious description of Coetzee's stylistic choices in the novels since *Disgrace*, because each is, in its own way, highly measured, as is all his writing, but it would be fair to say that the reintroduction of Elizabeth Costello in *Slow Man* was a gesture of abandonment, even reckless. In making that move, Coetzee must have decided to take a detached view of the likely reaction in many a reader.

Second-order questions predominate in Coetzee's third stage, then. In the letter to Auster he says that the passage into the third stage is brought on by boredom – by finding the overwhelming questions of one's youth no longer interesting enough. In the reflections of *Diary of a Bad Year*, the attenuation is ascribed to a weakening of desire. In their contexts, these explanations are equivocal – hyperbolic and ironic – and therefore not to be trusted. What they leave out is the power of circumstance. In Coetzee's real world, the circumstances governing the passage from the second stage into the third were momentous: he retired from full-time academic life, packed up his Cape Town home, and emigrated.

John Kannemeyer gives a thorough account of the reasons for Coetzee's decision to move to Australia, and of the choice of Adelaide in particular.[16] Only a brief summary is needed here. He and Dorothy had been visiting Adelaide and other Australian cities fairly regularly since 1990, and as early as 1995 Coetzee was in contact with immigration officials in Canberra. Through attorneys in Sydney, he eventually lodged a formal application for immigrant status in 1999, with assistance from Australian writers, notably David Malouf. Widely held assumptions about his departure being the consequence of the local reception of *Disgrace* (or of the ANC's references to it in the party's submission to the South African Human Rights Commission's hearings into the persistence of racism in the media in 2001) are therefore incorrect. The important soundings about emigration were taken before and during *Disgrace*'s completion, and the legal work was done well before the controversy erupted.

The fact is that South Africa is the country of Coetzee's birth, the country that has given him, by his own admission, the only place where he has felt truly at home, the Karoo. As a notoriously conflicted historical condition, South Africa has also shaped Coetzee's fiction and given it many of the qualities that make it distinctive, even if he has objected at times to being labelled a South African writer. But it is also true that Coetzee's intellectual connections are global in their reach (wherever European languages are spoken and written), and he has made homes in the United Kingdom, the United States, France and now in Australia. In his public statements about his relocation, Coetzee has tried to do justice to the complexity of the situation. He has acknowledged, 'leaving a country is, in some respects, like the breakup of a marriage. It is an intimate matter,' but he has also emphasized the attractions of Adelaide, saying that he has not left South Africa so much as he has *come to* Australia.[17]

The climate, the geography and the quiet life afforded by north Adelaide, ringed by the picturesque Adelaide Hills, suit Coetzee extremely well. He is often at work in the cultural metropoles of Melbourne and Sydney, but in Adelaide he is freer to define the terms of his existence. He is, of course, a public figure in Australia, as much as he is in South Africa, Europe and the United States; he is frequently called upon to lend *gravitas* to official functions, give readings and officiate at festivals; and he is involved in animal rights advocacy with the organization Voiceless. In all of these situations, Australians generally respect his stated preference for the quiet life. In his immediate circles, around the city and university, the tone is affectionate. It is difficult to imagine him leading an equivalent life in South Africa, where there are so many conflicted and conflicting claims on him.

Elizabeth Costello set out a series of arguments on what we have called second-order questions, but one theme in particular was announced in Coetzee's Nobel Lecture of 7 December 2003. Few critics have acknowledged its importance in these terms, but it is clear that Coetzee was signalling to himself and others that it represented new terrain on which he would be working.

'He and His Man' is about an author and his creations, or, to put it in the terms of *Diary of a Bad Year*, 'the difference between living in the real world and living in a world of representations'. The people who live in these worlds, who are represented in the story by Crusoe and Defoe, are proximate but distinct beings. The reports that the author, Defoe, sends in from his travels around England become the material of the character Crusoe's subjectivity. Defoe's realism thus becomes the fabric of Crusoe's inner life, realism reconfigured as autobiographical

John Coetzee and Dorothy Driver, Morialta Conservation Park, Adelaide.

fiction – a pattern that is borne out in much of Coetzee's career. The story ends on an expansive note, from which we can infer that Coetzee was looking to turn the ideas into a more developed project:

> he fears there will be no meeting, not in this life. If he must settle on a likeness for the pair of them, his man and he, he would write that they are like two ships sailing in contrary directions, one west, the other east. Or better, that they are deckhands toiling in the rigging, the one on a ship sailing west, the other on a ship sailing east. Their ships pass close, close enough to hail. But the seas are rough, the weather is stormy: their eyes lashed by the spray, their hands burned by the cordage, they pass each other by, too busy even to wave.[18]

It was with some reluctance that Coetzee ceded copyright in the lecture to the Nobel Foundation. His experience with the Costello stories was that it was only by reserving copyright that he was able to collect them later and, by doing so, give them the weight and purpose that he foresaw for them. He could well have seen the Nobel Lecture in the same light, but in the end the Nobel Foundation retained copyright and released the story in multiple forms, including streaming on the Internet.

The lecture was certainly unusual as Nobel lectures go. It was one thing to bring out Costello and her fictional world for public lectures on university platforms – even august ones like Princeton's Tanner Lectures – but it was another thing to air a piece of fiction on the global stage of the Swedish Academy. In introducing him, the Academy's permanent secretary, Horace Engdahl, felt that he had to prepare his audience. He referred to the irony of the situation in which Coetzee, whose 'reputation for reclusion' and critique of the author as public figure and celebrity were well known, now found himself in the gaze of the literary world. How would he direct the attention away from himself?[19] Coetzee began with the anecdote about reading *Robinson Crusoe* as a child, then launched into 'He and His Man'.

The novel he was writing at the time was *Slow Man*. The notes and fragments begin early in 2003, well before the events in Stockholm, but not long after the publication of *Elizabeth Costello*. In realist terms, *Slow Man* is appropriately about migration and belonging. It begins with a crisis when Paul Rayment, a naturalized Australian citizen with a French childhood, has a bicycle accident, which leads to a leg amputation. (That Coetzee himself was hospitalized after a cycling accident in Chicago in November 2002 would certainly have been a provocation.) Divorced, without children, Rayment falls in love, entirely quixotically, with the Croatian nurse and caregiver assigned to him by the welfare system, Marijana Jokić.

Rayment pursues his inappropriate feelings by offering to pay for Marijana's son Drago to attend an expensive private school. The gesture reveals that he needs the continuity provided by her children, as much as he desires Marijana's own attentions. The intrusion undermines the Jokićs' marriage and leads to a family crisis, in the course of which Drago pilfers some of the photographs in Rayment's prized collection, substituting photoshopped pictures of his own. The originals are by

Antoine Fauchery, a famous writer and photographer who worked in the mining camps of Victoria and New South Wales during the gold rush. Rayment intends to donate the collection to the National Library of Australia. As a photographer himself, Rayment is interested in Fauchery partly because it enables him to have an imaginative connection to Australian history, a connection that answers his own rootlessness. By the end of the novel, the originals are restored, and the Jokićs triumph over Rayment by graciously using their talents to build him a recumbent cycle that will enable him to regain his strength.

Such are the bare outlines of the story. There is much of Coetzee in it: not only obvious elements like the cycling and the photography, but the interest in the body and its vulnerabilities, the crisis that brings the character face to face with mortality, the transnationalism, and the sense of being cut off from one's past and from the future. *Slow Man* is the novel of Coetzee's emigration, a work that conscientiously sets out to explore the question of belonging to a new country, at a time of life when, in most middle-class lives, the primary concern is superannuation and its consequences. But as we have seen, Coetzee was no longer in a frame of mind to see this project through on such straightforward terms. If the novel was to engage him properly, the second-order questions would have to be on the surface.

Elizabeth Costello was still an active presence in this period, shuffling around Coetzee's house of fiction. Even after the publication of *Elizabeth Costello* in 2003, she made an appearance in an uncollected story, 'As a Woman Grows Older', in the *New York Review of Books* of 15 January 2004. So it is not altogether surprising that a third of the way into *Slow Man* (what became chapter 13), Elizabeth Costello appears at the door of Paul Rayment's flat. The most concentrated period in the writing of *Slow Man* was between July and December 2004. We can make the following circumstantial inference: in this period, when Coetzee reached what had become a familiar moment of doubt with *Slow Man*, when he reached that typical point of crisis at which the metafictional impulse asserts itself, on this occasion he opened the door and let Elizabeth Costello in.

She enters just at the point in the story when Rayment has declared his love for Marijana, precipitating a state of moral vertigo. The narrative changes gear at this point, from being a story of adjustments to external events to an inner, psychological drama of erotic and ethical entanglements. From this moment on, it will need an accomplished novelist to bring out all the implications of the story, so it is precisely the right moment for Costello to begin lecturing Rayment, 'You will have to make a stronger case for yourself.' She insists that he should become bolder, more emblematic: 'Push the mortal envelope,' she harangues.[20]

Thereafter, Costello takes over with an alternative to the story of the relationship with Marijana. The story she invents involves a parallel lover, the blind Marianna. A tryst is arranged and, in order to go through with it, Rayment has to agree to be elaborately blind-folded with flour-paste and lemon leaves and a stocking over his eyes, an implausible and rather literary game. It is Susan and Foe again, arguing over the story that will define her life; alternatively, it is Alonso Quixano, living out the story in which he is Don Quixote, knowing that it has all been scripted for him by Miguel de Cervantes. *Don Quixote* makes several appearances in the notes.

'Our friend advocated this,' says Rayment to the hapless, blind Marianna, 'because in her eyes it represents the crossing of a threshold. She is of the opinion that until I have crossed a certain threshold I am caught in limbo, unable to grow ... She probably has another hypothesis to cover you.'[21] Costello wants to transform the story in such a way that it acquires a deeper literary purpose, resisting her characters becoming 'like tramps in Beckett', 'wasting time, being wasted by time'.[22]

The contest between Costello and Rayment comes to occupy the centre of attention in *Slow Man*. It shifts the emphasis from an affecting story about migration, belonging and senescence to a comedy about meaning itself, a Beckettian shift, certainly. It was not always going to be that way, because in the drafts Coetzee had written a thoroughly consummated relationship between Rayment and Marijana, which would have put his erotic life more clearly at the centre. The Jokićs were also going to prove to be a more dubious conquest, pilfering from Rayment and abusing his hospitality more obviously.

In choosing the course that he did, Coetzee left in many a reader's mind uncertainty about where the novel's true focus lies: does it lie in the story about a man without roots who is jolted into a more conscious existence by an accident, or does it lie in the story of the novelist who is telling Rayment's story, and who struggles to subject her character to her own purposes? The novel contains both narratives, inviting us to keep them in mind at the same time, but for many readers that task was too much to ask.

In the papers of each of Coetzee's novels, we find ideas and resources that are taken up only in subsequent works, not necessarily in the novel on which he happens to be working. This is also true of the papers for *Slow Man*, in which we find Rayment reflecting,

> I have been given a new body, new and inferior, and that has made me a new person. Who I used to be ~~is just a memory. It is like what happens to us after, shall we call it~~ *the end,* ~~when we take on the new and better bodies that have been promised us. What we used to be~~ becomes just a memory, and a memory that fades fast ~~because after the end there is no nostalgia.~~

The phrases that Coetzee strikes out here, suggesting that they have no clear place in *Slow Man*, are Rayment's reflections on 'the end'. A few paragraphs later, still in the drafts, he adds,

> He is not ~~trying to restore~~ interested in restoring his body to functionality. On the contrary, he is tired of his body, looks forward to its final dissolution. There is nothing suicidal in that. He has a clear sense of being a soul with an undiminished soul-life.[23]

Some of the business that was left unfinished in *Slow Man* has been taken up in Coetzee's most recent novel, *The Childhood of Jesus* (2013).

Like *Waiting for the Barbarians*, it is set in a wholly invented milieu. In ways like aspects of *Life & Times of Michael K*, the characters are refugees, not from a recognizable historical situation but from a previous life of which they have no memory. They are survivors who find themselves making a new start, in an existence that could be described as an 'undiminished soul-life'. Their homes and mother tongues have been wiped away, and instead they are assigned new homes and a new language, Spanish. David, a boy of five, and his voluntary guardian, Simón, are in search of David's mother, whom Simón will know instinctively when he sees her, though he has never set eyes on her. In this story of instinctive optimism and new beginnings, their destination is the town of Novilla.

The literary touchstone for this story – and David's favourite book – is *Don Quixote*. Instead of drawing away from realism, which is what he does in writing *Slow Man*, Coetzee has used it, but also subdued it, turning its mirror to reflect the light of one of realism's founding texts on his material. It is a novel about a pristine mind, David's, and his efforts to understand a world that is less than ideal, a story that Cervantes would appreciate. Despite, or rather because of, his other-worldliness, David draws around himself a family who will follow him to a world they can all scarcely imagine.

We can't draw too many conclusions from Coetzee's latest novel about its place in the overarching narrative of his authorship, partly because the manuscript materials that might enable us to understand its genesis are not yet available to the public. We can be confident of one observation, however: *Slow Man* writes the story of migration as an ending, while *The Childhood of Jesus* writes it as a beginning.

NOTES

PREFACE

1 J.M. Coetzee, *Doubling the Point: Essays and Interviews*, ed. David Attwell. Cambridge, Mass.: Harvard University Press, 1992.

2 J.C. Kannemeyer, *J.M. Coetzee: 'n Geskryfde Lewe*. Johannesburg: Jonathan Ball, 2012.

3 J.M. Coetzee, *Summertime*. London: Harvill Secker, 2009.

4 Ian Hamilton, *Keepers of the Flame: Literary Estates and the Rise of Biography*. London: Hutchinson, 1992.

CHAPTER 1

1 J.M. Coetzee, *Elizabeth Costello*. London: Viking, 2003, p. 207.

2 J.M. Coetzee, *Life & Times of Michael K*. Johannesburg: Ravan Press, 1983.

3 Coetzee Papers, *Life & Times of Michael K*, 13 July 1981.

4 Orhan Pamuk, 'Other Countries, Other Shores', *New York Times Book Review*, 19 December 2013, www.nytimes.com/2013/12/22/books/review/other-countries-other-shores.html, pp. 1–3.

5 Ibid., p. 1.

6 Coetzee Papers, *Boyhood*, 11 May 1993.

7 Ibid., 19 June 1993.

8 Roland Barthes, *Roland Barthes*, trans. Richard Howard. New York: Hill & Wang, 2010, p. 41.

9 Ibid., p. 41.

10 Roland Barthes, 'The Death of the Author', trans. Richard Howard. UbuWeb Papers, n.d., www.tbook.constantvzw.org/wp-content/death_authorbarthes.pdf.

11 Geoffrey Wall, *Gustave Flaubert: A Life*. New York: Farrar, Straus, Giroux, 2001, p. 203.

12 Ibid., p. 203.

13 Roland Barthes, *The Preparation of the Novel*, ed. Nathalie Léger, trans. Kate Briggs. New York: Columbia University Press, 2011, p. 3.

14 Ibid., pp. 4–9.

15 Ibid., p. 16.

16 Coetzee Papers, *Master of Petersburg*, 14 May 1991.

17 Coetzee, *Doubling the Point*, p. 391.

18 J.M. Coetzee, 'What Is a Classic?', in *Stranger Shores: Essays 1986–1999*. London: Secker & Warburg, 2001, p. 3.

19 T.S. Eliot, 'Tradition and the Individual Talent' (1919), in *Selected Essays*. London: Faber & Faber, 1932, p. 21.

20 Ibid., p. 17.

21 Coetzee Papers, NELM, UCT Lectures, T.S. Eliot, 1974, p. 3.

22 Coetzee Papers, *Youth*, 15 January 1999.

CHAPTER 2

1 J.M. Coetzee, *Diary of a Bad Year*. London: Harvill Secker, 2007, pp. 195–197; Paul Auster and J.M. Coetzee, *Here and Now: Letters, 2008–2011*. New York: Viking, 2013, p. 65.

2 Auster and Coetzee, *Here and Now*, p. 73.

3 Coetzee Papers, *Summertime*, 1 May 2005.

4 Coetzee Papers, *Boyhood*, 13 December 1994.

5 These and subsequent details are drawn from the account given by Coetzee to John Kannemeyer as recorded in Kannemeyer's papers.

6 Coetzee Papers, *Youth*, 12 June 1999.

7 Coetzee Papers, *Summertime*, 18 March 2005.

8 Coetzee, *Doubling the Point*, pp. 342–343.

9 I am grateful to Rita Barnard for her help in what follows. See her 'Coetzee in/and Afrikaans', *Journal of Literary Studies* 25 (4), 2009, pp. 84–105.

10 Coetzee Papers, *Diary of a Bad Year*, 9 and 10 December 2005.

11 J.C. Kannemeyer, *J.M. Coetzee: A Life in Writing*. Johannesburg: Jonathan Ball, 2012, p. 557. Hereafter all citations are to the English edition.

12 'Doctoris Causa Honoris Lectio', *Iohannes Maxwell Coetzee*, Adam Mickiewicz University, Poznań, Poland, 2012, p. 87.

13 J.M. Coetzee, *Dusklands*. Johannesburg: Ravan Press, 1974, p. 61.

14 J.M. Coetzee, *Boyhood: Scenes from Provincial Life*. London: Secker & Warburg, 1997, p. 81.

15 J.M. Coetzee, *Youth*. London: Secker & Warburg, 2002, p. 127.

16 The current residents of Voëlfontein similarly use 'fountain' with reference to the spring, when speaking English.

17 Coetzee Papers, *In the Heart of the Country*, 4 December 1974.

18 Kannemeyer, *J.M. Coetzee*, p. 288.

19 Coetzee, *Summertime*, p. 54.

20 J.M. Coetzee, 'The Great South African Novel', *Leadership SA* 2 (4), 1983, p. 79.

21 J.M. Coetzee, *Disgrace*. London: Secker & Warburg, 1999, p. 117.

CHAPTER 3

1 Coetzee Papers, *Waiting for the Barbarians*, 30 May 1978.

2 For example, see also Joanna Scott and J.M. Coetzee, 'Voice and Trajectory: An Interview with J.M. Coetzee', *Salmagundi* 114/115, Spring–Summer 1997, pp. 82–102.

3 Coetzee Papers, *Doubling the Point*, 17 January 1989.

4 Coetzee Papers, *Dusklands*, 1 January 1970.

5 Ibid., 17 June 1972.

6 Oswald Spengler, *The Decline of the West* (1926), trans. Charles Francis Atkinson. London: Allen & Unwin, 1959, p. 37.

7 Coetzee, *Summertime*, p. 61.

8 Kannemeyer, *J.M. Coetzee*, pp. 18–21.

9 Ibid., p. 20.

10 Toy cattle and ox-carts made from bones and clay.

11 Coetzee Papers, *Dusklands*, 7 January 1970.

12 Coetzee, *Doubling the Point*, p. 52.

13 Coetzee, *Dusklands*, p. 61.

14 Coetzee, *Summertime*, pp. 58–59.

15 Kannemeyer, *J.M. Coetzee*, p. 192.

16 Ibid., p. 203.

17 Coetzee Papers, *Doubling the Point*, 17 January 1989.

18 Coetzee Papers, *Dusklands*, 11 June 1972.

19 Ibid., 2 July 1972.

20 Ibid., 9 March 1973.

21 Ibid., 15 March 1973.

22 Coetzee Papers, Notebook, *Waiting for the Barbarians*, 4 March 1978.

CHAPTER 4

1 Folke Rhedin, 'J.M. Coetzee: Interview', *Kunapipi* 6 (1), 1984, p. 10.

2 Coetzee Papers, *In the Heart of the Country*, 22 December 1974.

3 J.M. Coetzee, 'Nietverloren', in *Ten Years of the Caine Prize for African Writing*. Oxford: New Internationalist Publications, 2009, p. 21.

4 Ibid., p. 27.

5 Coetzee, *Doubling the Point*, pp. 393–394.

6 Coetzee, *Boyhood*, p. 80.

7 Ibid., p. 96.

8 Ibid., p. 82.

9 Coetzee, *Doubling the Point*, p. 97.

10 Coetzee Papers, *In the Heart of the Country*, 2 December 1974.

11 J.M. Coetzee, *White Writing: On the Culture of Letters in South Africa*. New Haven: Yale University Press, 1988, p. 49.

12 Coetzee, *Doubling the Point*, pp. 59–60. Coetzee goes on to say that the sources of this approach lie in film and photography. The novel is not written on the model of a screenplay, but it has in mind the filmic practices of Chris Marker and Andrzej Munk. Coetzee wrote a screenplay of *In the Heart of the Country*, but it was not the script used in Marion Hänsel's film version, *Dust*.

13 J.M. Coetzee, *In the Heart of the Country*. Johannesburg: Ravan Press, 1978, p. 20. English translation by J.M. Coetzee, from the Penguin edition, 1977, p. 20.

14 Coetzee, *In the Heart of the Country*, p. 21.

15 Coetzee Papers, *In the Heart of the Country*, 29 December 1974.

16 Coetzee, *In the Heart of the Country*, p. 138.

17 Coetzee, *Life & Times of Michael K*, p. 81.

18 Nadine Gordimer, 'The Idea of Gardening', *New York Review of Books*, 2 February 1984, pp. 3, 6.

19 Coetzee, *Life & Times of Michael K*, pp. 92–93.

20 Coetzee Papers, *Life & Times of Michael K*, 13 July 1981.

CHAPTER 5

1 Elements of this story have been told by Kannemeyer, Hermann Wittenberg and Peter McDonald, who are all duly acknowledged here. These elements acquire a different emphasis in the light of this previously unknown manuscript.

2 Coetzee Papers, Letter to David Gillham, 27 October 1972.

3 John Milton, *Areopagitica*, ed. J.C. Suffolk. London: University Tutorial Press, 1968, p. 88; also cited by J.M. Coetzee, *Giving Offense: Essays on Censorship*. Chicago: University of Chicago Press, 1996, p. 10.

4 Johan Jacobs, son of the customs official who made the decision. Personal communication, 10 December 2012.

5 Coetzee Papers, 'The Burning of the Books', 20 October 1973.

6 Ibid., 19 October 1973.

7 Ibid., 30 June 1974.

8 Ibid., 20 October 1973.

9 Ibid., 20 October 1973.

10 Ibid., 18 June 1974.

11 Peter McDonald, *The Literature Police: Apartheid Censorship and Its Cultural Consequences*. Oxford: Oxford University Press, 2009, p. 63.

12 Coetzee Papers, Letter to the Secretary for the Interior, 23 November 1974.

13 Coetzee Papers, Letter from Department of the Interior, 17 March 1974.

14 McDonald, *The Literature Police*, pp. 60–61.

15 Ibid., p. 61.

16 Ibid., p. 61.

17 Coetzee Papers, Letter to Peter Randall, 27 June 1975.

18 Coetzee Papers, Letter to Celia Catchpole, 31 May 1976. Also in Kannemeyer, *J.M. Coetzee*, p. 288.

19 Stephen Watson, 'Speaking: J.M. Coetzee', *Speak* 1 (3), 1978, p. 24.

20 Andrew van der Vlies, 'In (or From) the Heart of the Country: Local and Global Lives on Coetzee's Anti-pastoral', in Andrew van der Vlies, ed., *Print, Text and Book Cultures in South Africa*. Johannesburg: Wits University Press, 2012, pp. 178–179. Van der Vlies cites an interview he conducted with Mike Kirkwood in 2006.

21 McDonald gives an illuminating account of the policies and practices of Ravan Press, Ad Donker and David Philip in this period, which involved a continual parrying with the censors (*The Literature Police*, pp. 132–157).

22 Hermann Wittenberg, 'The Taint of the Censor: J.M. Coetzee and the Making of "In the Heart of the Country"', *English in Africa* 35 (2), 2008, p. 142.

23 Ibid., p. 142.

24 Ibid., p. 144.

25 McDonald's *The Literature Police* (particularly, for present purposes, pp. 303–320 on Coetzee's experience at the hands of the censors) is an authoritative account of the institutional history.

26 Coetzee Papers, Letter to Alison Samuel, 26 May 1977.

27 Coetzee Papers, Letter from Tom Rosenthal, 1 June 1977.

28 Coetzee Papers, Letter to Tom Rosenthal, 8 June 1977.

29 Coetzee Papers, Letter to Tom Rosenthal, 14 June 1977.

30 Coetzee Papers, Letter from Tom Rosenthal to Tim Manderson, 20 June 1977.

31 Coetzee Papers, Letter from Tom Rosenthal, 28 June 1977.

32 Coetzee Papers, Letter from Tom Rosenthal, 19 July 1977.

33 Coetzee Papers, Letter from Tom Rosenthal, 20 July 1976.

34 Coetzee Papers, Letter to Professor A. Coetzee (Director of Publications), 29 November 1982.

35 Coetzee Papers, Letter from A. Coetzee, 16 December 1982.

36 Coetzee, *Doubling the Point*, p. 299.

37 Kannemeyer, *J.M. Coetzee*, p. 660.

38 Ibid., p. 659.

39 Ibid., p. 659.

40 Coetzee, *Doubling the Point*, p. 298.

41 Coetzee, *Giving Offense*, p. vii.

42 Ibid., pp. 99–100.

43 Coetzee, *Doubling the Point*, p. 298.

44 Ibid., p. 298.

45 Coetzee, *Giving Offense*, pp. 37–38.

46 Ibid., p. 38.

47 Ibid., p. 38.

CHAPTER 6

1 Coetzee Papers, *Waiting for the Barbarians*, 27 January 1978.

2 Sigmund Freud, 'Psychoanalytic Notes on an Autobiographical Account of a Case of Paranoia' (1911), in James Strachey and Angela Richards, eds., *The Pelican Freud Library*. Harmondsworth: Penguin, 1979, pp. 213–215. Cited in Coetzee, *Giving Offense*, p. 198.

3 Coetzee, *Giving Offense*, pp. 198–199.

4 Coetzee Papers, Notebook, 'The Burning of the Books', 4 November 1974.

5 Ibid., 28 June 1974.

6 Ibid., 21 October 1974.

7 Ibid., 31 December 1974.

8 Coetzee, *Doubling the Point*, p. 142.

9 Coetzee Papers, *Waiting for the Barbarians*, 20 September 1977.

10 Coetzee, *Doubling the Point*, pp. 335–338.

11 Coetzee Papers, *Waiting for the Barbarians*, 20 September 1977.

12 Coetzee Papers, Notebook, *Waiting for the Barbarians*, 25 July 1977.

13 Ibid., 4 September 1977.

14 Ibid., 10 October 1977.

15 Ibid., 17 October 1977.

16 Robert Duncan, 'The Song of the Border-Guard', *The First Decade: Selected Poems 1940–1950*. London: Fulcrum Press, 1968, p. 135.

17 Coetzee Papers, Notebook, *Waiting for the Barbarians*, 6 November 1977.

18 Ibid., 6 November 1977.

19 Ibid., 25 December 1977.

20 Ibid., 27 December 1977.

21 Ibid., 6 October 1977.

22 Coetzee, *Youth*, p. 17.

23 Peter Lewis, 'Types of Tyranny', *Times Literary Supplement*, 7 November 1980.

24 Coetzee Papers, Notebook, *Waiting for the Barbarians*, 23 February 1979.

25 Coetzee Papers, *Waiting for the Barbarians*, 13 March 1978.

26 Coetzee Papers, Notebook, *Waiting for the Barbarians*, 25 July 1978.

27 Ibid., 19 February 1978.

28 Coetzee, *Doubling the Point*, p. 363.

29 Ibid., pp. 363–364.

30 Coetzee Papers, Notebook, 27 September 1978.

31 Coetzee Papers, Letter to Hans Zell, 8 May 1979.

32 Coetzee, *Doubling the Point*, p. 141.

33 Ibid., p. 142.

34 Coetzee Papers, Notebook, *Waiting for the Barbarians*, 18 September 1978.

35 Ibid., 21 February 1978.

36 J.M. Coetzee, *Waiting for the Barbarians*. Harmondsworth: Penguin, 1980, p. 6.

37 Ibid., p. 80.

38 Ibid., pp. 31–32.

39 Coetzee Papers, *Waiting for the Barbarians*, 1 January 1978.

40 Ibid., 4 January 1978.

41 Ibid., 13 January 1978.

42 Sigmund Freud, 'A Child Is Being Beaten: A Contribution to the Study of Sexual Perversions', *International Journal of Psychoanalysis* 1, 371–395, www.psykoanalytisk-selskab.dk/data/archive/kand--litteratur/A-Child-is-Being-Beaten—A-Contribution-to-the-Study-of-the-Origin-of-Sexual-Perversions.pdf, accessed 22 July 2013.

43 Coetzee, *Waiting for the Barbarians*, pp. 80–81.

44 Ibid., pp. 120–121.

45 Coetzee Papers, *Waiting for the Barbarians*, 14 September 1978.

46 Ibid., 24 October 1978.

47 Ibid., 19 February 1979.

48 Ibid., 15 September 1978.

CHAPTER 7

1 Coetzee Papers, Notebook, *Life & Times of Michael K*, from 17 October 1979.

2 Ibid., 10 November 1979.

3 Coetzee, *Doubling the Point*, p. 199.

4 Coetzee Papers, Notebook, *Life & Times of Michael K*, 9 June 1982.

5 Ibid., 31 May 1980.

6 Ibid., 6 June 1980.

7 Genadendal, meaning 'Valley of Grace', is a village 130 km east of Cape Town, originally an eighteenth-century Moravian mission to the Khoikhoi. It is close to Greyton, where Coetzee's mother owned a plot and where in this period Coetzee tried, unsuccessfully, to settle his parents after they retired.

8 Coetzee Papers, Notebook, *Life & Times of Michael K*, 9 June 1980.

9 Ibid., 9 June 1980.

10 Ibid., 9 June 1980.

11 Ibid., 9 June 1980.

12 Ibid., 10 June 1980.

13 Ibid., 14 June 1980.

14 Readers have speculated that behind 'MK' lies the armed wing of the ANC, Umkhonto we Sizwe. This is possible but remote because the material Coetzee was working with was from Kleist.

15 Coetzee Papers, Notebook, *Life & Times of Michael K*, 16 June 1980.

16 Ibid., 18 June 1980.

17 Ibid., 28 March 1981.

18 Ibid., 19 June 1980. Peter Horn is the only critic, to my knowledge, to have explored the influence of *Michael Kohlhaas* on *Michael K*. He notes that while Kleist affirms a bourgeois idea of freedom, Coetzee adopts 'an ethics of minimalism' that affirms freedom through 'the indestructible obstinacy of a human being in the image of a stone'. Peter Horn, 'Michael K: Pastiche, Parody or the Inversion of Michael Kohlhaas', *Current Writing* 17 (2), 2005, pp. 56–73.

19 Coetzee Papers, Notebook, *Life & Times of Michael K*, 13 December 1980.

20 Ibid., 9 December 1980.

21 Ibid., 21 October 1980.

22 Coetzee's son, Nicolas, began his formal education at a Waldorf school in Cape Town.

23 Coetzee Papers, Notebook, *Life & Times of Michael K*, 21 October 1980.

24 Ibid., 16 December 1980.

25 Ibid., 16 December 1980.

26 Ibid., 19 December 1980.

27 Ibid., 21 January 1981.

28 Ibid., 15 January 1981. This refers to Hendrik in *In the Heart of the Country*.

29 'It's been a long time since my grandmother was in Genadendal. Probably forty or fifty years. We're now trying to track down her old acquaintances. We are K – ... the K's have probably left or died out long ago – my grandmother wrote – but there was no answer. We've come a long way, from Cape Town.' (My translation.) Coetzee Papers, Notebook, *Life & Times of Michael K*, 11 January 1981.

30 Coetzee Papers, Notebook, *Life & Times of Michael K*, 2 March 1981.

31 Ibid., 19 June 1981.

32 Ibid., 9 May 1981.

33 Gordimer, 'The Idea of Gardening', p. 6.

34 Coetzee Papers, *Diary of a Bad Year*, 9 and 10 December 2005.

35 Coetzee Papers, Notebook, *Life & Times of Michael K*, 8 August 1981.

36 Ibid., 27 August 1981.

37 Ibid., 8 September 1981.

38 Ibid., 8 September 1981.

39 Ibid., 12 September 1981.

40 Ibid., 19 September 1981.

41 Ibid., 23 July 1981.

42 Ibid., 29 July 1981.

43 Ibid., 9 November 1981.

44 Ibid., 10 October 1981.

45 Ibid., 18 November 1981.

46 The title enters the notebook for the first time on 16 December 1981.

47 Coetzee Papers, Notebook, *Life & Times of Michael K*, undated entry.

48 Coetzee's rewriting of the Gospels in *The Childhood of Jesus* (2013) seems to revisit these notes on Bultmann. We recall that early title proposed for *Life & Times of Michael K*: 'The Childhood of Josef K'.

49 Coetzee, *Life & Times of Michael K*, p. 228.

50 Coetzee Papers, Notebook, *Life & Times of Michael K*, 23 January 1982.

CHAPTER 8

1 Coetzee Papers, *Foe*, 24 October, 1983.

2 Coetzee Papers, handwritten introduction, 'Nobel Speech', undated.

3 Coetzee Papers, *Summertime*, 18 May 2004.

4 Coetzee Papers, Notebook, *Foe*, 18 December 1982.

5 Ibid., 4 November 1983.

6 Ibid., 30 November 1983.

7 Ibid., 30 November 1983.

8 Coetzee Papers, *Boyhood*, 17 September 1993.

9 Coetzee Papers, Notebook, *Foe*, 24 October 1983 and 5 April 1984.

10 Ibid., 18 October 1983.

11 Ibid., 24 October 1983.

12 Ibid., 5 November 1983.

13 Ibid., 2 November 1983.

14 Coetzee Papers, *Foe*, 25 July 1983.

15 Ibid., 16 December 1983.

16 Ibid., 1 December 1983.

17 Coetzee, *Doubling the Point*, p. 248.

18 Coetzee Papers, Notebook, *Foe*, 17 March 1984.

19 Ibid., 4 October 1985.

20 Ibid., 4 October 1985.

21 J.M. Coetzee, *Foe*. Johannesburg: Ravan Press, 1986, p. 157.

CHAPTER 9

1 J.M. Coetzee, 'Speech at the Nobel Banquet', Stockholm, 10 December 2003, www.nobelprize.org/nobel_prizes/literature/laureates/2003/coetzee-speech-e.html, accessed 24 September 2012.

2 Coetzee, *Boyhood*, pp. 2–4.

3 Ibid., p. 81.

4 Ibid., p. 79.

5 Conversation with Sylvia Coetzee, 2 April 2012.

6 Coetzee, *Boyhood*, p. 162.

7 Coetzee, *Doubling the Point*, p. 394.

8 Coetzee, *Boyhood*, passim.

9 Conversation with Sylvia Coetzee, 2 April 2012.

10 Coetzee Papers, Notebook, *Age of Iron*, 16 June 1996.

11 J.M. Coetzee, 'Confession and Double Thoughts: Tolstoy, Rousseau, Dostoevsky', in *Doubling the Point*, pp. 251–293. Originally published in *Comparative Literature* 37 (3), 1985, pp. 193–232.

12 Coetzee Papers, Notebook, *Age of Iron*, 30 November 1986.

13 Ibid., 24 November 1986.

14 Ibid., 17 July 1987.

15 Ibid., 26 July 1987.

16 Coetzee Papers, *Age of Iron*, 26 August 1987.

17 Ibid., 28 August 1987.

18 Ibid., 29 August 1987.

19 J.M. Coetzee, *Age of Iron*. London: Secker & Warburg, 1990, pp. 15–16.

20 Ibid., p. 15.

21 Coetzee Papers, *Age of Iron*, 3 September 1987.

22 Ibid., 3 September 1987.

23 Coetzee, *Age of Iron*, p. 16.

24 Ibid., p. 17.

25 Coetzee Papers, *Age of Iron*, 19 September 1987.

26 Ibid., 7 August 1987.

27 Coetzee means a Parthian shaft.

28 Coetzee Papers, *Age of Iron*, 19 September 1987.

29 Coetzee, *Age of Iron*, p. 159.

30 Coetzee Papers, *Age of Iron*, 18 July 1987.

31 *Aeneid* 6, 327–330, for which Coetzee provides his own translation: 'It is forbidden to convey them past the bank of dread and over the snarling current before their bones have found rest in a burial place; instead they must roam here flitting about the river banks for a hundred years, and not until then are they accepted and find their way home to the pools which are now their heart's desire.' Coetzee Papers, *Age of Iron*, 14 and 15 May 1989.

32 Coetzee, *Doubling the Point*, p. 250. It is anomalous that Coetzee should refer to Mrs Curren as Elizabeth, because the name does not appear in the text of *Age of Iron*.

CHAPTER 10

1 Coetzee, *Summertime*, pp. 265–266.

2 Coetzee Papers, *Summertime*, 26 May 2003.

3 By the time she died, John and Philippa had been separated for ten years. She developed breast cancer after 1986, when the novel was under way, so the correspondence between her condition and the fictional Mrs Curren's would appear to be coincidental.

4 Coetzee, *Summertime*, p. 47.

5 Ibid., p. 6.

6 Coetzee Papers, *Summertime*, 31 January 2005.

7 Coetzee, *Boyhood*, p. 159

8 Coetzee Papers, *Boyhood*, 14 September 1994.

CHAPTER 11

1 J.M. Coetzee, *The Master of Petersburg*. London: Secker & Warburg, 1994.

2 Ibid., p. 121.

3 W.J. Leatherbarrow, ed., *Dostoevsky's 'The Devils': A Critical Companion*. Evanston: Northwestern University Press, 1999, p. 158.

4 Joseph Frank, "'The Master of Petersburg" by J.M. Coetzee', *New Republic*, 16 October 1995, pp. 53–57. The review was revised and published in J. Frank, *Between Religion and Rationality: Essays in Russian Literature and Culture*. Princeton: Princeton University Press, 2010, pp. 195–203. I quote the latter source.

5 J.M. Coetzee, 'The Artist at High Tide', *New York Review of Books*, 2 March 1995.

6 Frank, "'The Master of Petersburg" by J.M. Coetzee', p. 198.

7 Ibid., p. 199.

8 Ibid., p. 196.

9 Ibid., p. 201. Frank is persuaded that the style of the novel is based on Dostoevsky's story 'The Landlady', which is one, but only one, of Coetzee's intertexts.

10 Coetzee Papers, *The Master of Petersburg*, 14 May 1991, 3 June 1991.

11 Ibid., 3 June 1991.

12 Ibid., 3 June 1991.

13 J. Frank, *Dostoevsky: A Writer in His Time*, ed. Mary Petrusewicz. Princeton: Princeton University Press, 2010, pp. 622–625.

14 Joanna Scott, 'Voice and Trajectory', *Salmagundi* 114/115, Spring–Summer 1997, pp. 82–102. Quoted in Kannemeyer, *J.M. Coetzee*, p. 463.

15 Here I rely on Kannemeyer, *J.M. Coetzee*, pp. 452–457.

16 J.M. Coetzee, Letter to Howard Wolf, 7 September 1988, quoted in Kannemeyer, *J.M. Coetzee*, pp. 454–455.

17 Coetzee, *The Master of Petersburg*, pp. 20–1, 29, 33, 37, 105.

18 Coetzee Papers, *The Master of Petersburg*, 25 December 1992.

19 F. Dostoevsky, *The Notebooks for 'The Possessed'*, ed. E. Wasiolek, trans. V. Terras. Chicago: University of Chicago Press, 1968.

20 Coetzee Papers, *The Master of Petersburg*, 6 March 1991.

21 E. Wasiolek, Introduction to F. Dostoevsky, *The Notebooks for 'The Possessed'*, p. 17.

22 Ibid., p. 19.

23 H. Bloom, *The Anxiety of Influence: A Theory of Poetry*. New York: Oxford University Press, 1973.

24 Coetzee Papers, *The Master of Petersburg*, 3 June 1991.

25 Ibid., 14 May 1991.

26 Ibid., 29 January 1992.

27 Ibid., 3 November 1991.

28 Ibid., 19 September 1992.

29 Ibid., 6 August 1991.

30 Ibid., 29 January 1992.

31 Coetzee, *The Master of Petersburg*, p. 74.

32 Ibid., p. 249.

33 Coetzee Papers, *The Master of Petersburg*, 28 December 1992.

34 Coetzee, *The Master of Petersburg*, pp. 212–213.

35 Ibid., p. 213.

36 Coetzee Papers, *The Master of Petersburg*, 4 January 1992.

37 Ibid., 6 January 1992.

38 Coetzee, *The Master of Petersburg*, p. 235.

39 Ibid., p. 244. This final clause – or another version of it, 'everything is permitted' – resonates through philosophy from Nietzsche to Sartre, where it informs existential thought.

40 Ibid., p. 245.

41 Coetzee, *Diary of a Bad Year*, pp. 231, 233.

42 Coetzee Papers, *The Master of Petersburg*, 3 June 1991.

43 Coetzee, *The Master of Petersburg*, p. 249.

44 Ibid., p. 250.

45 Ibid., p. 250.

46 Mikhail Bakhtin, *Problems of Dostoevsky's Poetics*, trans. Caryl Emerson. Minneapolis: University of Minnesota Press, 1984, p. 51. I am indebted here to Patrick Hayes, *J.M. Coetzee and the Novel: Writing and Politics after Beckett*. Oxford: Oxford University Press, 2010, pp. 165–193.

47 The situation merits comparison with T.S. Eliot's famous analysis of Hamlet, to the effect that revenge drama was too flimsy a vehicle for Hamlet's distress over his father's death and his mother's sexual behaviour, and that Shakespeare had therefore not found a suitable 'objective correlative' for his theme. T.S. Eliot, 'Hamlet' (1919), in *Selected Essays*. London: Faber & Faber, 1951, pp. 145–146.

48 Coetzee Papers, *The Master of Petersburg*, 19 November 1991.

49 Ibid., 26 March 1992.

50 Ibid., 26 March 1992.

51 Coetzee, *The Master of Petersburg*, p. 221.

52 Ibid., p. 180.

53 Ibid., p. 181.

54 Ibid., p. 182.

CHAPTER 12

1 Coetzee Papers, Notebook, *Disgrace*, 24 October 1996.

2 Kannemeyer, *J.M. Coetzee*, pp. 484–485.

3 Ibid., p. 482.

4 Coetzee Papers, *Diary of a Bad Year*, 8 November 2005.

5 Coetzee, *Diary of a Bad Year*, p. 191.

6 J.M. Coetzee, 'Critic and Citizen: A Response', *Pretexts: Literary and Cultural Studies* 9 (1), 2000, p. 110. A reply to a position paper on the universities by the philosopher André du Toit.

7 Coetzee, *Disgrace*, p. 3.

8 Coetzee Papers, *Elizabeth Costello*, Public Readings, Stanford Humanities Center, 22 May 2001.

9 Thomas Hardy, 'The Convergence of the Twain', in Margaret Ferguson, Mary J. Salter and Jon Stallworthy, eds., *The Norton Anthology of Poetry*. New York: Norton, 2005, pp. 1156–1157.

10 Kannemeyer, *J.M. Coetzee*, pp. 538–545.

11 Coetzee, 'Critic and Citizen', p. 110.

12 Information provided by Crystal Warren, from the database of NELM, the National English Literary Museum, in Grahamstown, South Africa.

13 J.M. Coetzee, *The Lives of Animals*, ed. Amy Gutmann. Princeton: Princeton University Press, 2001.

14 J.M. Coetzee, 'Meat Country', *Granta* 52, 1995.

15 The UCT exam book containing the earliest drafts of *Disgrace* is inscribed 'autobiography'. However, this may not signify: since Coetzee was writing these projects at the same time, he could have swapped the stationery.

16 In the notebooks, the term 'realism' is often used pejoratively, as it is here, without the nuanced definition of the kind put forward in 'Realism', the first chapter of *Elizabeth Costello*.

17 Derek Attridge, *J.M. Coetzee and the Ethics of Reading: Literature in the Event*. Pietermaritzburg: University of KwaZulu-Natal Press, 2005, p. 191.

18 Coetzee Papers, Notebook, *The Lives of Animals*, 2 September 1995. I work from a later typescript in which the earlier notes are summarized.

19 He first made this argument in relation to *Burger's Daughter* in 'Into the Dark Chamber' (in *Doubling the Point*), where he relates it to the problem of representing torture.

20 Coetzee Papers, Notebook, *The Lives of Animals*, 28 May 1996.

21 Ibid., 16 May 1996.

22 Ibid., 26 July 1996.

23 Coetzee Papers, Notebook, *Disgrace*, 24 May 1996.

24 Coetzee, *Disgrace*, p. 112.

25 Ibid., pp. 55–56.

26 Coetzee Papers, Notebook, *Disgrace*, 19 July 1995. Coetzee is quoting from Barthes's *Selected Writings*. London: Fontana, 1983.

27 Coetzee, *Disgrace*, p. 66.

28 Coetzee Papers, Notebook, *Disgrace*, 23 September 1997.

29 Coetzee, *Disgrace*, pp. 50, 66.

30 Ibid., p. 199.

31 Coetzee Papers, Notebook, *Disgrace*, 21 April 1996. The note is later copied in typed extracts from the notebook dated 20 August 1997 and retained for later use. The parenthetical '(I too!)' is omitted.

32 James Joyce, *Ulysses*. London: Alma Classics, 2012, pp. 142–143.

33 Ibid., p. 143.

34 Coetzee Papers, Notebook, *Disgrace*, 6 May 1995. The 'expressive function' refers to Roman Jakobson's theory of the functions of language.

35 Coetzee, *Disgrace*, p. 166.

36 Ibid., pp. 107–108.

37 Coetzee Papers, Notebook, *Disgrace*, 17 and 19 February, 7, 9 and 11 March 1996.

38 Ibid., 11 March 1996.

39 This entry was made on a day Coetzee and I cycled through the Karkloof Valley near Pietermaritzburg. En route we passed through a foresters' camp, where cordial greetings were exchanged in isiZulu. Afterwards the conversation turned on how strange we would have seemed to the workers present, in lycra and cycle helmets.

40 Coetzee Papers, Notebook, *Disgrace*, 9 May 1996.

41 Ibid., 17 July 1997.

42 Ibid., 1 May 1997. *Slordig* is Afrikaans for 'unkempt'.

43 Ibid., 29 August 1996

44 Ibid., 29 August 1996.

45 Ibid., 31 August 1996.

46 Ibid., 18 May 1996.

47 Ibid., 9 January 1997.

48 Ibid., 9 January 1997.

49 Coetzee, *Disgrace*, p. 112.

50 Ibid., p. 156.

51 Ibid., p. 159.

52 Coetzee Papers, Notebook, *Disgrace*, 26 November 1996.

53 Ibid., 24 January 1998.

54 Ibid., 28 January 1998.

CHAPTER 13

1 Auster and Coetzee, *Here and Now*, p. 88.

2 J.M. Coetzee, *Slow Man*. London: Secker & Warburg, 2005, p. 40.

3 Coetzee, *Diary of a Bad Year*, p. 192.

4 Ibid., p. 193.

5 Ibid., p. 193.

6 Ibid., p. 193.

7 Auster and Coetzee, *Here and Now*, p. 88.

8 Coetzee, *Elizabeth Costello*, p. 1.

9 Coetzee Papers, Typescript drafts, *Diary of a Bad Year*, 22 December 2005.

10 Elleke Boehmer, 'J.M. Coetzee's Australian Realism', in Chris Danta, Sue Kossew and Julian Murphet, eds., *Strong Opinions: J.M. Coetzee and the Authority of Contemporary Fiction*. New York and London, Continuum, 2011, p. 5.

11 Coetzee Papers, *Diary of a Bad Year*, 22 December 2005.

12 Coetzee, *Diary of a Bad Year*, p. 192.

13 Coetzee Papers, *Diary of a Bad Year*, 22 December 2005.

14 Quoted in Coetzee Papers, *Diary of a Bad Year*, 22 December 2005. The same passage with elisions is quoted in the novel, p. 192.

15 Alternatively, *Diary of a Bad Year*, p. 192 and the draft of 22 December 2005.

16 Kannemeyer, *J.M. Coetzee*, pp. 535–539.

17 Ibid., pp. 540–541.

18 J.M. Coetzee, 'He and His Man', in Horace Engdahl, ed., *Nobel Lectures: Literature, 2001–2005*. Singapore: World Scientific, 2008, p. 56.

19 www.nobelprize.org/mediaplayer/index.php?id=716.

20 Coetzee, *Slow Man*, pp. 82–83.

21 Ibid., p. 112.

22 Ibid., p. 141.

23 Coetzee Papers, 'Notes and Fragments', *Slow Man*, undated. These notes are in typescript, and amended in pencil.

BIBLIOGRAPHY

Auster, Paul and J.M. Coetzee, *Here and Now: Letters, 2008–2011*. New York: Viking, 2013

Attridge, Derek, *J.M. Coetzee and the Ethics of Reading: Literature in the Event*. Pietermaritzburg: University of KwaZulu-Natal Press, 2005

Bakhtin, Mikhail, *Problems of Dostoevsky's Poetics*, trans. Caryl Emerson. Minneapolis: University of Minnesota Press, 1984

Barnard, Rita, 'Coetzee in/and Afrikaans', *Journal of Literary Studies* 25 (4), 2009, pp. 84–105

Barthes, Roland, 'The Death of the Author', trans. Richard Howard. Ubu-Web Papers, n.d., www.tbook.constantvzw.org/wp-content/death_authorbarthes.pdf

Barthes, Roland, *The Preparation of the Novel*, ed. Nathalie Léger, trans. Kate Briggs. New York: Columbia University Press, 2011

Barthes, Roland, *Roland Barthes*, trans. Richard Howard. New York: Hill & Wang, 2010

Bloom, Harold, *The Anxiety of Influence: A Theory of Poetry*. New York: Oxford University Press, 1973

Boehmer, Elleke, 'J.M. Coetzee's Australian Realism', in Chris Danta, Sue Kossew and Julian Murphet, eds., *Strong Opinions: J.M. Coetzee and the Authority of Contemporary Fiction*. New York, 2011

Coetzee, J.M., *Age of Iron*. London: Secker & Warburg, 1990

Coetzee, J.M., 'The Artist at High Tide', *New York Review of Books*, 2 March 1995

Coetzee, J.M., *Boyhood: Scenes from Provincial Life*. London: Secker & Warburg, 1997

Coetzee, J.M., 'Confession and Double Thoughts: Tolstoy, Rousseau, Dostoevsky', in *Doubling the Point*, pp. 251–293. Originally published in *Comparative Literature* 37 (3), 1985

Coetzee, J.M., 'Critic and Citizen: A Response', *Pretexts: Literary and Cultural Studies* 9 (1), 2000

Coetzee, J.M., *Diary of a Bad Year*. London: Harvill Secker, 2007

Coetzee, J.M., *Disgrace*. London: Secker & Warburg, 1999

Coetzee, J.M., 'Doctoris Causa Honoris Lectio', *Iohannes Maxwell Coetzee*, Adam Mickiewicz University, Poznań, Poland, 2012

Coetzee, J.M., *Doubling the Point: Essays and Interviews*, ed. David Attwell. Cambridge, Mass.: Harvard University Press, 1992

Coetzee, J.M., *Dusklands*. Johannesburg: Ravan Press, 1974

Coetzee, J.M., *Elizabeth Costello*. London: Viking, 2003

Coetzee, J.M., *Foe*. Johannesburg: Ravan Press, 1986

Coetzee, J.M., *Giving Offense: Essays on Censorship*. Chicago: University of Chicago Press, 1996

Coetzee, J.M., 'The Great South African Novel', *Leadership SA* 2 (4), 1983

Coetzee, J.M., 'He and His Man', in Horace Engdahl, ed., *Nobel Lectures: Literature, 2001–2005*. Singapore: World Scientific, 2008

Coetzee, J.M., *In the Heart of the Country*. Johannesburg: Ravan Press, 1978. English translation by J.M. Coetzee, Penguin, 1977

Coetzee, J.M., *Life & Times of Michael K*. Johannesburg: Ravan Press, 1983

Coetzee, J.M., *The Lives of Animals*, ed. Amy Gutmann. Princeton: Princeton University Press, 2001

Coetzee, J.M., *The Master of Petersburg*. London: Secker & Warburg, 1994

Coetzee, J.M., 'Meat Country', *Granta* 52, 1995

Coetzee, J.M., 'Nietverloren', in *Ten Years of the Caine Prize for African Writing*. Oxford: New Internationalist Publications, 2009

Coetzee, J.M., *Slow Man*. London: Secker & Warburg, 2005

Coetzee, J.M., 'Speech at the Nobel Banquet', Stockholm, 10 December 2003, www.nobelprize.org/nobel_prizes/literature/laureates/2003/coetzee-speech-e.html, accessed 24 September 2012

Coetzee, J.M., *Summertime*. London: Harvill Secker, 2009

Coetzee, J.M., 'What Is a Classic?' in *Stranger Shores: Essays 1986–1999*. London: Secker & Warburg, 2001

Coetzee, J.M., *White Writing: On the Culture of Letters in South Africa*. New Haven: Yale University Press, 1988

Coetzee, J.M., *Youth*. London: Secker & Warburg, 2002

Dostoevsky, Fyodor, *The Notebooks for 'The Possessed'*, ed. E. Wasiolek, trans. V. Terras. Chicago: University of Chicago Press, 1968

Duncan, Robert, 'The Song of the Border-Guard', *The First Decade: Selected Poems 1940–1950*. London: Fulcrum Press, 1968

Eliot, T.S., 'Hamlet' (1919), in *Selected Essays*. London: Faber & Faber, 1951, pp. 145–146

Eliot, T.S., 'Tradition and the Individual Talent' (1919), in *Selected Essays*. London: Faber & Faber, 1932

Frank, Joseph, *Between Religion and Rationality: Essays in Russian Literature and Culture*. Princeton: Princeton University Press, 2010

Frank, Joseph, *Dostoevsky: A Writer in His Time*, ed. Mary Petrusewicz. Princeton: Princeton University Press, 2010

Frank, Joseph, '"The Master of Petersburg" by J.M. Coetzee', *New Republic*, 16 October 1995, pp. 53–57

Freud, Sigmund, 'A Child Is Being Beaten: A Contribution to the Study of Sexual Perversions', *International Journal of Psychoanalysis* 1, 371–395, http://www.psykoanalytisk-selskab.dk/data/archive/kand--litteratur/A-Child-is-Being-Beaten—A-Contribution-to-the-Study-of-the-Origin-of-Sexual-Perversions.pdf, accessed 22 July 2013

Freud, Sigmund, 'Psychoanalytic Notes on an Autobiographical Account of a Case of Paranoia' (1911), in James Strachey and Angela Richards, eds., *The Pelican Freud Library*. Harmondsworth: Penguin, 1979

Gordimer, Nadine, 'The Idea of Gardening', *New York Review of Books*, 2 February 1984

Hamilton, Ian, *Keepers of the Flame: Literary Estates and the Rise of Biography*. London: Hutchinson, 1992

Hardy, Thomas, 'The Convergence of the Twain', in Margaret Ferguson, Mary J. Salter and Jon Stallworthy, eds., *The Norton Anthology of Poetry*. New York: Norton, 2005, pp. 1156–1157

Hayes, Patrick, *J.M. Coetzee and the Novel: Writing and Politics after Beckett*. Oxford: Oxford University Press, 2010

Horn, Peter, 'Michael K: Pastiche, Parody or the Inversion of Michael Kohlhaas', *Current Writing* 17 (2), 2005, pp. 56–73

Kannemeyer, J.C., *J.M. Coetzee: A Life in Writing*. Johannesburg: Jonathan Ball, 2012

Kannemeyer, J.C., *J.M. Coetzee: 'n Geskryfde Lewe*. Johannesburg: Jonathan Ball, 2012

Leatherbarrow, W.J., ed., *Dostoevsky's 'The Devils': A Critical Companion*. Evanston: Northwestern University Press, 1999

Lewis, Peter, 'Types of Tyranny', *Times Literary Supplement*, 7 November 1980

McDonald, Peter, *The Literature Police: Apartheid Censorship and its Cultural Consequences*. Oxford: Oxford University Press, 2009

Milton, John, *Areopagitica*, ed. J.C. Suffolk. London: University Tutorial Press, 1968

Pamuk, Orhan, 'Other Countries, Other Shores', *New York Times Book Review*, 19 December 2013, www.nytimes.com/2013/12/22/books/review/other-countries-other-shores.html

Rhedin, Folke, 'J.M. Coetzee: Interview', *Kunapipi* 6 (1), 1984

Scott, Joanna and J.M. Coetzee, 'Voice and Trajectory: An Interview with J.M. Coetzee', *Salmagundi* 114/115, Spring–Summer 1997

Spengler, Oswald, *The Decline of the West* (1926), trans. Charles Francis Atkinson. London: Allen & Unwin, 1959

Van der Vlies, Andrew, 'In (or From) the Heart of the Country: Local and Global Lives on Coetzee's Anti-pastoral', in Andrew van der Vlies, ed., *Print, Text and Book Cultures in South Africa*. Johannesburg: Wits University Press, 2012

Wall, Geoffrey, *Gustave Flaubert: A Life*. New York: Farrar, Straus, Giroux, 2001

Watson, Stephen, 'Speaking: J.M. Coetzee', *Speak* 1 (3), 1978

Wittenberg, Hermann, 'The Taint of the Censor: J.M. Coetzee and the Making of "In the Heart of the Country"', *English in Africa* 35 (2), 2008

INDEX